The Marketing Challenge

The EIU Series

This innovative series of books is the result of a publishing collaboration
between Addison-Wesley and the Economist Intelligence Unit. Our authors
draw on the results of original research by the EIU's skilled research
and editorial staff to provide a range of topical, information-rich
and incisive business titles. They are specifically tailored to the
needs of international executives and business education worldwide.

Titles in the Series

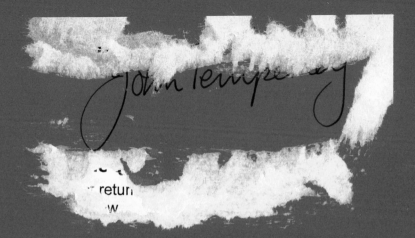

John Tempe...y

...return...
...w

The Marketing Challenge

Laura Mazur

Annik Hogg

The Economist
Intelligence Unit

 ADDISON-WESLEY PUBLISHING COMPANY

Wokingham, England • Reading, Massachusetts • Menlo Park, California • New York
Don Mills, Ontario • Amsterdam • Bonn • Sydney • Singapore
Tokyo • Madrid • San Juan • Milan • Paris • Mexico City • Seoul • Taipei

Many of the designations used by manufacturers and sellers to distinguish their products are claimed as trademarks. Addison-Wesley has made every attempt to supply trademark information about manufacturers and their products mentioned in this book.

The information in this book has been verified to the best of the authors' and publishers' ability. However, the authors and publishers cannot provide legal or absolute factual guarantees and they do not accept responsibility for any loss arising from decisions based on information contained in this book.

Cover designed by Pencil Box Ltd, Marlow, Buckinghamshire
incorporating photograph by Kerry Lawrence
and printed by The Riverside Printing Co. (Reading) Ltd.
Text designed by Valerie O'Donnell.
Line diagrams drawn by Howie Twiner.
Typeset by Meridian Phototypesetting Limited, Pangbourne.
Printed in Great Britain at the University Press, Cambridge.

First printed 1993.

British Library Cataloguing in Publication Data
A catalogue record for this book is available from the British Library.

Library of Congress Cataloging in Publication Data
Mazur, Laura.
    The marketing challenge / Laura Mazur, Annik Hogg.
        p.   cm.
    Includes bibliographical references and index.
    ISBN 0-201-63191-1
    1. Marketing--Management.   2. Marketing--Europe--Management.
    I. Hogg, Annik.   II. Title.
    HF5415.13.M3686   1993
    658.8--dc20   93-15369
                                                                               CIP

Preface

The creation of an integral marketing culture with an international perspective is a major challenge for any business, especially one operating in Europe. Yet it is ironic that in the run-up to the year 2000 when 'the market' dominates corporate thinking as never before that 'marketing' is still underrated and confused so often with selling or advertising. The arguments about the need to improve quality, boost productivity and foster innovation have in the main been won. But what marketing is, and what it needs to be, is to a large extent an unresolved issue. Outdated notions persist.

Marketing should be the whole operation of the company as it tries to figure out not only how to sell what it makes, but what to make and what to sell. Marketing starts the process rather than ends it. It is the homework that a company has to do to work out what its target market wants. On the functional level, areas like purchasing and production are equally as important as functional marketing. But strategic marketing must be the driving force of the company. It is what management should be all about.

The annals of corporate literature are littered with organizations that have failed to define even basic questions like 'to whom are we trying to sell?' They carry on offering products or services that are not very good or in any way superior to those from their competitors. Perhaps it is the very simplicity of the notion that success is based on getting to know the customers and their real needs that scuppers so many companies. Business is complex; the world is changing rapidly; the organization is a maze of complexity. How can it be simple? But that is what the successful companies are trying to do: cut through the noise, formulate a clear vision of the market and how to be positioned in it, eject cumbersome hierarchies and rigid management planning and proceed on the basis that the only certain premise is change.

What this book sets out to do is examine the common issues that are faced by companies. They fall into several interrelated areas: the stimulus to change and organizational responses; marketing strategies and marketing programmes; and managing information and culture. Different industrial sectors need to formulate their responses to particular changes in their marketing environment, but the common challenges faced by all are:

- Understanding the global setting in which the company operates;
- Dealing with markets that are both global and yet able to split into smaller segments;
- Deciding what elements constitute strategic marketing;
- Organizing for marketing advantage;
- Developing a clear brand strategy. The most important asset a company has, apart from its people, is its brands and what they stand for. This includes the corporate image;
- Translating strategies into programmes of promotion, sales and pricing;
- Exploiting information technology (IT) both for structural flexibility and as a way to harness the customer database for competitive advantage;
- Recruiting and keeping marketing management with a global/European outlook;
- Driving a lasting marketing culture through the whole organization.

A clear theme emerges from the companies interviewed for this book. In the best, most forward-looking ones marketing has not been kicked upstairs but has marched vigorously into the highest office. Marketing is the primary business function. It forces the organization to work from the outside in, instead of the inside out. Successful companies are devising and 'owning' their strategies for survival and growth and looking for help in implementation rather than being force-fed strategic visions from external experts. After all, strategies can be copied rapidly; it is in the implementation, the details, where winning lies.

While these concerns apply to markets on a global basis, the onset of a Europe as an integrated trading bloc has acted as a catalyst in rethinking marketing strategy and reorganizing the company to implement that strategy. Dealing with a European market that is set to get both broader and deeper has become a major corporate preoccupation. The emergence of a market that is large, could get even larger as other European countries enter the EC, and yet is full of microsegments that might or might not have certain similarities mirrors what is happening on a global scale and is forcing some painful readjustments and reorganization for companies, particularly those that have relied heavily on their home markets being protected by both regulatory and cultural barriers. Companies from all parts of the globe are using Europe as a testing ground for organizational solutions that can be emulated elsewhere.

That reorganization is causing major corporate headaches for companies of all sizes: how do you streamline both strategic and tactical marketing strategy to avoid wasteful overlap and confusion, and at the same time ensure that local subsidiaries retain enough autonomy to be able to respond to local conditions? Some companies are in the midst of setting up structures based on a system of matrix management which is supposed to encourage collaboration and avoid hostile confrontation of the 'not-invented-here' type. Others are breaking up headquarters and assigning world-wide responsibilities for product groups to those parts of the world best suited to handle them.

The problem is that very few companies are in the fortunate position of being able to plan their organizations on a blank piece of paper. The great majority already have assets on the ground, plant, employees, customers, cultures and technologies that combine to provide something near the desired commercial result. The first question that has to be asked is not what type of organization should be adopted, but how should the organization change to face the challenges of the 1990s?

The balancing act of trying to be centralized while localized also confronts organizations with what is the most important task (and probably the hardest) facing any business: the creation of a true marketing culture that touches every part of the company. This cannot be done quickly, nor can it be carried out under the wrong circumstances: it takes a five- to ten-year commitment, at least. Moreover, the chief executive must believe in it, understand it, and want it, or it will not go anywhere. There has to be a commitment to 'marketing marketing': converting everyone to the understanding that they all work for the customer.

Nevertheless, there is still a vital role for competent senior marketing specialists:

- They are at the sharp end in dealing with customer needs, so they can be used to spread the gospel of the market throughout the organization. This book will show how some companies have already begun that process.
- They understand both intellectually and pragmatically the role of promotion and how to integrate all the different aspects of the marketing mix to enhance the value of the products or services.
- They can act as explorers, creating the 'tomorrows' of their companies with new ideas.
- They can act, at a senior level, as 'consultants' to chief executives.

The least that a new attitude to marketing can do for business is re-inject it with the sense of creativity and challenge that may have been smothered by corporate rigidity. The difficulties companies face in the modern world, not only from equally talented competitors but also from social and environmental challenges which have to be met head on, should not be underestimated. It is unlikely that companies will be able to plan within a stable framework; the unexpected is never far away. Good marketing practice, however, will at least ensure that survival is an option.

Structure

This book is based on three management reports researched and written between 1989 and 1991. Because of that, some of the executives quoted might have changed jobs – those that are known to have moved are described as 'former' – while corporate structures might have altered as well. But the purpose of the book is not to describe current corporate events but to examine underlying trends and analyse the role of marketing in the corporate environment, describing the challenges facing marketing professionals, with a focus on the management of change. There are also a number of case studies drawn from 'best practice' which, although they deal with issues of European marketing management, highlight themes applicable to any complex market.

The book is organized into four main parts. The first, The Global Setting, looks at the main trends which will affect marketing and a global framework that demands the companies be both centralized yet decentralized.

The second part, Marketing Strategies, considers those elements which comprise strategic marketing, how companies are organizing for marketing advantage. Brand strategies are also covered, with a particular focus on getting the portfolio in shape to cope with the Single European Market.

The third part, Marketing Programmes, homes in on the more specific aspects of promotion, sales and pricing programmes.

The final part, Managing Information and Culture, looks at the critical implications for marketing, both strategically and tactically, of the application of IT. Equally important, it examines the human factors, including recruitment and establishing a marketing culture.

Each chapter concludes with a summary for ease of reference and a checklist to enable the reader to assess his or her own company against the analysis of best practice.

The Marketing Challenge has been compiled from three Economist Intelligence Unit reports: *Marketing 2000, Organising for Marketing Advantage* and *Marketing Strategies for Global Growth and Competitiveness.* All three reports are based on extensive interviews with major companies operating in Europe.

Laura Mazur
Annik Hogg
June 1993

References

Economist Intelligence Unit. (1991). *Marketing 2000.* (March) London: Economist Intelligence Unit
Economist Intelligence Unit. (1990). *Organising for Marketing Advantage.* London: Economist Intelligence Unit
Economist Intelligence Unit. (1990). *Marketing Strategies for Global Growth and Competitiveness.* (October) London: Economist Intelligence Unit

Contents

Executive summary

(1) Marketing strategy has to take account of political, economic and social trends. That does not mean putting undue emphasis on long-term – or even medium-term – forecasts, which often prove to have been unreliable after the event. But it does demand acknowledging the existence of factors which, if identified, could be a source of survival and opportunity if taken into account, or harmful if ignored. The difficulty all companies face is to balance the understanding of the bigger picture with the exploration of increasingly complicated markets that require a deeper and more refined understanding.

Some of the major trends that need to be taken into account include:

- Globalization
- Political upheavals
- Demographic shifts
- Environmental and ethical concerns
- Technological change
- Asia and Japan as an economic force
- Europe as a Single Market.

(2) Being responsive or efficient or a quick learner used to be enough for a company to create competitive advantage. That is no longer the case. The strategic requirements now are multidimensional, where global economies of scale need to be matched with in-depth local market knowledge, and where centralization of shared goals and values is not allowed to dampen local enthusiasms or initiative. What companies have to grasp is that it is no longer a question of 'either/or', of globalization/localization, centralization/decentralization.

(3) The balance of power has shifted to the market with a vengeance. The nature of demand, the multiplicity of choice, the rise of affluence and the availability of information have all contributed to that shift. The result is that companies must take a number of critical strategic concepts into account, including:

- Developing the strategic framework
- Carrying out a marketing audit
- Competitive analysis
- Clarifying the strategic role of the centre
- Measuring marketing effectiveness.

(4)   Many companies are increasingly becoming convinced of the need to coordinate their marketing across Europe, although the rationale is usually rather more complex than for manufacturing. National markets cross-subsidize the effective implementation of marketing plans in a number of complex ways:

- They provide opportunities for learning and feedback to other markets;
- Market networks can be used to leverage good ideas and exploit innovation rapidly;
- Market networks help to fight competitive battles through increasing options of attack and defence and also through generating the required cash flows;
- The strength of the network itself is a competitive advantage, in many service industries, for example, providing a 'halo' effect to a particular brand.

(5)   The building of brands which attract a loyal and lucrative consumer following has been a familiar concept and one developed by consumer goods companies over a long period of time. But the increasingly sophisticated concepts are spreading throughout businesses of all types because of several key trends which include:

- The evolution of Europe from separate national markets into one trading area which nonetheless comprises quite distinct segments and which demands a careful evaluation of the brand portfolio;
- The increased emphasis on getting higher margins from creating the added value attributable to premium brands;
- The success of some niche brands;
- The rise of distributors' own brands;
- Corporate branding;
- The evolution of brand valuation.

(6)   Getting the marketing communications right is crucial. The best-laid strategic plans and organizational charts will prove of little use if not translated into the sharp end of promotion and sales. The problem of the global/local divide applies just as much to how companies actually reach their customers.

(7)   The globalization of marketing has put tremendous pressure on multinational pricing systems. Over the past few decades, as companies moved from purely domestic operations to exporting and then to overseas manufacturing and marketing, they had to transform their pricing structures. Those structures, originally set up to function in a single-market setting, have had to be adapted to the much greater heterogeneity of the international environment. Executives of internationally oriented firms must now grapple with many questions to which there are no simple or precise answers.

(8) The slow arrival of information technology (IT) into that last bastion of IT ignorance, the marketing function, has deep implications for marketing both strategically and tactically. Closing the information loop so that real-time, integrated data about customers flows around the company effectively ends reliance on inert geographical structures and enables the corporation to 'think global, act local' in the truest sense. The application of IT to marketing at all levels will enable information to function as the central nervous system in the corporate organism, reacting to stimuli from both within and without the structure.

(9) No company can hope to meet the challenges facing it without finding and motivating the right people to provide marketing expertise. Issues of recruitment at both the middle and senior level on an international scale are increasingly complex, with the restructuring demanded by the European market in particular presenting companies with a daunting personnel task not least, making managers of varing nationalities think European.

But while this has to be at the top of the agenda in the short term, it has to be underpinned by a long-term commitment to foster the corporate culture that makes everyone in the company face outward and think marketing and customers. An integral part of that effot is coming to terms with what the role of the marketing director and marketing department will be in a marketing-led organization.

About the authors

Laura Mazur is a business writer and editorial consultant. She graduated from Smith College in the US in economics, and has an MA from the University of London. She has been a business journalist since 1978 and was editor of *Marketing* magazine in the UK from 1986 to 1989. Now freelance, she is the author of management guides on marketing and public relations published by the Economist Intelligence Unit. She is also project director of the European Marketing Council for The Conference Board Europe.

Annik Hogg is Head of the Marketing School in the Faculty of Business and Law at Kingston University. She has experience working with a wide variety of international companies, especially American but also European and Japanese, on the development of European marketing strategies. Her work and consultancy interest lead Annik Hogg to specialize in International Marketing teaching and research. She is currently involved in Pan European research projects, examining the cross-cultural factors influencing demand in wine and rice.

PART ONE

The global setting

1

Marketing trends

Introduction

'Probably 75% of changes in markets is because of big trends, not market trends. But 75% of the effort is often spent looking within markets. This can be a mismatch.'

Barrie Staniford, marketing director, The Henley Centre.

Marketing strategy has to take account of political, economic and social trends. That does not mean putting undue emphasis on long-term – or even medium-term – forecasts, which often prove to have been unreliable after the event. But it does demand acknowledging the existence of factors which, if identified, could be a source of survival and opportunity if taken into account, or harmful if ignored. The difficulty all companies face is to balance the understanding of the bigger picture with the exploration of increasingly complicated markets that require a deeper and more refined understanding. Solutions devised for the European arena and described in this book could provide a template for other parts of the globe.

Some of the major trends that need to be taken into account include:

- Globalization
- Political upheavals
- Demographic shifts
- Environmental and ethical concerns
- Technological change
- Asia and Japan as an economic force
- Europe as a Single Market

Globalization

Globalization is an overworked word that was first popularized in a provoca-tive thesis by Professor Theodore Levitt of the Harvard Business School who said that the world is becoming standardized and homogeneous and companies should follow suit. While it has since been extended to 'go global, but act local' it is still a valid description of the trend for companies to have a presence in more of the world. A company could lose out if it operates only in Europe and misses out on the technological developments of Japan, or the huge market opportunities offered by the US and Canada. These three land masses are often referred to as the 'triad' of global markets.

Globalization describes a process that has been steadily gaining ground over the last decade, characterized by the internationalization of business opportunities and threats and stimulated by factors like modern communica-tions, shrinking domestic markets, converging consumer demands in the devel-oped countries and the ability to meet these demands quickly and efficiently. Additional impetus has come from the erosion of national barriers, financial deregulation and shifting cost structures as companies have internationalized their operations for economies of scale in production and distribution.

The emphasis now has to be on product differentiation on a large scale, flexible manufacturing and rapid innovation to service a more discerning and demanding customer before the competition does. Attention is being focused more on what sort of products are made, rather than how they are made. Higher added value is the key. That means combining low-cost standardization with local adaptation on an international scale.

The other side of the globalization coin is the pronounced and growing homogeneity among certain groups, particularly business executives, the brand-hungry young and the wealthy. Brands like Rolex watches, premium Scotch whiskies and Hertz rental cars are found undifferentiated all over the world. These are matched by youth brands like Levis, Coca-Cola, Benetton clothing and McDonald's restaurants. These last two global brands rely on central quality control but handle local tastes by franchising nationally. More similarities among discrete population groups will grow over the next 10–20 years: spotting them offers unrivalled marketing opportunities.

The trend to globalization, however, is constantly under threat from the forces of protectionism and bilateralism. While the European Community countries, grappling with powerful recessionary forces and vexed questions of how to deal with the former Eastern bloc countries, have put some of the uni-fying measures on hold, the march toward a single market cannot be halted. The signing of the North American Free Trade Agreement (Nafta) would create a market whose combined 1992 Gross Domestic Product equalled $6200 billion, while Asia and Japan are forming the third apex of the trade triangle.

Potential protectionism in the 1990s will thus be on a much larger scale, between powerful economic blocs rather than countries. This could have a dampening effect on what has been vigorous trade activity over the last decade. In 1989, for example, world trade in goods increased by about 7%, more than double the rise in production, although it slipped by almost 2% in 1990 because of recession in key parts of the developed world (Tables 1.1 and 1.2). International direct investment has also risen markedly during the last ten years. Outward investment by the top five Organization for Economic Co-operation and Development (OECD) countries, in fact, grew by almost 60% to $419.3 billion between 1981 and 1988, while the respective figures for inward investment were 75% and $107.5 billion.

According to a report from the United Nations Department of Economic and Social Development (1992), foreign direct investment is beginning to overtake international trade as the driving force behind globalization of the world economy. During the second half of the 1980s, foreign direct investment (FDI) grew four times faster than domestic output and two-and-a-half times as fast as exports. The total stock of FDI world-wide now stands at $1.7 trillion. The EC, US and Japan accounted for 70% of world inflows. And while industrial internationalization will be affected during the first half of the 1990s because of the economic downturn, forecasts predict an upturn in the latter half.

Political upheavals

The swift and unforeseen collapse of the centrally planned economies in Eastern Europe has created what futurologists call a paradigm shift in global development. The potential chaos resulting from the break-up of the former Soviet Union and the rise in ethnic conflicts – evidenced in the extreme in the former country of Yugoslavia – have rapidly ended hopes of a new and more stable world economic order, but they in no way compare to the magnitude for potential catastrophe engendered by the Cold War. It means, however, that the 'what-if' scenarios companies face are markedly different. All predictions are dangerous; nevertheless, the consensus seems to be that the long-term global outlook tends more to the bullish than the bearish, although a severe short-term recession is already present in many parts of the developed world and for Western Europe a massive influx of refugees from war-torn areas is bound to have an impact on economic development.

But the fact that half of Western gross national product (GNP) is concentrated in services or consumer non-durables is reckoned by economists to signal fewer dramatic blips over the next decade. The joker in the pack could be what was the Communist Bloc. The enormous sums needed to stabilize the individual countries as they make the transition to market economies will have

Table 1.1 World trade: volume change by region, 1980–90 (annual % change).

	1970	1971	1972	1973	1974	1975	1976	1977	1978	1979	1980	1981	1982	1983	1984	1985	1986	1987	1988	1989	1990
Exports																					
Developed market economies	10.3	5.5	8.6	13.6	8.4	−4.4	11.3	4.5	6.7	6.2	4.6	2.4	−2.1	2.3	9.6	3.9	1.2	5.4	7.9	7.3	5.4
North America	8.9	0.4	9.1	20.5	5.7	−3.2	5.3	1.8	11.3	7.3	7.5	−2.0	−9.3	−2.5	9.8	0.4	1.0	10.2	15.3	8.3	7.9
Western Europe	10.1	6.0	8.5	11.2	8.1	−5.9	12.6	5.0	5.5	6.8	0.8	2.8	1.1	2.9	7.6	5.1	2.0	4.1	5.6	7.4	3.9
Southern Europe[a]	17.5	12.6	15.9	14.7	3.9	−1.9	14.2	6.7	12.0	8.4	7.8	7.5	12.9	7.1	17.6	6.6	−3.3	12.4	1.7	12.2	8.3
Japan	15.8	18.3	6.4	6.8	20.5	−0.2	21.1	8.6	0.7	0.2	17.1	10.7	−2.3	8.7	15.8	4.9	−0.6	0.4	4.4	5.0	5.6
Developing economies[b]	9.6	7.0	12.1	8.3	1.5	−8.7	13.9	2.6	0.6	5.1	−9.0	−5.5	−6.9	1.7	6.9	0.5	8.3	11.9	11.4	6.9	3.7
Oil-exporting countries[c]	18.1	10.2	4.6	8.9	2.1	−14.0	13.4	0.4	−4.2	2.8	−15.8	−13.9	−14.1	−4.7	—	−3.8	11.9	3.2	13.7	8.1	4.1
Non-oil-exporting countries	5.0	4.9	17.0	8.0	0.3	—	14.6	5.1	6.3	9.3	2.1	4.7	0.2	6.7	11.6	3.2	7.2	15.2	10.7	6.5	3.5
Eastern Europe and the Soviet Union	7.8	5.3	6.1	12.3	4.4	4.4	8.3	9.5	4.8	3.8	2.3	2.3	4.9	5.5	4.6	−1.0	4.4	2.4	4.3	−0.9	−11.6
Eastern Europe[d]	10.7	8.6	11.0	9.3	7.0	7.0	7.9	8.0	6.7	7.9	3.1	2.7	5.3	8.0	7.0	2.5	−1.2	1.4	3.6	−1.9	−7.9
Soviet Union	6.1	3.2	2.7	14.4	2.6	2.5	8.6	10.6	3.4	0.6	1.6	1.9	4.5	3.3	2.5	−4.3	10.0	3.3	4.8	—	−13.1
TOTAL	10.0	5.9	9.4	12.1	6.2	−5.0	11.8	4.3	4.9	5.8	0.7	0.2	−3.0	2.3	8.5	2.7	3.4	7.0	8.6	6.7	3.8
Imports																					
Developed market economies	9.9	5.5	10.7	11.9	0.8	−7.7	14.8	4.0	6.2	7.3	−1.7	−1.9	−0.8	4.7	11.8	5.9	7.3	7.2	7.7	7.3	5.1
North America	2.0	9.0	14.1	6.9	1.0	−10.5	18.5	8.5	8.8	2.2	−6.8	2.6	−7.5	10.5	23.2	9.0	10.1	3.3	5.7	5.6	2.9
Western Europe	12.2	4.7	8.3	11.1	1.0	−5.8	14.4	1.7	5.1	9.5	1.0	−4.6	1.9	2.7	6.4	5.1	5.6	6.8	7.0	7.2	5.6
Southern Europe[a]	17.4	11.1	12.4	12.6	2.8	0.7	11.1	8.9	−0.1	5.7	6.9	6.1	7.9	3.4	10.6	6.4	—	38.5	9.5	16.1	11.0
Japan	18.7	−0.4	13.9	30.6	−0.7	−12.2	8.9	2.5	6.6	11.4	−5.1	−2.2	−0.6	1.2	10.5	—	10.5	9.0	16.6	8.3	5.8
Developing market economies[b]	8.8	8.8	3.9	14.0	18.4	6.5	5.7	10.9	6.3	2.0	9.3	8.0	−4.3	−3.3	2.4	−0.3	−2.6	6.8	11.6	8.0	3.0
Oil-exporting countries[c]	6.6	11.5	13.4	18.5	26.8	45.2	23.6	22.4	0.3	−10.2	17.2	22.7	−1.8	−12.6	−7.9	−9.9	−20.3	−5.5	8.3	5.0	2.7
Non-oil-exporting countries	9.2	8.4	2.3	13.0	16.8	−1.6	0.7	6.9	8.8	6.4	6.8	2.2	−5.0	1.5	6.9	3.3	4.1	10.3	12.4	8.7	3.1
Eastern Europe and the Soviet Union	11.4	6.8	11.8	13.2	7.9	8.5	6.8	3.4	8.4	2.0	3.9	0.4	1.7	4.0	4.1	5.3	−0.6	1.0	3.6	5.0	−5.1
Eastern Europe[d]	14.0	7.5	8.2	12.1	13.0	4.3	6.7	5.2	5.0	2.7	1.3	−4.3	−5.3	4.0	3.9	5.8	4.8	3.4	3.3	1.2	−8.6
Soviet Union	7.8	5.9	17.2	14.6	1.0	14.8	7.0	0.9	13.3	1.1	7.5	6.4	9.7	4.0	4.4	4.7	−6.0	−1.6	4.0	9.3	−1.4
TOTAL	9.7	6.4	9.2	12.5	5.3	−3.5	12.2	5.5	6.3	5.8	1.1	0.5	−1.5	2.8	9.2	4.4	4.5	6.7	8.3	7.3	4.0

[a] Includes Economic Commission for Europe (ECE), OECD or World Bank estimates for certain subperiods for Portugal, Turkey and Yugoslavia.
[b] IMF definitions for developing countries.
[c] IMF definition covering Algeria, Indonesia, the Islamic Republic of Iran, Iraq, Kuwait, Libyan Arab Jamahiriya, Nigeria, Qatar, Saudi Arabia, the United Arab Emirates and Venezuela.
[d] Excludes Yugoslavia.

Sources: IMF, *International Financial Statistics*, February 1992 for the developed market economies; IMF, *IFS Supplement on Trade Statistics* (Supplement Series No. 15) and *World Economic Outlook*, May 1991 for developing countries; ECE secretariat calculations, based on national sources for Southern Europe and the East European economies. *Note:* for market economies and Eastern Europe, weights for aggregations are US dollar trade shares in 1985.

Table 1.2 World trade: value by region, 1970–90 ($ billion).

	1970	1971	1972	1973	1974	1975	1976	1977	1978	1979	1980	1981	1982	1983	1984	1985	1986	1987	1988	1989	1990
Exports																					
Developed market economies	215.1	240.8	286.6	390.1	525.1	560.1	623.2	707.6	849.1	1042.2	1228.7	1210.1	1145.9	1132.9	1208.9	1251.1	1463.2	1710.9	1953.9	2089.9	2414.6
North America	59.4	61.9	70.4	97.3	133.9	142.9	157.4	166.7	194.3	244.7	293.3	311.4	287.7	282.4	314.2	309.8	317.5	352.3	439.0	484.1	520.2
Western Europe[a]	131.9	149.4	180.3	246.0	322.7	348.0	383.4	443.1	535.4	667.4	771.5	713.7	685.1	669.1	684.3	721.8	887.4	1067.1	1181.6	1255.5	1513.7
Southern Europe[b]	4.6	5.4	6.9	9.8	12.9	13.3	15.1	16.7	21.2	27.8	33.4	33.4	34.7	34.5	40.7	42.4	47.6	60.2	68.4	76.5	93.1
Japan	19.3	24.1	29.1	37.0	55.5	55.8	67.3	81.1	98.2	102.3	130.4	151.5	138.4	147.0	169.7	177.2	210.8	231.3	264.9	273.9	287.6
Developing market economies	55.3	64.2	75.6	113.3	238.3	221.9	265.8	300.0	317.5	457.4	583.3	438.4	471.6	448.4	403.4	509.6	586.1	652.9	717.6	737.5	803.1
Oil-exporting countries[c]	17.4	22.6	26.3	40.2	131.3	120.8	146.5	159.3	155.6	236.4	300.8	178.8	173.1	154.8	100.9	121.2	120.6	148.5	177.6	158.6	178.1
Non-oil-exporting countries	38.0	41.6	49.3	73.1	106.9	101.1	119.3	140.7	161.9	221.0	282.5	259.6	298.5	293.6	302.5	388.4	465.5	504.4	540.0	578.9	625.0
Eastern Europe and the Soviet Union	32.6	35.5	42.2	55.6	71.5	87.0	71.2	82.5	92.3	111.9	128.0	132.3	135.9	134.1	134.4	131.5	137.5	143.8	144.0	142.8	138.2
Eastern Europe[d]	19.8	21.7	26.8	34.3	43.0	51.8	42.0	46.9	52.4	62.0	70.0	71.9	71.7	70.5	72.0	74.2	77.4	80.4	82.0	80.5	79.1
Soviet Union	12.8	13.8	15.4	21.4	28.5	35.2	29.2	35.5	39.8	49.9	57.9	60.4	64.2	63.6	62.4	57.3	60.0	63.4	62.0	62.3	59.1
TOTAL	303.1	340.5	404.4	559.1	834.9	869.0	960.2	1090.1	1258.9	1611.5	1939.9	1780.8	1753.3	1715.5	1746.6	1892.3	2186.8	2507.5	2815.4	2970.2	3355.9
Imports																					
Developed market economies	224.6	249.5	299.0	410.1	585.6	589.0	679.7	770.1	888.6	1140.4	1368.9	1296.0	1215.4	1199.3	1310.4	1344.7	1523.3	1805.5	2037.9	2199.5	2540.3
North America	56.6	64.8	78.9	97.9	145.1	142.0	172.7	202.5	232.3	278.9	319.5	343.4	313.0	334.7	424.2	433.1	467.8	517.0	572.3	612.7	639.0
Western Europe[a]	139.8	154.8	183.3	255.5	350.4	359.0	409.2	461.0	540.0	705.0	846.3	750.1	711.0	682.1	693.2	722.0	860.9	1047.0	1173.2	1254.6	1510.9
Southern Europe[b]	9.2	10.1	12.9	18.2	28.1	30.2	32.9	35.2	36.4	46.7	61.8	59.6	59.9	56.1	56.9	59.1	67.1	90.4	105.1	122.5	155.1
Japan	18.9	19.8	23.9	38.4	61.9	57.9	64.9	71.3	79.9	109.8	141.3	142.9	131.5	126.4	136.2	130.5	127.6	151.0	187.4	209.7	235.4
Developing market economies	55.6	63.0	68.3	95.5	156.6	181.0	194.1	233.0	280.5	343.9	456.1	515.2	475.9	447.8	450.2	423.0	413.8	457.1	553.4	601.6	674.5
Oil-exporting countries[c]	8.9	10.5	13.2	19.1	30.9	50.9	63.1	83.9	94.7	98.0	131.5	158.1	160.4	142.3	126.0	105.1	91.8	91.1	104.1	99.0	113.5
Non-oil-exporting countries	46.7	52.6	55.2	76.4	125.8	130.1	130.9	149.1	185.8	245.8	324.6	357.1	315.5	305.5	324.2	317.9	322.0	365.9	449.3	502.5	561.0
Eastern Europe and the Soviet Union	33.1	36.0	43.6	58.0	77.4	100.2	81.3	89.3	101.5	117.8	133.4	134.8	127.1	122.0	120.7	125.2	132.7	132.8	135.9	143.1	148.9
Eastern Europe[d]	21.3	23.5	27.5	37.0	51.4	61.4	50.6	57.1	63.0	73.4	81.2	77.9	70.0	66.7	66.7	70.5	72.7	79.0	77.8	78.1	84.0
Soviet Union	11.7	12.5	16.1	21.0	25.9	38.8	30.8	32.2	38.5	44.4	52.2	56.9	57.1	55.4	53.9	54.8	55.0	53.8	58.0	65.0	65.0
TOTAL	313.2	348.5	410.9	563.6	819.6	870.3	955.1	1092.4	1270.6	1602.0	1958.5	1945.9	1818.4	1769.2	1881.3	1892.9	2069.8	2395.4	2727.2	2944.1	3363.6

[a] Austria, Belgium-Luxembourg, Denmark, Finland, France, the Federal Republic of Germany, Ireland, Italy, the Netherlands, Norway, Sweden, Switzerland and the United Kingdom.
[b] Greece, Portugal, Spain and Turkey.
[c] IMF definition covering Algeria, Indonesia, the Islamic Republic of Iran, Iraq, Kuwait, Libyan Arab Jamahiriya, Nigeria, Qatar, Saudi Arabia, the United Arab Emirates and Venezuela.
[d] Including Yugoslavia.

Sources: IMF, *International Financial Statistics*, February 1992 and ECE secretariat calculations, based on national publications for the countries of Eastern Europe and the Soviet Union, using consistent rouble/dollar crossrates for recalculation of trade flows denominated in transferable roubles.

a marked impact on global savings. The capital sums involved (excluding the former Soviet Union) over the next few years could be as high as £80 billion.

Dominating many company executives' thoughts since the peoples' revolutions of 1989 is Central and Eastern Europe, and the rapidly changing prospects these regions now offer. It is too early, and events are moving too fast, for companies to have made significant changes to their structures to allow them to develop the new opportunities opening up. However, the extension of the definition of 'the European market' eastward needs to be kept in mind when formulating a corporate view of Europe. The unification of East Germany with West, alongside the growing links with countries like Poland, the Czech and Slovak republics and Hungary could begin to shift the centre of European economic gravity eastward. As a result, Brussels may lose some of its popularity to Vienna or Berlin as a base for a European regional presence.

Demographic shifts

Most industrialized countries are facing the same trends:

- The decline in the number of young people;
- The rise of the over 55s – the single fastest-growing age group in most industrialized countries is 50–54;
- The slowing of population growth as a whole.

For example, the EC is projected to grow in terms of population by only 4% to the year 2020. That compares to 18% for Africa and 58% for Asia. While the undeveloped world suffers higher infant mortality rates and life expectancies are shorter, the sheer size of its population will have a major effect on global balance (Tables 1.3 and 1.4).

In terms of marketing opportunity, of course, numbers have little significance on their own. Less tangible factors like lifestyles and attitudes have to be incorporated into strategic plans. However, the fact that by the year 2000 India, with its rapidly growing middle class sector of the population, could contain 100 million consumers for goods and services beyond essentials cannot be ignored. The best opportunities will probably be in those countries which combine both high population plus high income growth, notably in the Asia–Pacific regions.

A dramatic shift in age groups is underlined by projections for Europe. The 1989 Eurostat age pyramid looks very different from that of 1960 (Figure 1.1). The 1960 pyramid shows both the baby boom years of 1946–60, and the effect of two world wars. The 1989 pyramid highlights the sharp drop in the birth rate which began in the mid-1960s and speeded up in the mid-1970s. The demographic trends are projected up to 2020 (Figure 1.2). According to Eurostat, only three-quarters of the number of children that would be needed to replace the present generation are actually being born.

Table 1.3 Population of the major regions of the world, 1950–2020 (million)[a].

	1950	% of total	1970	% of total	1988	% of total	2000	% of total	2020	% of total
Europe	393	16	460	12	496	10	509	8	514	6
of which: EC 12	260	10	303	8	324	6	332	5	323	4
USSR	180	7	243	7	283	6	308	5	343	4
USA	152	6	205	6	246	5	266	4	295	4
Latin America	165	7	285	8	430	8	540	9	719	9
Africa	224	9	363	10	610	12	872	14	1,441	18
Asia	1,376	55	2,101	57	2,996	59	3,698	59	4,680	58
of which: Japan	84	3	107	3	122	2	129	2	130	2
China	555	22	804	22	1,089	21	1,286	21	1,460	18
India	358	14	555	15	797	16	1,043	17	1,375	17
Oceania	13	1	19	1	26	1	30	0	37	0
WORLD	2,516	100	3,698	100	5,112	100	6,251	100	8,062	100

[a] According to United Nations' geographic definition.
Source: Eurostat.

What companies need to come to terms with is the effect of these age bulges on their goods and services. Older populations tend to have higher discretionary incomes, are mainly house owners, and are people who will not only have the freedom to spend, but the freedom to withhold that spending until they get what they want.

The European statistics also illustrate other demographic trends in the industrialized world, including the change in the proportion of females to males (Table 1.5), the increase in one-parent households (Joseph Rowntree Foundation, 1993), and the inexorable decline in marriage, despite a slight rise in 1988 (Figure 1.3). This has implications not just for marketing strategy, but for human resources planning as well. For instance, while the number of

Table 1.4 Main demographic indicators, 1985–90[a].

	Births '000	Natural increase	%<15	%>65	Life expectancy Males	Females	Total fertility	Infant mortality	Population
Europe	6,426	1,117	20	13	70.9	77.6	1.74	13	97
of which: EC 12	3,874	643	19	14	72.0	78.6	1.60	9	144
USSR	5,198	2,209	26	10	65.0	74.2	2.38	24	8
USA	3,687	1,900	22	13	71.9	79.0	1.83	10	16
Latin America	12,372	8,890	36	5	63.4	68.8	3.61	56	8
Africa	26,936	18,015	45	3	50.3	53.6	6.23	106	7
Asia	81,984	54,850	33	5	60.9	62.6	3.45	73	50
of which: Japan	1,393	541	19	12	75.4	81.1	1.70	5	221
China	22,507	15,195	26	6	68.0	70.9	2.36	32	58
India	25,999	16,838	37	4	57.8	57.9	4.30	99	109
Oceania	513	308	27	9	66.4	71.3	2.57	26	3
WORLD	137,488	87,666	33	6	60.0	63.0	3.44	71	19

[a] According to United Nations' geographic definition.
Source: Eurostat.

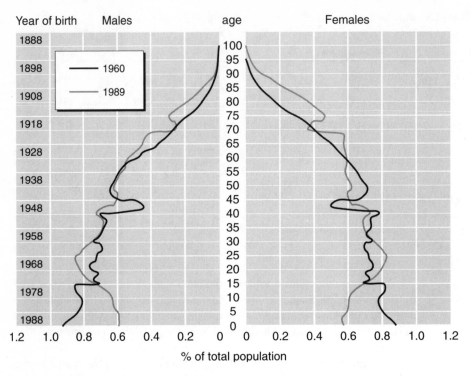

Figure 1.1   Age pyramid for the EC, 1960 and 1989 (estimated). *Source:* Eurostat.

Table 1.5   Proportion of males to females in the EC, 1995–2020 (% of age group).

	1995	*2000*	*2010*	*2020*
Age group				
0–19				
Males	25.4	24.8	23.5	21.8
Females	22.9	22.5	21.4	19.7
20–39				
Males	31.4	30.1	26.1	25.2
Females	29.1	27.8	23.8	23.1
40–59				
Males	25.4	26.4	29.7	29.4
Females	24.4	25.5	28.6	28.0
60+				
Males	17.8	18.7	20.8	23.6
Females	23.6	24.2	26.3	29.2
of which 75+				
Males	–	–	6.0	6.6
Females	–	–	10.1	10.7

Source: Eurostat.

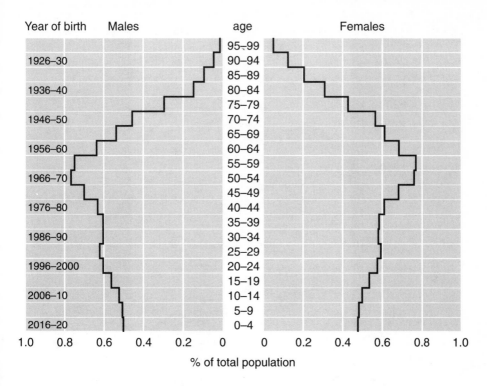

Figure 1.2   Age pyramid for the EC, 1926–2020. *Source:* Eurostat.

Brazil's 15–24 year olds has increased by 12% in five years to 1986, the number of what was West Germany's 15–24 year olds has declined so fast that German electronics conglomerate Siemens has predicted that if current trends continue it will need to hire the entire output of the country's engineering graduates – although these shortages could be somewhat alleviated by access to skilled East German engineers.

Table 1.6   Population of Eastern Europe, 1988.

Country	Total population (million)	Aged under 15 (%)
Bulgaria	9.0	22
Czechoslovakia	15.6	24
East Germany	16.7	19
Hungary	10.6	22
Poland	37.8	25
Romania	22.9	25
Yugoslavia	23.4	25
USSR	284.0	26

Source: EuroBusiness.

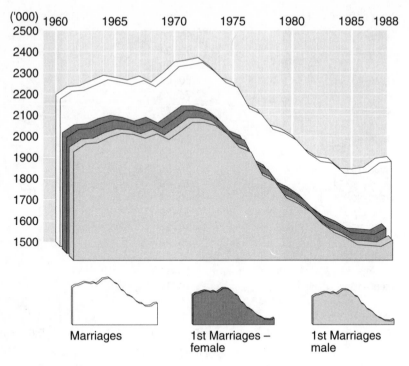

Figure 1.3   Number of marriages in the EC, 1960–88. *Source:* Eurostat.

Indeed, over the long term Eastern Europe could be a source both of a skilled workforce and new consumers, although the lack of an infrastructure demands that companies move very cautiously. As Table 1.6 shows, by the mid-1990s there could be a substantial pool of people in their 20s. There is also likely to be a foreshortening of the classical market evolution from essentials to conveniences to luxuries. The prevalence of Western media and the brand-hunger of a population fed on a diet of blandness and greyness will mean that, as discretionary incomes rise, so too will a demand for the best products and services.

Environmental and ethical concerns

The tremendous upsurge in environmental consciousness is a major social force that will not go away. Any marketing strategist worth his or her salt will make sure the company at least hears and acts on the environmental message.

Widespread environmentalism means not just a 'clean' product, but a change in attitudes. It turns the spotlight on basic issues such as energy, transport, waste products, raw materials and methods of production. The 'green' bandwagon was at first dismissed as a fad, sparked off by amongst other issues the discovery of a hole in the ozone layer, the destruction of part of the Alaskan coastline by the spillage of 11 million gallons of oil from the Exxon oil tanker, the *Valdez*, animal testing, food scares, and the destruction of the Amazonian rain forest. These increasingly global concerns are not just a reaction against 'consumerism', but a fundamental questioning of methods of industrial production, energy consumption and chemical use.

> 'It is possible that with all these enormous changes (in population, use of fossil fuel) concentrated into such a short period of time, we have unwittingly begun a massive experiment with the system of this planet itself.'

A quotation from a green manifesto? No – it is from a speech given by the former UK prime minister, Margaret Thatcher, to the Royal Society in 1988.

In Europe, the EC is formulating a number of measures to deal with the environment, including taxes on air and water polluters and a labelling scheme based on the German 'Blue Angel' system which is given to products which fulfil tough standards of environmental friendliness. Mandatory environmental auditing, packaging and recycling are also not far off.

Companies should not neglect the opportunities: the head of the UK Confederation of British Industry (CBI)'s Environmental Health and Safety Group has estimated that there could be a potential world-wide market of £100–£150 billion for environmentally friendly products and technologies. But there is far more to it than that: companies that are branded as consistent polluters, or environmental enemies, whether in products or processes, will start to see the effect not only on their bottom line, but in their ability to recruit staff.

Some companies have gone well beyond the stage of spouting green aphorisms. Chemicals giant ICI, for instance, has committed itself to spending £1 billion over the next five years to reduce its output of harmful wastes by at least 50%. And it has gone one step further by linking managers' pay to how well they meet environmental performance targets, following the example of Exxon which set up an environmental evaluation system after its oil spill disaster.

The Swedish experience demonstrates how foresight, combined with a social conscience, can work through to real competitive advantage. Sweden's environmental laws are among the toughest in the world; many of its industries are well along the path of cleaning up their act. Almost 7% of total corporate investment is for environmental protection, while the Swedish paper and pulp industry is reckoned to be the world leader in its sector in dealing with pollution. As the head of Sweden's third biggest forestry company has pointed out, it is natural to improve the production process from an environmental point of view in order to gain competitive advantage in the future.

Other countries lag well behind. A recent report by DRT Ross Europe Services on European managers' attitudes to environmental issues in the chemical, heavy engineering and consumer goods industries showed that, generally speaking, the British, French and Belgians were far behind the Germans, Dutch and Danes in areas like managerial responsibility (having a board member responsible for environmental issues), product strategy and setting standards for their suppliers.

Environmental concern among the public at large is at different stages of development in different countries. The first stage is usually awareness, accompanied by the feeling that it has little to do with individual actions. That then grows into a desire to see 'something' done by governments, institutions and companies. In the final stage 'greenness' becomes personalized and consumers demand products that really do make a difference. The lead time between these stages is now shortening. What took four years in Germany, say, could happen far more rapidly in less developed countries, for example Spain and Portugal, and in Eastern Europe, where pollution is a monumental problem.

This should also be put into the wider context of corporate behaviour as a whole. Questions of morality, of how companies act in the broadest sense, are slowly beginning to have an impact on how people view products and services of all sorts. An unprecedented amount of information means that corporate audiences are both larger and smarter. Companies have to justify their actions not only to shareholders but to employees, customers, the communities in which they operate and governments. And this spreads beyond their environmental policies to how they treat their employees, the companies' activities in the Third World, community involvement and, with sensitive products like alcohol and tobacco, how serious they are about discussing the potential dangers.

Technological change

The impact of new discoveries can be almost impossible to foresee or predict. Quantum leaps can occur, but there are signposts along the way that might give some clues to developments in areas like electronics, biotechnology and medicine which might affect the company. It might appear enough to keep abreast of developments in IT, or innovation in a company's own sector, but what might seem inapplicable technological discoveries could have a real and unforeseen impact on a business.

For example, what would happen to the detergents markets if ultrasonic washing machines which only need water to clean clothes become a reality? If laser surgery becomes sophisticated enough to repair defective eyesight permanently would the contacts lens industry disappear? What about cameras that don't need film, or the impact on computers of biochips? Remember the classic story of the drill manufacturer who thought he made drills, until laser technology showed him his product was really holes.

Getting to grips with technology is not just a matter of keeping a close watch on R&D efforts, however. Not only are global communications blurring the old boundaries between markets, but IT is dramatically changing how goods and services are actually created and delivered. As Regis McKenna (1991), the well-known Silicon Valley venture capitalist, has argued,

> 'So pervasive is technology today that it is virtually meaningless to make distinctions between technology and non-technology businesses and industries: there are *only* technology companies. Technology has moved into products, the workplace and the marketplace with astonishing speed and thoroughness. Seventy years after they were invented, fractional horsepower motors are in some 15 to 20 household products in the average American home today. In less than 20 years, the microprocessor has achieved a similar penetration.'

Asia and Japan as an economic force

'What the chairmen of Ford and IBM are really worrying about is the Japanese.' That remark, overheard on a flight from London to Paris, highlights one of the major preoccupations of the West, one that can neither be shrugged off nor ignored: the economic power of the Pacific Rim countries, with Japan as its centre.

The question is will it be an unavoidable threat or an exciting opportunity in the 1990s? To which the answer is 'both'. While some of the countries in the region are less well developed, or having a hard time economically in the short term, the potential power of the region, powered by Japan as the economic engine, has to be reckoned with (Table 1.7), not just as a viable location for low-cost manufacturing or raw materials, but as a source of new markets and new capital. In 1988, for example, Taiwan, once a key target for assembly operations, was the second largest investor, after Japan, in mainland China, Thailand and Malaysia, and the largest in the Philippines. Average Asian personal consumption is estimated to be growing at 5–10% a year.

The Japanese continue to hold the centre stage. They have conquered the world in such industries as ships, steel, cars (the Japanese have between 20 and 30% of the US car market), microelectronics and consumer electronics. They are rapidly adding investment in the West to exports. Now, however, they are trying to come to terms with the less tangible concept of added value. While they have set world standards in quality of design, of manufacturing and of service – ironically, based on ideas imported several decades ago from the US –

Table 1.7   GDP growth in South-East Asia, 1989–94 (real % change).

(Real % change)	1989[a]	1990[b]	1991[c]	1992[c]	1993[c]	1994[c]
Australia	4.1	1.7	1.9	3.1	3.2	3.1
China[d]	3.5	3.0	2.9	4.7	6.4	7.2
Hong Kong	2.5	1.8	4.7	6.3	3.9	2.7
India	6.3	6.4	5.9	6.0	5.3	5.2
Indonesia	6.0	5.4	5.5	6.1	5.5	5.1
Japan[e]	4.9	4.3	4.0	4.3	3.8	3.5
Malaysia	8.5	6.7	7.0	7.5	7.0	6.5
Pakistan	5.6	5.1	5.3	5.5	5.4	5.2
Philippines	6.0	4.8	5.5	5.7	5.5	5.0
Singapore	9.2	6.3	6.5	7.3	6.6	5.9
South Korea	6.1	5.7	7.1	7.4	7.1	7.1
Sri Lanka	2.3	5.1	6.1	7.1	6.8	6.5
Taiwan	7.4	7.3	6.5	7.0	6.5	7.0
Thailand	12.4	9.0	8.0	7.9	7.6	7.5

[a] Actual.
[b] Estimates.
[c] Forecasts.
[d] NMP (net material product).
[e] GNP.

Source: Business International.

they are now struggling to come to grips with the idea of local nuances and of branding, not just offering clever options and features.

Dealing with the less tangible issues of Western consumer needs and wants is new to the Japanese and will not be easy for them. But Western consumer goods companies cannot afford to underestimate their long-term intentions and determination (nor their huge corporate asset base). As Miles Colebrook, chief operating officer of J. Walter Thompson noted, 'The Japanese will plug, plug and plug away. If it doesn't work in three years, then they will start again.' Remember, he warned, that the world press laughed at Honda when it first entered grand prix racing in the 1960s. Now it is a dominant force.

Cosmetics is a good example. Shisheido, one of the major Japanese cosmetics companies with (mainly) home sales of £1.75 billion, is pouring massive resources into both R&D and promotion to get market share in Europe. It already claims 10% of the Italian market, while it is building a factory in France to gain a more permanent foothold. It is following the same pattern as its counterparts in cars and consumer electronics: using the muscle built up in the huge home market sales to power the push abroad.

Kao, the Japanese company often compared to Procter & Gamble, is following a similar strategy with household products. One of the reasons Kao bought US hand lotion maker Jergens was to get at its distribution channels as a way to grab market share. If the latest thesis from Michael Porter of Harvard Business School (Porter, 1990) on the importance of national comparative advantage in attaining international success is correct, few Western sectors can afford to be complacent.

The Japanese are not, of course, unbeatable. Doggedness, determination, a well-thought-out strategy and a deep pocket can take the battle to Japan's domestic market. Coca-Cola has done it by painstakingly setting up a massive distribution system, after accepted wisdom said it would not work. It is now number one in the soft drinks market. Kodak is another well-documented case study. Having been walloped by Japanese rival Fuji in its American and European market, it returned to Japan in 1984, spending $500 million in the process. Its patience and persistence has been rewarded with sales of well over $1 billion. And with the Japanese love of Western brands, some Western retailers have penetrated the market, from the globally active Toys-R-Us to upmarket menswear designer Paul Smith.

What the Japanese do have is a view that says a product or service can always be improved. This is almost a self-driven quality that makes them compete against themselves and their own standards. Toshiba and its move into laptop computers is a notable example of this. Between 1986 and 1990 it had produced over 30 models in order to explore all possible market segments and iron out any product problems. By 1991, it had discontinued more laptop models than some of its slower competitors had launched.

Another Japanese strength is the huge capital base that can be exploited to make a string of investments in other Western countries in their bid not to get locked out of the other trade blocs. That investment is no longer just in assembly plants either. Eisai, a major Japanese pharmaceutical company, is investing £50 million over the next 15 years to build and run a new pharmaceutical research laboratory at University College, London. In another industry, several major Hollywood studios are in the hands of Japanese firms which will allow them to use film as 'software' for their hardware. While acceleration of such ventures could attract more Western criticism and fear, on their part the Japanese will have to prove they can profitably manage the Western mentality and cultural diversity.

Japan also faces problems at home, including an ageing population, an increased interest in leisure among younger Japanese coupled with a demand for improvement in the quality of life, a growing disenchantment with the workings of the political system and more competition from its Pacific neighbours.

Europe as a Single Market

The date '1992' has become as much a source of boredom as symbol of momentous change. That should not obscure what is going to be one of the most exciting – and daunting – business challenges of the next 10–20 years. How can companies prepare for a market of such size and yet such diversity? The boundaries, currently defined by the 12 EC members, will, over time, stretch to the European Free Trade Association (EFTA) countries (who will inevitably be sucked into the Single Market sphere) and ultimately, Eastern

Table 1.8 EC: total consumer spending, 1979–94 (Ecu billion).

	1979	1984	1989	1990	1991	1992	1993	1994
Belgium	48.2	65.0	88.1	94.8	100.3	105.3	111.1	117.1
Denmark	25.6	37.2	49.4	51.9	53.9	56.3	58.8	60.9
France	234.1	382.8	515.7	551.0	575.0	608.4	642.8	676.4
(West) Germany	297.0	446.9	583.2	634.5	685.5	738.0	791.2	843.2
Greece	16.9	27.7	33.2	36.0	39.0	41.5	44.3	46.8
Ireland	7.3	13.2	17.3	18.9	20.3	21.7	23.0	24.6
Italy	158.3	326.9	486.4	526.8	557.1	599.1	651.8	696.0
Luxembourg	1.7	2.5	3.4	3.7	3.9	4.1	4.4	4.6
Netherlands	66.4	93.5	120.8	129.4	137.8	145.7	154.3	163.8
Portugal	9.5	17.2	26.3	28.9	32.1	35.2	38.5	41.8
Spain	88.9	129.0	215.0	235.2	255.5	269.0	289.9	308.4
UK	175.6	335.2	483.4	482.8	505.6	541.1	583.2	626.8
TOTAL	1,129.7	1,877.7	2,622.2	2,793.8	2,966.0	3,165.4	3,393.4	3,610.3

Source: Economist Intelligence Unit (EIU).

Europe. Management guru Peter Drucker believes that Europe will gradually become the world's leading economic power, not only because of its size and affluence but also because of its political power and market dynamics.

According to one report by The Economist Intelligence Unit (EIU, 1990), the EC consumer market, excluding the former East Germany, will be worth Ecu 3600 billion ($4730 billion) by 1994 (Table 1.8). Including the contribution from the former East Germany, this could mean that the total market by then will be almost as big as that of the US. But that market will be a multitude of different segments in different product areas at different stages of development (Tables 1.9 and 1.10).

The EIU report predicts that housing and leisure will be key areas of growth, while the decline of overall spending on food will be matched by rising demand for luxury and convenience foods. The latter will become more important as more mothers are enticed back to work. That will be accompanied by a growing demand for products that are of high quality, individualistic and reflect environmental concerns.

The big puzzle will be to find the right organization to profit from such a large but fragmented area, and knowing when to harmonize and when to exploit the differences. The internal market programme is probably the least important of the reasons for the current restructuring activity among companies. Crucial differences will persist for several decades. A more simple stimulus is the growing realization that an effective approach to European markets is not just a vital prerequisite of corporate health: it can provide the key to powerful competitive advantage. And lessons learned in Europe can be applied elsewhere.

The combined impact of the EC's decision to remove the remaining non-tariff barriers to free trade and competition within the Community may be summarized as follows:

- The gradual harmonization of standards will increase the quantity and range of products sold across national boundaries. Companies are therefore

Table 1.9   EC: breakdown of private consumption by main categories, 1990–94 (% of total based on 1990 price Ecu equivalent).

	1990	1991	1992	1993	1994
Food	17.5	17.3	17.2	16.9	16.7
Non-alcoholic beverages	0.5	0.5	0.5	0.5	0.5
Alcoholic beverages	1.3	1.3	1.3	1.2	1.2
Tobacco	1.8	1.7	1.7	1.6	1.6
Clothing and footwear	7.6	7.5	7.4	7.4	7.3
Housing	13.8	13.9	14.0	14.0	14.1
Energy	3.8	3.7	3.7	3.6	3.6
Furniture and equipment	6.2	6.3	6.3	6.3	6.3
Household operation	2.0	2.0	2.0	2.0	2.0
Health	5.4	5.5	5.6	5.6	5.7
Leisure and education	8.6	8.6	8.7	8.7	8.8
Personal transport	5.0	4.8	4.9	5.0	5.1
Hotels and catering	7.4	7.4	7.5	7.5	7.5
Personal care	2.0	2.0	2.1	2.1	2.1
Other	17.2	17.4	17.4	17.5	17.6
TOTAL	100.0	100.0	100.0	100.0	100.0

Source: Economist Intelligence Unit (EIU).

rationalizing their production between, typically, two or three plants covering the whole region in order to take advantage of the new economies of scale possible. Company subsidiaries that once controlled their own manufacturing now have to draw their products from a central source. This means a new degree of coordination with fellow subsidiaries.

- The physical distribution of goods is being concentrated on a few central warehouses, with major implications for internal systems.

Table 1.10   EC: consumer spending by main sector, 1990–94 (Ecu billion; 1990 prices).

	1990	1991	1992	1993	1994
Food	489	515	543	574	603
Non-alcoholic beverages	13	14	15	16	17
Alcoholic beverages	37	38	40	42	43
Tobacco	49	51	53	55	57
Clothing and footwear	212	223	236	251	265
Housing	386	412	442	475	508
Energy	105	110	116	123	129
Furniture and equipment	174	186	199	214	229
Household operation	57	60	64	68	73
Health	151	163	176	190	205
Leisure and education	240	256	275	296	317
Personal transport	138	143	155	170	182
Hotels and catering	208	221	237	255	272
Personal care	57	60	65	70	73
Other	481	515	552	594	634
TOTAL	2,794	2,966	3,165	3,393	3,610

Source: Economist Intelligence Unit (EIU).

- Companies are putting resources behind products and brands that have international status or potential as well as having to find methods of accommodating both international and local brands.

In addition, issues such as differential pricing will place new demands on companies. For example, Ecosystem is a French auto dealer that specializes in buying vehicles for domestic customers in the cheapest European market. Wide discrepancies exist between France, Belgium, Denmark, Germany and so on, which manufacturers explain away by the need to conform to different national technical standards. Peugeot has been typical in trying to keep its markets segregated, and in May 1989 instructed its agents in Belgium and Luxembourg not to supply Ecosystem. The European Commission, however, insisted that Peugeot supply Ecosystem with up to 1200 autos a year (Ecosystem's purchase volume before the ban) pending a detailed investigation. Pressure on the manufacturers is expected to increase.

A growing number of companies are responding to the challenge of the European market so far with an accelerated pace of acquisitions and alliances in a search not only for scale, but, in consumer goods, for local brand names and distribution networks. Figures show that European cross-border transactions more than doubled in 1990 from £15 billion to £32.2 billion. Japan has quadrupled investment in Europe in the last year or so, while the stock of direct investment by the US almost trebled between 1977 and 1988 to $126 billion. That is matched, however, by direct investment by EC companies in the US, which soared in the same period from $19 billion to $194 billion.

While some European industries, like chemicals and consumer electronics, are concentrating on core industries and shedding peripheral interests, others, notably Daimler-Benz and BMW, are meeting the challenge of the Single Market by diversification into other areas. Europe is most likely to follow the general pattern of markets and support only a certain number of big groups, with a number of energetic and innovative niche players. Those European middle-sized companies still anchored in their national markets could be most at risk and be squeezed out since they will not have the advantage of size or flexibility.

This trend to fewer but bigger groups on a European-wide scale is already notable in several industries, including food, cars and media. Even retailers are showing distinct signs of internationalization and concentration.

Food

Three groups are becoming dominant: Swiss-based Nestlé, Anglo–Dutch Unilever and French-based BSN, though US conglomerate Philip Morris, since its purchases of Swiss coffee and confectionery group Jacob Suchard on top of the acquisitions of General Foods and Kraft in the US, is making a powerful bid for a strong European market presence.

Cars

Volume car makers are scrambling to make acquisitions or forming strategic alliances to get to critical mass, push down the cost base and be able to sport a full model range. Volvo/Renault is one of the more recent alliances, while Ford and General Motors have acquired Jaguar and Saab respectively. Fiat is fast forming alliances with car companies in what was the Eastern bloc, as is VW–Audi.

Retail

The retailers, both non-food and food – the latter of which has in the past been one of the most domestic of industries – are moving inexorably along the path of internationalization, employing a combination of investment, organic growth and buying alliances (Table 1.11). European food retailers, to the consternation of food manufacturers, have been particularly busy on both the European and world stage. It has been estimated that foreign ownership could account for a quarter of the US food retailing industry, while throughout the 1980s Spain and Italy have both proved attractive because of the potential for expansion (Table 1.12).

This reflects what has already begun to occur at a national level in some countries; in the UK, for instance, the top five retail chains account for 50–80% of the major food manufacturers' business. That, plus the increasing sophistication of own-label products, has put heavy pressure on margins and has often meant the elimination of brands that stand in third and fourth place. Yet another development to worry suppliers is the determination of some retail sectors to discount the prices of what have been seen as premium luxury goods. In the UK, for example, several store chains are acquiring makes of luxury perfume on the grey market and selling it at much cheaper prices than other more traditional outlets.

Retailers are noticeably improving their strategic marketing skills. As George Wallace, chief executive of international retail consultancy Management Horizons, noted,

> 'Marketing for retailers historically meant advertising. In the last five years, however, it has taken more of a front seat, where the objective is much more about defining the mission of the company.'

As retailers join hands across Europe to boost their buying power further, this trend to concentration can only increase. It will not only affect consumer goods companies; it will also have an impact on the producers of industrial goods and services who supply them.

Table 1.11   Major European food alliances, 1990.

Group	Members	Country	Group	Members	Country
Sodei	GIB	Belgium	European	Markant	Germany
	Paridoc/Docs de	France	Marketing	Markant Food	Netherlands
	France		Distribution	Marketing	
Eurogroupe	GIB	Belgium		Selex Gruppo	Italy
	Rewe-Liebbrand	Germany		Selex Ibérico	Spain
	Vendex	Netherlands		Sodacip	France
European Retail	Ahold	Netherlands		Uniarme	Portugal
Alliance	Argyll	UK		Zev-Zentrale/	Austria
	Casino	France		Julius Meini	
incorporating:			Di-Fra	Arland	France
Associated	Ahold,	Netherlands		Francap	France
Marketing	Allkauf	Germany		Louis Delhaize	Belgium
Services	Casino	France		Monoprix/SCA	France
	Dansk			Montlaur	France
	Supermarked	Denmark		Rallye	France
	ICA	Sweden	Deuro	Asda	UK
	Kesko	Finland		Carrefour	France
	La Rinascente	Italy		Makro	Netherlands
	Mercadona	Spain		Metro	Germany/
	Migros	Switzerland			Switzerland
			Nordisk	Cooperative	UK, Denmark,
			Andelsforbund	organizations	Finland, Iceland,
					Norway, Sweden

Sources: Corporate Intelligence Group: *Marketing* magazine; *Financial Times.*

Media

Cross-border ownership is advancing in media as well. While some of the biggest groups, like Rupert Murdoch's News International, are very big and dominant in certain markets, they have not yet made significant inroads in Europe as a whole, although the joint venture between British-based publisher Reed and Dutch group Elsevier marks a major step in a Euro-direction. The

Table 1.12   European retail market, 1989.

	Population (million)	Total retail sales[a] ($ billion)	Sales per person ($)	Total retail outlets[b] ('000)	Persons per outlet
France	56.0	253	4,518	418	134
West Germany	62.0	273	4,403	415	149
Italy	57.7	278	4,818	871	66
Spain	39.1	107	2,737	540	72
UK	57.2	215	3,759	343	167

[a]Estimates are for 1989 sales and have been adjusted to exclude motors and fuel.
[b]Number of outlets based on the latest year census data for separate fixed retail businesses.

Sources: Eurostat, Management Horizons.

increase of cross-border holdings of companies like the Italian-based Fininvest and Bertelsmann from Germany shows that their tentacles are spreading. This concentration of media power is being accompanied by media fragmentation as new channels and media vehicles proliferate.

Summary

There are major trends that companies should keep in mind when formulating their strategies. The main concern is not to let 'information overload' obscure the big picture. These trends are:

- Globalization and the complications it is bringing to the economic scene;
- The change in the world political order;
- The ageing of the population, the growing participation of women in economic activity, and the nascent opportunities in the as yet undeveloped economies;
- The implication of environmental and ethical concerns;
- The impact of changing technologies;
- Asia and Japan as an economic threat and opportunity;
- Europe as a powerful Single Market and the potential for eastward expansion;
- The concentration of retail power;
- Media concentration and, concurrently, media fragmentation.

Checklist

The following questions highlight some of the key areas that companies should consider in terms of the global setting.

Looking globally, has your company:

(1) Identified the social, political and economic trends that could have a long-term impact on corporate strategy?

(2) Filtered through the potential implications into corporate thinking?

(3) Analysed the company's options in light of markets that are both more global and yet increasingly localized?

(4) Taken a position on countries in South-East Asia as potentially lucrative new markets and/or a source of determined competition ?

(5) Established its approach to the European Single Market?

(6) Assessed the implications in Europe of increasing concentration and of the fact that markets tend to support only a few big players in each sector? Survival in Europe?

References

DRT Europe Services. (1990). *European Managerial Attitudes to Environmental Issues*

Economist Intelligence Unit. (1990). *Consumer Spending Patterns in the European Community*. London: Economist Intelligence Unit

Joseph Rowntree Foundation. (1993). *One Parent Families: Policy Options for the 1990s*

McKenna, R. (1991). Marketing is everything. *Harvard Business Review,* Jan/Feb

Porter, M. (1990). *The Competitive Advantage of Nations*. London: Macmillan

United Nations Department of Economic and Social Development (1992). World Investment Report 1992. UN Publications

2

The paradox of centralization/ decentralization

Introduction

Being responsive or efficient or a quick learner used to be enough for a company to create competitive advantage. That is no longer the case. The strategic requirements now are multidimensional, where global economies of scale need to be matched with in-depth local market knowledge, and where centralization of shared goals and values is not allowed to dampen local enthusiasms or initiative. What companies have to grasp is that it is no longer a question of 'either/or', of globalization/localization, centralization/decentralization.

That emphatically does not mean that all companies have to be global. There is nothing especially heroic in being global if there is no competitive pressure to be so. The pursuit of a multidomestic strategy – where companies do not exploit synergies between operations in the countries where they are located – can be entirely legitimate. Some industries, however, simply cannot compete multidomestically, when others are achieving competitive advantage by operating globally.

Modern methods of manufacturing and distribution using both communications links and just-in-time (JIT) delivery mean that where and how you make is rapidly becoming secondary to what you make. Flexible manufacturing techniques enable volume plus almost individually crafted products, while distribution can be subcontracted out to 'womb-to-tomb' operators like TNT. That means that management attention should be turned to market need and innovation.

Italian clothes manufacturer and retailer Benetton illustrates the speed and fine tuning modern methods can bring. Benetton, which operates through a system of franchises, has almost 6000 retail shops in over 80 countries. Its flexible manufacturing system allows the company to make most of the clothes economically in a basic grey, and then dye them at the last minute according to the colours demanded world-wide. The company can judge colour demand by a sophisticated data retrieval system which tells it what colours are selling best and where.

That is only one example, of course. In general the challenges facing companies are complex and wide-ranging. The previous chapter highlighted the long-term trends which should be fed into strategic calculations. This chapter examines the issues that need to be faced in the global battle including:

- Balancing centralization/decentralization
- The challenge of the European Single Market
- Taking a regional approach
- Regional authority
- The demands of the product
- The demands of the customer
- The potential of strategic alliances.

Balancing centralization/decentralization

For many years the conventional wisdom purveyed by business school professors, management consultants and some corporate executives has been that decentralized marketing is the path to success for multinational companies. According to this line of thinking, centralization may be acceptable, even necessary, for certain management functions, such as R&D, manufacturing and finance, but marketing requires the company to stay abreast of customer needs and preferences in many countries. Therefore, the argument goes, marketing decision making should proceed as much as possible through a decentralized, bottom-up approach.

In the past centralized marketing management has more often been the approach of industrial companies rather than consumer products companies. The rationale was that industrial corporations could devise global or country-'unspecific' marketing programmes and apply them fairly uniformly to diverse markets because the products were relatively uniform. Since steel or mining equipment, for example, could be manufactured to essentially the same specifications for a number of markets around the world, it was assumed that the products could be marketed similarly in many countries. Conversely, it was widely thought that marketing strategies for consumer goods had to be country specific to take account of the significant differences that exist in national and cultural tastes. These traditional theories are breaking down.

There are, of course, some real differences among companies in the handling of the centralization/decentralization issue. In every industry, successful companies can be found at nearly every point along a spectrum ranging from strict centralization to total decentralization. In short, neither centralization nor decentralization is necessarily superior. Rather, every company must find the balance that best suits its needs and management style.

In considering the issue of centralization, it is also important to differentiate between centralization of operations and centralization of control. Most multinationals are indeed decentralized operationally, that is, their overall business and marketing strategies are carried out locally. The one possible exception to this general rule is an export strategy. Depending on the products involved, a company may be able to export to certain foreign markets from its home country, relying on logistical support from independent local enterprises, such as agents or distributors. Such a situation is most feasible when the manufacturer is in a nearby country with similar channels of distribution and no major language or cultural differences. A French company can more easily export to Belgium without maintaining a Belgian presence than it can to, say, Brazil. Similarly, some US companies have been able to export to Canada without establishing operations there, but they would be foolhardy to try to do so almost anywhere else.

Decentralization of control – that is, goal setting, determination of strategy and measurement of performance – is another matter. Whether and how many of these functions should be delegated to foreign subsidiaries are hotly contested issues among corporate executives, even those in the same industry or the same company. In practical terms, however, the central headquarters almost always is the measurer of performance because it is the parent company whose money is at risk and that must produce results satisfactory to stockholders. Frequently, the parent company also sets the targets, both financial and market oriented (such as market share, unit sales, and so on), that its overseas affiliates must try to reach.

Most multinationals agree that some centralization (in addition to basic goal setting and performance measurement) is necessary. Even companies that preach the merits of decentralization believe it would be ludicrous for each foreign operation to make marketing decisions in total isolation. Avoiding duplication of effort, realizing the cost savings that come from economies of scale, emulating the successful aspects of another group's strategy – all these and more are benefits that central direction can bring.

A somewhat special case is that of companies seeking a single global image either for the entire company or for particular brands. A relatively high degree of centralization is necessary in order to obtain a consistent image across many national boundaries. Companies such as Coca-Cola, PepsiCo, IBM and Mercedes-Benz are instantly recognized world-wide because they have pursued strategies that emphasize the sameness of the product and the company everywhere. A company that has not stressed its corporate image as much as its specific brands is Britain's Grand Metropolitan, whose Smirnoff vodka and Häagen-Dazs ice cream are well known in dozens of countries, even though the company itself is not. In all these cases, the goal has been to transcend political and economic barriers and national, ethnic and cultural differences, and the means of doing so is a centrally planned and coordinated global marketing programme.

The challenge of the European Single Market

Many companies are viewing the European market as a tough testing ground in meeting the challenge of being both centralized and decentralized on a global scale. Designing an organization for a complex entity like Europe demands a crystal clear understanding of the strategy it is designed to implement. Changing market conditions, profitability, manoeuvrability and productivity must all be taken into consideration and reflected in the grand design.

To be sure, in the current interim period companies still encounter barriers that retard the shift to pan-European strategies. First, each country still has its own currency, thanks in part to the UK's refusal to yield to pressure from its EC partners on this subject. Second, countries continue to maintain their own languages and national identities, conditions that will no doubt persist indefinitely and that dwarf any cultural differences among states in the US. Finally, content and safety standards are not yet harmonized, and there is real disagreement as to whether they will be even by the year 2000.

Nevertheless, as the integration of the EC nears, its implications are permeating virtually every corporate function. A number of firms have begun to reshuffle their organizational structures in order to improve integration of their diverse European manufacturing and marketing operations. There is always a danger, of course, that managements will be tempted into the assumption that a regimented and coordinated pan-European organization is necessary for long-term profitable growth. However, the need to control, coordinate and actively manage the European structure, whatever its shape, is unavoidable and springs from any or all of the following:

- The limited ability or experience of the local management;
- The need to maximize returns from R&D and product ideas;
- The economies of scale derived from large-scale manufacturing and distribution;
- The cumulative strength of international branding;
- Utilization of the available management talent and ideas;
- Serving international customers;
- The economies of centrally produced advertising and international advertising media;
- The increasing speed needed to exploit innovations across markets before rivals seize the initiative.

Some rationalization of production across Europe has generally been seen as the first, relatively straightforward step in integrating European operations. For cars, computers, pharmaceuticals, chemicals and so on, this has usually been done from the outset, but in household appliances, photographic products and other fast-moving consumer goods (fmcg), only in the past decade have the benefits of automation grown large enough and certain enough to justify the investment and overcome the country managers' resistance.

Even so, consultants warn, the benefits may not be easily attained for the following reasons:

- Rationalized production implies rationalized products, which the customer may not easily accept.
- Producing too many variants from a single plant for local markets quickly reduces the economic benefits.
- Central or regional control of production makes the company less flexible and less sensitive to customers' needs and preferences.
- The scope is limited for development projects aimed at local market niches.
- Rationalized production is heavily dependent on efficient distribution.
- Rationalized production results in a serious reduction in the country manager's role and job satisfaction. If the centre plans to coordinate the marketing of individual products, country managers may well feel their jobs are being shot from under them.

Different companies, of course, face different problems. As Francis Huggins, marketing director of Zanussi UK, the Italian white goods manufacturer owned by Swedish Electrolux, said, you have to ask yourself:

(1) Are you a manufacturer who makes and sells only in a local (that is, national) marketplace? If you are, then you follow the rules of that market and gear production to its demands.

(2) Do you sell in the UK but your manufacturing bases are spread throughout Europe? Then different rules apply and you have to respect the manufacturing base's culture, abilities and so on.

This is a subtle point which has great relevance to the type of product finally offered to the consumer. As Huggins pointed out,

> 'If I go to a factory and start talking about the temperature requirements of a refrigerator to store fresh fruit and vegetables, are we all talking the same language? No. Not because no one understands what a fresh lemon is. But the *degree* of freshness and what freshness is in the first place changes entirely depending on where you are. In Spain or Italy, for instance, a fresh lemon is one from the tree, put into a box, and taken to the supermarket.'

> 'In the UK, consumers won't accept a lemon unless it is geometrically perfect, yellow all over, shiny, and with a little label saying that this is

a first class lemon. You have to throw half the lemons you have away, polish the best ones, put the label on, wrap them in tissue paper and put them into a box. That lemon has different temperature requirements.'

Taking a regional approach

Pushing responsibility away from the centre and nearer to the market is, however, in some instances, a step of only relative significance. A European regional head office in Geneva, Brussels or London can become a mushrooming centre of corporate power in its turn. Many have been cut back, along with the global headquarters, but there is an opposite tendency for some to be set up from scratch or to grow further as the trend toward coordinating European marketing and sales accelerates. Distance and the size of individual markets, the continuing need to consider and manage each one separately and cultural factors usually dictate that a regional office be set up as:

- A focus for the national subsidiaries to ensure that their views and preferences are given due weight by the company's central management;
- A performance monitor, to check what results should be expected from each subsidiary;
- An interpreter of central direction as it affects subsidiary managements;
- A vehicle for managing whatever is pan-European about the product – technical specifications, packaging, advertising, servicing multinational customers, liaison with the EC, as well as finance, manufacturing and research;
- A vehicle for joint ventures and acquisitions and a base for operations in Eastern Europe.

Case 2.1 PepsiCo Inc.

PepsiCo Inc., headquartered in Purchase, New York, sells relatively homogeneous consumer products, the kinds that are most suitable for an international division. The company has continued to use this organizational approach, but with some significant modifications of the classic model. For instance, it has

continues

continued

made its regional subdivisions very strong, in order to be close to rapidly changing markets.

PepsiCo moved to create strong regions in response to its number-two image in many foreign markets. The management believed that by establishing six geographic business units within a single international subsidiary (Pepsi-Cola International), it could better unify and refine its international marketing strategies. Pepsi-Cola International, located in New York, comprises six regional subdivisions: Western Europe (headquartered in London); Middle East/Africa (Cyprus); Asia–Pacific (Singapore; responsible for all countries in the region except China and Hong Kong); Canada (Toronto); India/China/Eastern Europe, based in Hong Kong, covers China, India, Hong Kong, Eastern Europe and the former Soviet Union; and Latin America (Rio de Janeiro, Brazil). Each region is headed by a president who reports directly to the president of Pepsi-Cola International. The regional presidents are also corporate senior vice presidents. The president of Pepsi-Cola International reports directly to Roger Enrico, president and chief executive officer of PepsiCo Inc., and operates out of PepsiCo's corporate headquarters.

According to the company, the changes are designed to help increase sales overseas by moving operations and executives closer to the point of sale, particularly in Europe and Asia. 'Through this new structure, we are strategically positioned to seize the abundant opportunities of the 1990s and beyond,' said Enrico, 'The new units will operate with a clear charter to develop and build our business in local markets across the world.'

For some this represents a reversal of an earlier trend to de-emphasize European headquarters, stress individual-country operations. General Motors, for instance, began early when it reorganized its European subsidiary in 1986, creating a new Zurich office to oversee plant operations, marketing and public relations throughout Europe. Gillette, in 1987, restructured its European operations along product lines, rather than geographically, and folded its 15 European units into one central marketing operation. Using this set-up the company can launch the same products with the same prices, advertising and similar packaging throughout the Community.

Matsushita Electric Industry Co. is one of the many Japanese companies that are seeking to establish solid production bases in Europe. However, becoming an EC insider has not been easy, say company spokesmen. Until 1988, most of Matsushita's production in Europe was carried out in so-called 'screwdriver' plants: virtually 100% of the components were imported from Japan and assembled locally. With the approach of EC market integration, pressure for localization intensified; moreover, moves by European makers to formulate unified industrial standards gave rise to fears that entry for the firm's Japan-designed finished products and components could be blocked.

Matsushita's solution was completely to revamp its business operations in Europe, a costly and complex undertaking, but one that the company felt was its only alternative. In conjunction with the reorganization of Matsushita's global operations in 1988–89, the Osaka-based firm established Panasonic Europe in the UK as the European regional headquarters, with a mandate to fully localize operations and build a strong manufacturing and sales base in the EC market that will increasingly rely upon local suppliers. Besides having full autonomy in formulating and executing its own marketing strategies, Panasonic Europe also manages most of Matsushita's nearly 30 manufacturing, sales and finance subsidiaries in 13 European countries (plus two operations in Africa). Since the reorganization, Panasonic Europe has also participated in the formation of the Siemens Matsushita Components GmbH & Co. joint venture to produce a wide range of passive electronic components. Each of Matsushita's manufacturing facilities in Europe has plans under consideration to set up technology development functions to localize design and component supply further, according to a company spokesman.

Case 2.2 The Japanese subsidiaries in the UK

The contradictions inherent in setting up a global/local approach to the market are seen in a 1986 study conducted by Peter Doyle, professor of marketing at Warwick University in the UK. He found that of 45 subsidiaries operating in the UK of US, Japanese and UK parents, the Japanese subsidiaries were more successful than their rivals in similar markets (and often run by UK managers with similar backgrounds) because:

- They were more autonomous, but subject to often daily, informal monitoring rather than a formal control system.
- Reporting was concerned with the whole product-market situation: 'The overriding financial focus of top management in American and British companies appeared to be a key reason for the lack of well-thought-out marketing strategies in their business, and their consequent disappointing performance in the market.'
- Organizations were structured around individual products and geographical markets.
- The Japanese subsidiaries were better at differentiating the segments of their market and targeting each one specifically.

continues

continued

> Doyle also found that '47% of British and 40% of US companies (vs 13% of the Japanese) acknowledged that they were unclear about the main type of customers in the market and what their needs were.' Another problem in the case of the US subsidiaries was that marketing decisions were often made by European or international committees outside the UK, and with little effort being made to differentiate among the European countries. 'Thus when the Japanese concentrated their marketing investments on the high-potential customer groups in the UK, the British and Americans tended to spread theirs thinly across the entire market,' concluded Doyle.

Seiko Epson, the Japanese computer and peripherals manufacturer, has also recently established a regional operational headquarters – Epson European Operations Centre Ltd, in London – to coordinate the firm's growing activities in Europe. As with most Japanese firms, Epson's first foray into the European market was through the establishment of sales offices to market the firm's products and coordinate distribution in key country markets during the late 1970s and 1980s. At present, the company has five sales offices in Europe – specifically in the UK, Germany, France, Spain and Portugal. Each office is responsible for the country in which it is located as well as for two or three other countries. For instance, the UK office covers Denmark, and the German office covers Switzerland and Austria.

The regional HQ will also be responsible for overseeing the localization of the company's European manufacturing operations. Beginning in 1981, the firm established three manufacturing plants, commencing with SNW Uhrenwerk GmbH (to make high-grade metal watch casings) in Dusseldorf, followed by Epson Engineering (France) SA (terminal printers) in 1985 and Epson Telford Ltd in the UK (terminal printers, personal computers and related parts) in 1987.

Other non-European multinationals gearing up for the Single Market include:

- Acer, the Taiwan-based computer company. Over 30% of the firm's $686 million in sales comes from Europe now, even though Acer's first foray into the market occurred in 1985 with the establishment of a subsidiary in West Germany. Since then, Acer has set up subsidiaries in France, the Netherlands and the UK and will shortly set up shop in Spain and Italy – all coordinated by Acer Computer GmbH, the regional headquarters operation sited in Dusseldorf. Stan Shih, Acer's chairman of the board, added that 'we are aggressively recruiting more and more European managers to help us expand.' Acer plans to set up a manufacturing site in one of the 12 EC nations, with at least some of the financing to come from a planned Eurobond issue. Direct acquisitions are also a major component of Acer's

European game plan: in 1989, the Taiwan firm purchased CE-TEC Data Technology GmbH in West Germany and the Dutch personal computer company, Kangaroo Computer SB.

- Colgate–Palmolive began its integrated pan-European operation by transforming its European operations into a full-scale company with total P&L responsibility.
- Allen-Bradley, a division of Rockwell International, took the same route as Colgate–Palmolive. The division's need for a more consistent and uniform sales support strategy across the continent spurred Allen-Bradley to adopt a functional pan-European organization.
- Sonoco Products, a manufacturer of packaging materials for both consumer and industrial markets, began to move its European headquarters from Manchester to Brussels in 1987, in large part to force a more pan-European orientation.
- Partly because of 1992, Sony established a European headquarters in Cologne in 1986 and quickly made its top European managers key players in the parent company. (Sony also wanted to foster better world-wide coordination and rationalization of its operations.) Other Japanese manufacturers, such as Hitachi and Fujitsu, have also begun to strengthen the role of their European headquarters.

European firms are also repositioning themselves in order to be more effective in their markets. For example, Ciba-Geigy, the Swiss pharmaceutical company, plans to replace its current European marketing strategy with one that will take advantage of the region's trade liberalization. Presently, each European country operation directs its own local marketing, designs its own labels and packages and formulates its own advertising campaigns. One reason the company has used independent marketing strategies is that pharmaceutical packaging and marketing standards differ from country to country.

With the advent of consistent pharmaceutical marketing standards came Ciba-Geigy's new pan-European strategy, which called for uniformity in the packaging, design, logo and label for each product. Only the language in which the labels are printed may differ among markets, and even there the variations will be minimized by using more symbols and fewer words. Pharmaceutical products will be produced in the least costly locations in Europe for shipment to the other EC countries.

The European sales effort will be handled by language-based teams. Thus, there will be separate sales departments for Europe's German-speaking areas, English-speaking areas and so on. Although this approach will generally accommodate national boundaries, it will also transcend them in some cases; for example, the French-speaking salesforce will cover not just France but also Luxembourg and the French-speaking parts of Belgium.

Grand Metropolitan, the British food, beverage and retail conglomerate, decided several years ago that in order to succeed after 1992, it would have to be well positioned in the EC as a whole, not just in individual European countries. To improve its competitive position the company entered into several joint ventures and engaged in a number of acquisitions. Its strategy was to align itself with other European companies that were trying to establish pan-European operations and that had strong presences in markets in which it was unrepresented. For example, the company purchased Metaxa, a Greek alcoholic beverage producer, to give the Cinzano and Cointreau brands, in Grand Met's Hublein division, greater access to Greece and Germany.

One major incentive for non-European companies to plan their European strategies carefully and fully was the fear that the EC will erect barriers to outside trade after 1992. This expectation, sometimes called the 'Fortress Europe' theory, postulated that in place of the local trade barriers that existed between countries, the EC as a whole would erect one large barrier around itself. Under this scenario, the most likely way the Europeans would keep out foreign goods would be through local content and/or local manufacturing rules.

Whether to escape any Community-wide barriers that may be set up or simply to take advantage of post-1992 opportunities, a large number of US and Japanese companies are trying to attain insider status. This is an urgent concern for many Japanese multinationals because they are relative latecomers to Europe, especially in manufacturing. (A striking exception to the latecomer characterization is Sony, which began to establish manufacturing and assembly plants throughout Europe 15 years ago and had eight by the end of 1989.)

To paraphrase several Japanese executives, 'We don't believe the EC will turn itself into Fortress Europe, but it is still prudent to become an "insider", just in case.'

Regional authority

Most regional heads have specific profit responsibility with country managers reporting direct to them, but their degree of independence from the global headquarters and the extent of their involvement with the marketing and sales of the national companies vary widely. While IBM in Paris (like Rank Xerox, near London) was sharply curtailing the activities of its large regional office, Levi Strauss, with a small unit in Brussels, shouldered half the marketing burden for its European operations. Procter & Gamble's 600 staff in Brussels (including technicians) appeared to be growing in influence, but such a large regional office may become a rarity as better ways are found of coordinating and dispersing marketing operations. For example, both 3M and ICI, as it faces demerging, have begun to slim down their Brussels offices. In 3M's case, it has created European Business Units run from whichever country is deemed the centre of expertise for the various product groups.

Some companies find it advantageous to extend the central authority through the regional head office. Union Carbide, for instance, recently reshaped itself into a holding company with three main world-wide product divisions – carbon products, gases, and chemicals and plastics. All three now operate their own sales subsidiaries in the main national European markets (some are still being established) to facilitate the process of acquisition and divestment. But the three all centre their European operations firmly on Geneva, where business directors conduct the marketing, set the prices and select the source of their products for the whole of Europe. Country managers are left to build relationships with client companies according to plans laid down in Geneva. European sales of Union Carbide's chemicals and plastics increased by 25% in 1989.

Japanese electronics company Canon does not interpose regional authority between the larger European subsidiaries and Tokyo. The president of Canon Europa, Takeshi Mitarai, explained his role:

> 'The Big Three subsidiaries (France, Germany and the UK) report their daily activities on sales, purchasing, price negotiations etc., direct to Tokyo, but their profit is reported to me. I report to the president for sales, profits and finance.... Generally speaking, they run their own businesses – I just check the monthly financial data.'

The smaller operations do report to Mitarai, and 'many times, I ask them, "please keep more profitable" ' – indicating a light, supervisory hand on the controls. Some five years ago, the Big Three reported through the Europa office, but the inefficiency involved in shipping products to Europe led to the present ambiguous system – untidy by US standards, but effective. In Tokyo, the reporting lines are simply not a big issue, and as one Canon main board director remarked a few years ago, 'We're quite flexible. We have a permanent employment system, and we know each other very well, so we do not need formal channels.'

Case 2.3 The Japanese and centralization

The following tables (Tables 2.1 and 2.2), taken from *The White Paper on International Trade 1989 – Rapid Progress in Structural Adjustment*, by H. Aoki (the former director of the International Trade Research Office of the International Trade Policy Bureau of the Ministry of International Trade and Industry) of the Japan Economic Foundation (published in the Tokyo-based *Journal of Japanese Trade and Industry*, 1 September 1989), delineate the extent to which Japanese companies have delegated authority on key functions to their overseas subsidiaries. (This article does not indicate the scope, methodology or time frame of the survey.) According to the survey, the widest

continues

---

continued

range of autonomy allowed by Japanese parent companies to their local operations was in decisions on promotion and performance rating systems (in line with adjustment of personnel management to local cultures), supply sources for raw materials and parts, production and inventory volumes, and marketing strategy. The authority most zealously guarded by Japanese corporate headquarters was in the appointment of officers and in decisions on corporate finances (for example, dividend payouts, long-term fund raising, capital expansions), R&D plans and plant and equipment investments or expansions.

However, the imperative for centralized management among Japanese companies became truly apparent when compared with the management of foreign-affiliated enterprises in Japan. While parents still controlled over half of decisions regarding the appointment of officers and long-term funding, their local subsidiaries in Japan seemed to exercise far more control over determination of production and inventory volume, sourcing, sales price and marketing, personnel management and even R&D. The comparison also revealed that relatively more control over marketing and pricing was held by Japanese corporate headquarters than by non-Japanese firms: about 60% of decisions on marketing strategy and selling prices could be made by local subsidiaries of Japanese firms, while over 80% of subsidiaries (even in joint ventures) of foreign firms could do so.

Table 2.1 Delegation of authority in overseas subsidiaries of Japanese corporations and Japanese subsidiaries of foreign enterprises: management of foreign-affiliated enterprises in Japan.

	% of decisions made by		
	Overseas parent company	Subsidiary in Japan	Japanese parent company
Decisions on marketing strategy	10.2	80.3	9.5
Decisions on production and inventory volume	2.9	92.6	4.4
Decisions on supply sources for raw materials and parts	7.4	86.7	5.9
Decisions on product specifications	22.2	74.1	3.7
Decisions on sales price	5.2	87.3	7.5
Decisions on promotion and performance rating systems	1.4	84.2	14.4
Plant and equipment investment plans	48.4	41.8	9.8
Research and development plans	29.9	64.6	5.5
Appointment of officers	53.5	22.8	23.8
Decisions on dividend payouts	46.4	39.3	14.3
Decisions on long-term fund raising, including capital expansion	50.00	33.3	16.7

Source: White Paper on International Trade (1989).

Table 2.2   Delegation of authority in overseas subsidiaries of Japanese corporations and Japanese subsidiaries of foreign enterprises: management of wholly owned overseas subsidiaries.

	% of decisions made by	
	Japanese parent company	Overseas subsidiary
Decisions on marketing strategy	43.3	56.7
Decisions on production and inventory volumes	32.8	67.2
Decisions on supply sources for raw materials and parts	24.4	75.6
Decisions on product specifications	61.7	38.3
Decisions on sales price	36.1	63.9
Decisions on promotion and performance rating systems	21.8	78.2
Plant and equipment investment plans	82.6	17.4
Research and development plans	85.5	14.5
Appointment of officers	95.9	4.1
Decisions on dividend payouts	89.3	10.7
Decisions on long-term fund raising, including capital expansion	92.7	7.3

Source: White Paper on International Trade (1989).

The demands of the product

It is vital that corporate structures keep pace with any changes in the marketing structure demanded by the products or the underlying technology. There can be serious consequences when business drifts away from the groups' rigid structures. Equally damaging is the allied risk that the structure does not allow new technologies the management focus and freedom they need to develop. The classic product divisions widely used to make the existing business manageable carry the attendant risk that promising developments that don't fit in could be frozen out.

This problem has given rise to a number of 'intrapreneurial' techniques aimed at fostering and building new innovative businesses around the technology coming out of the central labs. The Swedish plastics group Perstorp is a keen advocate of such methods, which have accounted for much of its growth in recent years. The UK-based electronic instruments company Eurotherm, a world leader in many fields of temperature and process control, has grown steadily over the past 25 years in the face of competition from giants like Honeywell and Foxboro Yoxall. A factor crucial to its success has been its policy of spinning off each promising new development into a separate subsidiary at the earliest practical moment, and relying on highly motivated and autonomous managers to build it into a worthwhile business alongside the others.

The rapid rate of technological change in certain industries like electronics, combined with the increasing investment demanded and shorter payback period, means that companies have to ensure that product breakthroughs are quickly and effectively exploited throughout the group. In the past, many companies have tightened the central control of their operations for this purpose. Now, for many the preferred course is to maintain local autonomy but increase the level of communication and intragroup cooperation to ensure willing, enthusiastic and imaginative support for new developments elsewhere.

Technological change does not always come in clearly labelled packets, however. As the following examples from the chemical and computer industries show, effective exploitation required imaginative local application and the organization to support it.

In the chemical sector, to help escape the slow growth and vulnerability to economic cycles of the commodity chemical business, many of the world industry leaders have concentrated on developing markets for specialty or effect chemicals, from dynamite to anaesthetics. But these products require much more sophisticated marketing and selling, and often close contact with the customer to develop solutions to his or her technical problems. This is one of the factors behind the decision by ICI to spin off its pharmaceuticals business and focus more strongly on its core products like paints, explosives and specialized plastics.

Du Pont has set up a number of marketing groups with executives drawn from different product divisions to focus on all of the chemical needs of a specific industry, such as cars or electronics. Du Pont also hopes that these groups will help overcome the traditional isolationism of the company's product divisions, and encourage the transfer of technology from, say, composites to fibres.

Two separate technological developments have affected computer marketing profoundly in the past few years. First, the move down the size and unit value scale, while maintaining computing power, has meant the end of direct selling for the ubiquitous PCs, and a rising proportion of sales of all sizes of computers, even mainframes, through intermediaries. Second, open systems, particularly in Europe, are overtaking the proprietary software that so effectively kept customers loyal. With open systems, customers are free to choose the hardware and software from whichever manufacturer suits them.

IBM has therefore had to learn about serious marketing the hard way, and pushed 8000 people out of national headquarters into branch offices to be nearer to customers. With the executives has gone a fair measure of authority and power.

Whatever companies decide their stance in European markets should be, they must be prepared to change tack rapidly to meet altered circumstances. As one executive remarked, 'If you read about it, it's too late.' The environmental challenge is just one issue that has demanded a rapid response from detergent manufacturers, for example, with the action matched to differing levels of concern in the various European countries.

Companies also have to increase the flow of new models onto the market, cutting development time. 3M's vice president for its European marketing subsidiaries, Edoardo Pieruzzi, said that for the company's prolific new product programme, it has now adopted a 'planned roll-out approach – but we'll have to get faster.' For Colin Brown, group director in charge of European household and toiletry products at Reckitt & Colman, selling in Europe's different markets meant that 'unless you're coordinated, you'll be late somewhere.'

This does not imply a large coordinating staff, however. 'We run Europe with four people,' said Brown. Country managers are left firmly in charge of their own markets, but when the group finds a successful product anywhere that has potential in a wider market, it is rolled out as quickly as possible. One example was the Magic Mushroom, an Airwick air freshener that originated in the US. It was successfully introduced into the UK, and then launched onto 14 other European markets in 18 months, each one requiring some element of national difference as well as international harmonization.

It is significant that most companies find the coordination process for new products much quicker and easier than for the old-established ones, and companies like 3M, which expects 30% of its sales in any year to come from products that are four years old, score for that reason. New products have the advantages that:

- The technical requirements of each market can be designed into the product from the outset;
- The market positioning can be planned in advance, therefore avoiding many harmonization problems over distribution channels, advertising and so on;
- Organizational attitudes do not have a chance to harden around products.

Changing these once the product has become established in a number of markets will be a laborious and expensive process. In its challenge for the European detergents market, the Japanese Kao may need vast resources to outgun established players such as Procter & Gamble and Unilever, but at least it has the advantage of starting from scratch.

The demands of the customer

A growing corporate preoccupation is meeting the multinational demands of customers. Chemicals, computers, copiers – all have a high proportion of users with operations in more than one country. Even in food products and toiletries, 8–10 international buying groups are already being formed with the prime purpose (in the manufacturers' view) of extracting ever larger discounts based on Europe-wide turnover.

One of the furthest developed is the European Retail Alliance (ERA), set up in 1989 by Argyll (the UK foods group that owns the UK grocery chain Safeway), the French supermarket chain Casino and the largest Dutch food retailer Ahold. ERA in turn owns 60% of Associated Marketing Services (AMS), headquartered in Zug, Switzerland, which is planning a joint label and common purchasing of major items like wine and petfood (see Table 1.11, page 22). It is intended that suppliers of a particular product will pay AMS, say, 1% of their total sales to its members. In return, suppliers will be able to increase their sales of the product, and cut costs by, for example, all members agreeing on a common formulation for private label use.

Traditional geographical organizations where country managers are responsible for pricing are in obvious difficulty in cross-frontier negotiations. But even groups with strong international product divisions face problems when the negotiations extend across divisional boundaries. Depending on industry, the following areas can be affected:

- Country managers' profit responsibilities;
- Central and local manufacturing, and distribution facilities;
- Ordering procedures and credit arrangements (in the grocery trade, the customary payment period ranges from 15 days to 120 days across European countries);
- Aftersales service;
- Management information systems.

The Swiss chemical/pharmaceutical company Roche clearly foresaw the trend as it will affect its vitamins, flavours and fragrances product areas. With the help of the Boston Consulting Group, it is currently re-examining its whole corporate structure, anticipating that the big food manufacturers could have one central buying operation for the whole of Europe within the next few years.

Roche believes that it will have to build Eurosales teams that deal with this one central organization. For such large customers, there will no longer be local teams in individual countries with the main marketing and sales responsibility. And as customers centralize, orders will become bigger, meaning that customers will have more sophisticated demands. Roche sales and marketing teams will have to develop a broader approach to satisfy a wider range of tastes.

Indicative of the way the 'one-customer, one-price' trend is developing, in 1990 four European airlines – Swissair, SAS, Finnair and Austrian Airlines – collectively requested the European Airbus consortium and the US McDonnell Douglas to tender for up to 240 narrow-bodied, twin-engined aircraft. The purpose was to obtain price reductions by agreeing a common specification.

The traditional response of many multinational companies to the increasing Single Market awareness of customers has been to increase head office coordination. But companies were also firmly committed to lean head offices and decentralized power. Roche's stated intention was typical of many: 'The local organization should have as much responsibility as possible to handle local business. We consider that a strength of Roche.'

In many industries, central purchasing is only just beginning to make itself felt, with many suppliers handling no more than a fraction of business in this way. There is a wide recognition that the organizational answers they have so far arrived at are only partially effective.

The potential of strategic alliances

Buying groups like ERA are one part of the growing trend toward strategic alliances across Europe as a way to secure competitive advantage, share costs, leapfrog into new markets or protect existing ones. Strategic alliances are nothing new – by the end of the last decade the car industry was already involved in a confusing and almost impenetrable array of alliances across the world (Figure 2.1).

These alliances are appearing in a variety of forms, from full-blown joint ventures and mergers, to cooperation agreements in areas like licensing, technology and R&D agreements, long-term buyer–seller agreements and market alliances. They can help companies:

- Gain competitive advantage with less risk and expense than going it alone;
- Gain economies of scale if the partners are in the same sector;
- Share development costs;
- Swap technical know-how;
- Gain a wider presence – helpful where takeover targets are thin on the ground;
- Overcome cultural and language barriers;
- Enter complementary product lines;
- Enlarge distribution reach.

But if the failure rates for alliances between companies in the same country are often as high as one-third, the very nature of cross-border marriages provides even greater opportunity for failure. The most commonly touted example took place years ago: the spectacular failure of the Dunlop–Pirelli merger in the 1970s. Other more recent ones, like Italian computer maker Olivetti's alliance with US communications group AT&T to foster mutual market penetration, faltered from a lack of a clear strategy. But the number of new alliances continues to grow across a range of sectors:

- Coca-Cola and Nestlé are joining forces to develop the international market for 'ready-to-drink' tea and coffee, which currently only sell in significant amounts in Japan.

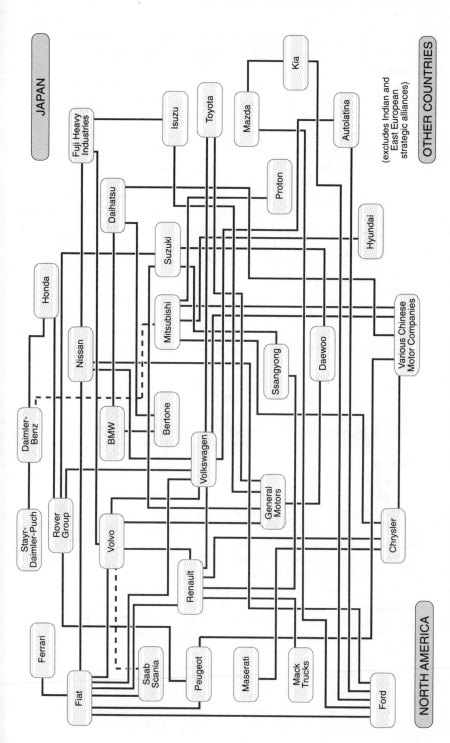

Figure 2.1 Strategic alliances within the motor vehicles industry, 1989. *Source:* PA Consulting Group.

- US domestic appliance manufacturer Whirlpool has taken a 53% stake in Dutch electronics group Philips' white good business to leapfrog into the European market.
- Volvo and Renault have exchanged shareholdings to give them more R&D muscle and a more coherent product policy (see Case 5.4, page 139).
- The *Independent* newspaper has formed links with Italy's *La Repubblica* and Spain's *El Pais* in a £21 million deal to invest in the expanding European media.
- Consumer goods group Procter & Gamble has formed a joint venture with Italian arch rival Fater in nappies which will give the combined group almost 60% of the UK market and up to 90% of the Italian market and lead to further cooperation in other paper products around Europe.
- British Telecom and IBM are forming a partnership to supply a full range of advanced communications and information services to business customers around the world.

In the countries of the former Communist bloc, for political reasons joint ventures are likely to figure prominently, since perceived national interests exercise just as powerful a tug as in the West. However, several companies, the Swedish giant Electrolux among them, do not conceal their dislike of joint ventures because of the confusion in objectives and control that is a common feature.

As for organic expansion in Eastern Europe, German groups like Siemens or Volkswagen have to consider what was East Germany as part of their domestic market. But even though there is political unification, Eastern Germany may for most companies justify separate organizational structures for some years to come, owing to its economic and political heritage.

Most non-German multinationals are, like NCR, reacting cautiously to developments. For the time being, NCR is simply extending its structure eastward by setting up branch offices in Poland, the Czech and Slovak republics, Hungary and so on, via its West German subsidiary. Many managements, however, may find that the European region will still need to be subdivided because of size, either geographically (northern and southern states, for example) or economically (by GNP per head).

Soaps and detergents group Colgate–Palmolive has decided to take the plunge with a separate organization for the whole of Central and Eastern Europe (except for East Germany, which will be handled by the West German subsidiary). As Brussels-based Brian Bergin, president of Colgate–Palmolive Europe, explained:

> 'A whole different set of circumstances applies in Eastern Europe now. There's a lack of business skills, and revenue and profit will be different. Therefore, a firm line has to be drawn [between Colgate–Palmolive's East and West European organizations].'

Bergin argued that although the business environment is in some senses 'simpler' than in the West, 'the risk of getting caught is greater.'

Making a success of alliances between companies of whatever complexion requires a clearly defined strategy, which is regularly refined, re-assessed and managed with commitment. Specific goals and time scales help. Given the relatively closed nature of much corporate ownership of many European companies, which often prevents hostile acquisitions, alliances can be one of the few ways to enter a market successfully.

Japanese companies typically buy minority shares in European firms in keeping with their desire to make only 'friendly' investments and minimize possible negative public opinion. For example, Honda Motor Co. announced, in July 1989, that it would acquire 20% of Britain's Rover Group PLC. Perhaps because it was mindful of the effect of this news (Honda is the first Japanese car maker to own a piece of a European car company), the company announced at the same time that it would soon construct its first major plant in Europe (in Swindon, England).

Not everyone thinks they are a good idea. A powerful note of dissent has been struck by Harvard Business School Professor Michael Porter, whose views on comparative advantage, most recently laid out in *The Competitive Advantage of Nations* (1990), were that these sorts of ventures can discourage real competitive edge and encourage complacency. In an interview in the PA Consulting Group's *Journal for Management*, he argued:

> 'The big concern that I have regarding 1992 is that European companies and policy makers will squander this opportunity and essentially nullify its impact. On the company side, we already see firms scurrying around to merge as quickly as possible, with as many firms as possible. In a variety of industries, we see alliances among all the leading competitors. On the government side, there are signs that this type of behaviour is going to be allowed. There is evidence that companies are hedging because they fear being losers, and governments are hedging because they fear that their industries may lose. What I fear is a blunting of the dynamic forces through a heavy level of intervention. This could lead to a return to the quasi-cartels that were prominent in Europe before World War II.'

Case 2.4 *The merger maelstrom*

Fear of takeover, and the generally tougher investment climate in most financial centres, have prompted some multinationals, particularly those originating in the US, to reorganize their European operations as part of a major

continues

continued

exercise to improve financial performance. Deciding what are the core businesses is now the customary first stage in the remedial action; second comes divestment of what are deemed to be peripheral activities; last is reorganizing the core to make it leaner and more effective – or simply better able to support the debt burden that may have been incurred.

Gillette, a victim of 'greenmail' in the mid-1980s and still vulnerable to market adventurers, was forced in defending itself to triple its corporate debt to reach a peak debt/equity ratio of nearly 200%. In an attempt to recover its poise, it has divested itself of a long string of businesses, the latest announced in January 1990, aimed at cutting costs in the remaining European shaving and male toiletries businesses by heavily centralizing its marketing in a North Atlantic Shaving & Personal Care Group. The effectiveness of this latter move will be measured in part by the success of its 19-nation launch this year of the new wet-shaving system, Sensor.

Kodak has not suffered so severely from corporate raiders, but much of the impetus behind its reorganization in the 1980s came from the imperative need to improve its financial performance.

Where acquisition rather than divestment is the priority, a tighter organization may again be required, but for a different reason. Successful acquisitions in today's competitive conditions require:

- A clear strategic sense based on a careful analysis of the group's strengths and weaknesses;
- A united management team attuned to decisive action;
- Painstaking field intelligence to locate possible targets and assess their strengths and weaknesses, and therefore the potential 'fit';
- Mobilization of cash and other financial resources to enable the group to mount the bid.

Unilever, for all its financial success, boasted none of these in the 1960s. It had relied largely on the organic growth of its highly autonomous and widely spread operating subsidiaries. Financial management was similarly relaxed, and one or two small but significant takeover bids in the UK failed. But by the late 1970s, it had set up a US regional headquarters, and bought critical mass in the US marketplace with the purchase of National Starch, paying what was then the highest price ever for a US company by a foreigner.

Ten years later, with a much tighter central management team, it mounted a rapid and ultimately successful bid for the Chesebrough-Pond's personal products group, having earlier been beaten to the draw for Richardson-Vicks by its arch rival, Procter & Gamble. It has since built on that purchase with the acquisition of Elizabeth Arden and Fabergé from their US owners.

Such acquisitions raise vital questions about how they should be attached to the existing structure. Much depends on the company's overall strategy and management style, as well as the more obvious considerations of line of busi-

continues

continued

ness, size and location of the acquired assets and so on. In the Chesebrough-Pond's case, Unilever determined to amalgamate the purchased operations with its existing Elida Gibbs personal care business, but whether Chesebrough-Pond's was merged into Gibbs or vice versa depended on which unit was the larger in each European country.

By contrast, when the US food group Heinz bought the Weight Watchers (WW) operation in 1978, there was considerable internal debate as to how such a distinct business should be fitted into Heinz's world-wide organization. At the time of the takeover, WW's slimming foods and Heinz's own products were sold through largely similar outlets.

As a result, if the two were merged, Heinz's marketing skills could be expected to expand WW's sales. However, Heinz decided to separate the 'classroom group' (essentially about organizing educational weight loss programmes in the community) from the high street operations. Heinz's senior vice president, Europe, Paul Corddry, explained that grocery products like ketchup, baked beans, baby foods and the WW range require a hard sell to make an impact in the supermarkets. A small coordinating group was appointed from both sides at the operating level. Now WW provides an operating income of over $100 million annually.

Summary

- Being responsive or efficient or a quick learner used to be enough for a company to create competitive advantage. That is no longer the case. The strategic requirements now are multidimensional, where global economies of scale need to be matched with in-depth local market knowledge, and where centralization of shared goals and values is not allowed to dampen local enthusiasms or initiative.
- Europe is a catalyst for these forces. The issues that companies have to face in the battle for competitive survival in the European market include:
  - balancing the need to be both centralized to exploit organizational synergies and economies of scale while keeping abreast of local needs;
  - shifting from a country-oriented stance to one that exploits regional understanding;
  - keeping pace with any changes in the marketing structures demanded by the products or the underlying technology;
  - meeting the multinational demands of customers;
  - considering the potential for strategic alliances.

Checklist

The following questions highlight some of the key areas that companies should consider in terms of the global setting.

In the light of what are now multidimensional strategic requirements, has your company:

(1) Formed a view on the approach needed to balance centralization and decentralization that best suits its needs and management style?

(2) Begun integration of some functions already happening across Europe?

(3) Established the degree of responsibility to be given to regional offices?

(4) Analysed the extent that the competition is restructuring to deal with global markets and the European Single Market in particular?

(5) Created structures flexible enough not to hamper the rapid development of new products or the exploitation of technological development across the markets and organization?

(6) Ensured that the ability exists to deal with international customers demanding a simplified approach to international dealings?

(7) Examined potential strategic alliances to enhance competitive advantage?

(8) Developed a policy for managing strategic alliances?

References

Aoki, H. (1989). The White Paper on International Trade 1989 – Rapid progress in Structural Adjustment. *Journal of Japanese Trade and Industry,* September. Tokyo

Doyle, P., Saunders, J. and Wong, V. (1986). A comparative study of Japanese marketing strategies in the British market. *Journal of International Business Studies*, **17**, (1)

Porter, M. (1990). *The Competitive Advantage of Nations.* London: Macmillan

PART TWO

Marketing strategies

3

Critical strategic concepts

Introduction

Marketing is an overused, but often misunderstood word. What it should not mean is promotion or selling, although they are part of it. What it should be is the orientation of the organization – and therefore of all the people in it – to its internal and external relationships.

Marketing as a professional management function has its roots in the 1960s, when US marketing experts like Philip Kotler, now Northwestern University's S.C. Johnson and Son distinguished professor of international marketing, began to define marketing as a set of principles, a philosophy which said that companies have to figure out what the target market wants. While consumer goods companies understood this to a certain extent, for most industrial sectors selling what you made was the guiding rule. And, with buoyant markets, it usually worked.

The balance of power has shifted to the market with a vengeance. The nature of demand, the multiplicity of choice, the rise of affluence and the availability of information have all contributed to that shift. Companies – and there are still many of them around – which use 'marketing' interchangeably with promotion or selling are obscuring from themselves the fact that marketing cannot be regarded as simply tactics or techniques.

This has been said countless times, but rigidity, bureaucracy and fear of change often prevent the message from permeating through to the top of the corporation. Top management needs to understand that marketing is not a science, nor an art – nor a budget black hole – but an attitude: it is the ability to stand back and take an objective look, enhanced by both experience and vision, at what has to be done to the products in their marketplace to make a profit.

It sounds simplistic. But if there is any common theme in the writings and sermons for success from the influential management gurus like Peter Drucker, Michael Porter, Tom Peters and Kotler himself it is that companies have to work from the market *in*, rather that from the company *out*, in devising their strategies.

This chapter examines those critical concepts which are fundamental to marketing strategies, including:

- Developing the strategic framework
- Carrying out a marketing audit
- Competitive analysis
- Clarifying the strategic role of the centre
- Measuring marketing effectiveness.

Developing the strategic framework

In terms of strategic planning this approach to the market by no means signals the end to a formal approach to long-term planning. On the contrary, translating the corporate mission into a coherent, strategic framework is more important than ever. What has changed is the style of the plan, a style that has to be far more flexible and dynamic. Rolling five-year budgets made up of numbers are being replaced by more 'goal-oriented' plans like 'We have to be number one in the market'. In many companies there is an increasing concern that planning systems grow of their own accord and become too bureaucratic. Models are used to give insights but not answers; they can be a superficial analysis matched to a budget. What is called strategic planning is really becoming more about strategic management. The view that says strategy is a plan and has to be implemented is taking a pounding. Instead, companies are beginning to focus on their 'core competences' and how best to exploit them fully. So while broad guidelines will be set at the most senior level with perhaps some input from specialist long-range planners, the real plan comes from divisional levels based on careful investigations of the organization's markets and its role in them.

This is alien to executives brought up in the school of the financial budget as plan. While Tom Peters has attracted criticism for an occasionally glib approach, there is a lot of truth in his assertion (Drucker *et al.*, 1990) that,

'Over the years we have developed a style of doing business that is detached, calculating, dispassionate, analytical, methodological, dull and hard. My own hypothesis about tomorrow's survivors is that they will be fast, intuitive, opportunistic, hustling, caring, trusting, empathizing, cheer leading, emotional, mistake making and action taking.'

These principles apply to all companies, whether they sell directly to consumers or to other businesses. Production-led organizations, particularly those in very complex new technologies, will find it hardest to make the shift. Engineers are used to being in charge of their own destiny. But, as Peter Stauvers, strategic marketing manager at Case Communications – which deals in a specialist IT niche where volumes are small – pointed out,

'The only difference between us and other companies is the amount we spend on research and development. Like other companies, we are getting much closer to our customers, and have to spend more time on promotion, distribution, branding and customer service.'

For some the solution is to import marketing skills from the consumer goods sector, as the Mercury case study shows.

Case 3.1 Mercury

Deregulating the UK telecommunications industry has, like financial services, resulted in a raft of new, eager competitors keen to take advantage of sophisticated technology and lure customers increasingly frustrated at what has been a monopoly service from British Telecom. Companies like Mercury Communication have entered the £13 billion telecoms market to meet this perceived consumer need by offering new products and services.

So far, cellular phones have been at the forefront of innovation. But an even greater revolution is on the way in the shape of personal communications networks, a radio-based portable system based on digital technology in line with a pan-European standard which – put simply – would allow people to have phone numbers rather than places. Last year the government awarded licences to three operators to set up personal communication networks (PCN) as a competitor to what are called the 'hardware' networks in the UK. One of them was Mercury Personal Communications, renamed One-2-One in early 1993.

This was the context into which Mercury Personal Communications' marketing director Roy Doughty brought strategic marketing skills honed to a sharp edge from years in consumer goods. It was not, he admitted, easy: the company was new, the investment breathtaking – setup costs were estimated

continues

continued

at about £1 billion – and he had as yet no product to show potential customers. But what he did have was a fascinating – and daunting – marketing challenge.

Having been in the telecoms industry a relatively short time after working in companies like Duracell, where he was chief executive, and latterly household goods maker Prestige, he believed that

> 'marketing people are still something of a rarity in telecoms. It has been an industry driven by features and not benefits for many years; companies have loaded in engineering features and then pushed them into the marketplace and the marketplace either misunderstood them because they were so complicated or communicated badly, or rejected them because the benefits they wanted didn't line up with the features.'

Doughty said the marketing job had three main attractions for him:

- Mercury has made it plain it will be driven by consumer need – a phrase relatively new to the telecoms industry;
- The phones and service will be sold directly to the consumer. Currently cellular phones are sold through middlemen called service providers;
- There is the tough challenge of changing behaviour and getting people who associate mobile phones only with 'yuppies' to become users of the new products when they finally appear.

An even trickier task is to ensure that the marketing culture spreads throughout the company:

> 'In telecoms people have generally not understand marketing and think it is advertising, which is what used to be the case in the 1960s. That has meant it is technology- and engineering-driven so when they believe that they have a technical solution to a perceived problem, "advertising" is asked to communicate that.'

The great advantage in building up a company from scratch was that Doughty could inculcate a marketing culture from the start.

Doughty insisted that his mission was the same as it was in his other jobs: define what people want, distinguish between features and benefits, find a sustainable competitive advantage, get the right positioning and make a profit. Doing the research needed to get the project working is hard, of course, without having a product to show.

That research has to be very sophisticated, from qualitative behaviourial and lifestyle studies to quantitative programmes. The findings are then compared with the original business plan. The character of the research is determined by a few distinctive features:

- It is a marketplace where there is a plethora of products but with people confused about what all the offerings are;
- It is characterized by a degree of 'techno-fear';

continues

continued

- It is a market with enormous penetration – who does not have a telephone? – but one without frequency of either purchase or, in many cases, usage;
- The usage itself is many-layered, from business calls, to offpeak time, and is characterized by a lack of consumer understanding of the cost/benefit of the service.

Doughty's marketing strategy was the same as that in an established consumer goods company, although with added elements of complexity:

- Ensuring that the product and service reflect what people will and can use by making a product that will have the power of a small personal computer seem user-friendly;
- Overseeing all the services that go into setting up a telephone company from scratch, including coping with regulatory bodies at both a national and regional level;
- Organizing sales and distribution – complicated by the fact that the PCNs will be aimed at a mass market with many different segments;
- Outlining the brand strategy, formulating a promotional package and briefing outside agencies;
- Determining the pricing structure: will people pay a premium for such mobility?

Doughty has not worked alone, but has brought in marketing muscle from outside to use as a 'bolt-on' resource that not only gave him the horsepower he needed while recruiting and building up his team but enabled him to keep challenging the assumptions of the original plan.

His promotional strategy will need to be carefully thought out. Not only will his agency need the creative clout to devise promotions that will help change behaviour, and make such a novel concept acceptable, but it will also have to display rigorous media planning skills to deal with what will have to be a very complicated market.

The stakes are high, but the marketing challenges are invigorating. Doughty did not minimize the enormity of the job before him. It revolved around several crucial factors:

- The ability of the shareholders to provide funds over a very long term;
- A regulatory framework that stays consistent;
- Fierce competition, not only from makers of other systems like cellular phones, but from other countries, notably Japan.

The starting point in developing a market-led strategy lies in a change of attitude. As Anne Ferguson, director of corporate communications at chemicals group ICI said,

'To me the most important thing, and what ICI is addressing, is how do you take marketing and make it permeate a business so that there is a change of attitude. That is what is critical. It does not mean taking marketing as some sort of fancy function, but to say that your entire business has to be market-oriented.'

It matters very little whether you ask: What is the role of marketing in strategy? or What is the role of strategy in marketing? The answer is the same: it is to grow profit. Several main principles must be followed to reach that objective.

- Select the markets that are growing and select the markets for growing; look at demographics, customer attitudes and lifestyles, technologies.
- Aim for market share, not just through prices and products but through people.
- Recruit people with the right values, train them and motivate them.
- Increase markets.
- Get the cost base down, through an intelligent and integrated use of information technology.
- Do not just rationalize production and cut lead times, but increase the information flow to the customer and create added value which will enable premium prices.

Juggling what can seem to be conflicting concepts demands a fundamental rethinking of the role of the senior management. This will be either exciting or terrifying to corporate leaders, depending on their ability to cope with change on an unprecedented scale. Company chief executives have to become leaders, missionaries, innovators, motivators. Military-style hierarchies will be increasingly less effective. Peter Drucker compared it to being the conductor of an orchestra. That in turn requires a structure or organization that does not dominate people but is fluid and able to be exploited for the common objectives, one that is a means to an end, not the end in itself.

This isn't anarchy, although it might seem so to those used to comfortable, static structures. Nor is it the ultimate solution. Companies have to adapt themselves according to what market they are in, and at what stage of the learning curve they are at. A certain type of management style which suits a young, fast-growing business would probably be unsuitable for one with a flattening growth curve. But the underlying principles are the same. The head of the company has to be the champion who ensures that everyone remains focused on the strategic vision. ICI is a good example. When chairman Denys Henderson took over in 1987, he wanted to make his mark and have an effect on long-term performance by making ICI more market-oriented, and has carried that vision through to the point where the two main ICI businesses of chemicals and pharmaceuticals are being demerged. It boils down to a very simple axiom, as director of corporate communication Ferguson pointed out:

'No customer, no business. If you look back, ICI was not market-driven but centred around skills like engineering and production. Now there is nothing wrong with that. Many people think that when you become more market-oriented you go from one extreme to the other and no longer put an emphasis on those skills.

'This is very wrong. What you should say is how do you make use of those skills in the marketplace. You no longer use them for their own sake, and that may be the difference. In the past ICI would say we are wonderful engineers, this is the best product available and therefore people will like it.'

There are two points to keep in mind:

- Measurements should not just be financial ratios, but include other, less tangible aspects like levels of customer satisfaction and employee turnover;
- Any planning has to have built-in flexibility and shouldn't exist for its own sake.

If all companies are equally proficient at developing a marketing strategy, how can one win over the others? According to Philip Kotler,

'I believe it won't be the companies that have developed better strategies, in so far as strategies can be copied rapidly. It will be the companies that carry out "marketing" more thoroughly.'

In other words, success will be in the details, in linking planning with implementation.

Case 3.2 NCR

NCR is a major provider of IT systems and services, offering the world's broadest line of industry-standard computer systems. The company established its first sales agency in England, in 1885, one year after the founding of the business, in Dayton, Ohio. Today NCR Europe employs about 13,000 people on the continent, nearly all Europeans. The company's two largest plants are in the UK and Germany, and it has major systems engineering and integration centres in Denmark and the Netherlands. NCR Europe, which covers the EC, European Free Trade Association (EFTA) countries and the East European countries, accounted for one-third, or $2 billion, of the parent

continues

continued

company's total revenues of $6 billion in 1988, and Europe's share of world-wide sales is growing.

NCR has taken the EC's 1992 changes as an opportunity for a stem-to-stern rethinking of the way it does business in Europe. Although NCR had an infrastructure in place in Europe for many years for gathering market and competitor information, management decided in 1987 that to cope with the EC's plans for full integration, more information and guidance were necessary than the basic system was set up to supply. To manage its approach to 1992, NCR developed a four-phase, multi-year undertaking called 'Project 1992'.

For Phase I, completed in late 1988, NCR retained the European arm of Hill & Knowlton, the multinational public relations firm, to analyse the effect of European integration not only on the IT industry but also on six target industries that are heavy users of NCR products. The Phase I findings were broad but provided enough detail to allow NCR's management to focus on a dozen or more key issues.

Phase II involves two parallel activities. First, about a dozen issues have been assigned to NCR experts (known as issue 'owners'). The issues include, for example, manufacturing, law, marketing, telecommunications standards and subjects related to suppliers. The owners have defined the scope of their assigned issues and have made preliminary recommendations on the position NCR should take on each issue.

Second, company executives have commissioned the Battelle Institute, a multinational technology research and consultancy firm based in Columbus, Ohio, to work with NCR issue owners to develop scenarios for Europe and the European IT industry throughout the 1990s, using a cross-impact matrix methodology supported by the institute's exclusive BASICS-PC software. The methodology uses a wide range of expert judgement and takes account of the interrelationships among the various issues, events and time frames inherent in the EC programme. It also allows for changes over time so that the scenarios do not become outdated.

Battelle and NCR developed the first set of scenarios for the European Community in the summer of 1989. They produced an *ad hoc* update to the scenarios following the fall of the Berlin Wall in November 1989. During the spring and summer of 1990, they produced a comprehensive revision of the EC scenarios that incorporated new expert input, more definitive factors for the EC's relationship with EFTA and the East European countries and a time frame that extended to the end of 1995. They have also developed a separate, but related set of scenarios covering the economic development of Eastern Europe and its implications there.

Phase III, which began in the autumn of 1989, concerned the implementation and monitoring of the issue owners' recommendations. To guide this phase, the company's board of directors provided the broad perspective needed to bring the highly focused opinions of the issue owners into balance.

continues

continued

Along with their recommendations, issue owners identified key indicators that should be monitored. They established the 'threshold values' of the indicators so that NCR line managers will recognize significant deviations from the original assumptions and take appropriate and timely action. Phase III is likely to continue through the 1990s and possibly beyond.

Phase IV is being introduced while Phase III is under way and, like the latter, will go on for several years. In Phase IV NCR proposes to develop planning partnerships with leading companies in the targeted industries to focus on their IT need in the new European market. NCR views this phase as especially important because it will help the company plan its R&D to meet customer needs from the outset. It also represents an opportunity for the company to lever the project into a marketing tool that will have business value both for itself and for its customers.

Carrying out a marketing audit

A marketing audit should be carried out within the context of the overall strategic investigation. According to Kotler *et al.* (1989), who pioneered the concept of the marketing audit, it is 'a comprehensive, systematic, independent, and periodic examination of a company's – or business unit's – marketing environment, objectives, strategies, and activities with a view to determining problem areas and opportunities and recommending a plan of action to improve the company's marketing performance.' The 10 most common problems market audits turn up, according to Kotler are:

(1) Insufficient knowledge of customers' behaviour and attitudes.
(2) Failure to segment the market in the most advantageous way.
(3) Lack of a marketing planning process.
(4) Price-cutting rather than improvements in value.
(5) Failure to have a market-based product-evaluation process.
(6) Misunderstanding the company's marketing strengths and how they relate to the market.
(7) Narrow, short-term view of advertising and promotion.
(8) Tendency to view marketing as involving only advertising or sales.
(9) Organizational structure that is incompatible with the marketing strategy.
(10) Failure to invest for future development, particularly in the area of human resources.

The following sample of the key elements of an international marketing audit, written by marketing consultants Edward Lucaire, is an 'international' interpretation of a similar general marketing audit outline that was developed by Kotler.

Sample outline for evaluation of marketing performance
(1) Macroenvironmental considerations
   (a) Demographic – Are the demographics in the country shifting favourably for the product or service? If not favourably, can the product/service be altered to adapt to the demographics?
   (b) Economic – Are the economic conditions right (in terms of earnings, prices, discretionary income, and so on) for the people to afford or continue to afford the product?
   (c) Natural – Are there natural resources available, if needed, to make the product locally? Is there a shortage or an abundance?
   (d) Technological – Can the country handle the high-tech aspects of the business? Have the employees handled the high-tech aspects in the past?
   (e) Political – Has the political climate changed enough to affect the overall business (for example, anti-foreign sentiments) or specific products (for example, birth control pills, devices)?
   (f) Cultural – Have the values changed sufficiently to accept the product? Are there relevant religious aspects (for example, objections of Catholics, Muslims to birth control?)
(2) Task environment considerations
   (a) Markets – Does the market or segment thought to be there actually exist? Is it growing fast enough to justify keeping the product?
   (b) Customers – Are customers perceiving the product properly? And the perception of the parent company?
(3) Competitors – Have the competitors done well? If so, why? Are there indigenous brands?
   (a) Distribution and dealers – Are there enough distribution outlets? Can additional ones be located and bought?
   (b) Suppliers – Are there adequate numbers of suppliers and are they sophisticated enough to handle the product? Has the ad agency properly positioned the product? Is the agency using the right media?
   (c) Publics – Are certain publics (for example, environmentalists) adversely affecting the performance of the product? Are they using the right media?
(4) Marketing strategy
   (a) Business mission – Is it feasible in the UK (for example), given the initial or historical results?
   (b) Marketing objectives and goals – Can they be achieved?
   (c) Strategy – Has the strategy worked? If not, what elements have to be changed? Do some elements work better than others in the target country or region?
(5) Marketing organization
   (a) Formal structure – Is the marketing hierarchy appropriate or does it have to change to accommodate the culture, for example, adapt to a consensus decision mode?

(b) Functional efficiency – Are the various divisions working harmoniously? Is reporting to a foreigner (often the case) a problem? Do the executives need more training?

(6) Marketing systems

(a) Marketing information – Is the information/intelligence dependable? Is it coming in as fast as it should? Are the suppliers reliable? Are they affiliated with an international organization or network?

(b) Marketing planning – Is the system working and effective?

(c) Marketing control – Are the marketing elements being monitored and evaluated on a regular basis? Is each problem area being diagnosed properly and addressed quickly?

(d) New product development – Are new product opportunities and line extensions being sought out on a regular basis?

(7) Marketing productivity – Are the products making enough money to justify the investment in the short term? In the long term? Can future costs be cut?

(8) Marketing functions

(a) Product – Does the product fill a niche in the country? Is it better than existing products? Is the product being positioned optimally? Can other features be added to better suit the product to the country's or region's preference?

(b) Price – Does the price justify the value in the country? How can the price/value relationship be enhanced?

(c) Distribution – Are there sufficient distribution outlets? If not, what existing outlets can be utilized? Any new outlets?

(d) Advertising, sales, promotion and publicity – Do the home country ads, positionings, price-offs, and so on work in other countries? How much media exposure did the advertising get? What percentage of the population has seen the advertising? Has the publicity potential been fully exploited? Do sales-promotion techniques (money-off coupons, retailer discounts, and so on) work well?

(e) Sales force – Is the sales force selling? Are they sufficiently motivated with commissions, incentives? Do they know how to sell the product?

Competitive analysis

Competitive analysis should be at the heart of strategic planning, since gaining and keeping competitive advantage over rivals is what ensures survival. But the concept of competitive advantage is not straightforward – competition itself is unlimited and international and companies have to assess carefully both the actual and potential competitive forces surrounding them.

There are a number of well-defined sources of competitive advantage (Day and Wensley, 1988). For example, companies can maintain leading market positions with superior skills and resources. Skills can include superior engineering or technical skills, or an ability to respond quickly and effectively to change. Superior resources can cover the scale of the manufacturing facility, the location, distributional networks and so on. And the adroit company will lever these skills and resources to gain positional advantages in terms of lower relative costs and/or differentiating the business by creating perceived superiority.

Faced with the increasing ferocity of Japanese attacks on such a wide range of industries, however, some observers argue that 'laundry lists' of strategic typologies like product life cycle, product portfolios and the experience curve have precluded mainly Western management from being truly innovative in a global sense. As Gary Hamel and C.K. Prahalad argued (1989), companies have to emulate the Japanese by not merely developing a strategic plan that matches resources and opportunities but by creating a vision of strategic intent which comprises a focus on winning, on motivation of all the workforce through communication of company goals, and is used as a basis for optimum resource allocation among different countries and sectors. While the emphasis in strategic planning is on trimming ambitions to match available resources, they pointed out, the emphasis in the latter is to lever resources to reach seemingly unattainable goals: as when Japanese earth-moving manufacturer Komatsu set out to 'Encircle Caterpillar' and copier-maker Canon to 'Beat Xerox'.

The authors have discerned four successful approaches to competitive innovation by the Japanese to build global businesses and which Western management would do well to emulate:

(1) Building layers of advantage by continually improving existing skills and learning new ones: once the Japanese began to lose labour and capital cost advantages in the 1960s, they poured effort and investment into process technology and quality standards.
(2) Searching for loose bricks by analysing the conventional wisdom in the market and finding a base of attack just outside the territory occupied by the industry leaders: as the Japanese TV industry did in the US by first concentrating on small-screen and portable televisions, thus establishing a base from which to attack the colour TV market.
(3) Changing the rules of the game – as Canon did when it took Xerox on in the copier market, both in terms of product development and distribution.
(4) Competing through collaboration: as Chapter 2 shows, the formation of strategic alliances both across industry borders and within sector boundaries is increasing.

Analysing areas of longer-term competitive advantage should be accompanied by analysis of competitors' sales and marketing efforts on a regular basis.

Advertising and promotion campaigns, discounting practices, relationships with distributors and various other aspects of marketing are important indicators of competitive activity, although details are often difficult to ascertain. Doubly difficult is obtaining accurate competitive numbers – market share, advertising expenditures and the like. To make matters worse for multinationals, the data from country to country are rarely comparable. (Both the International Advertising Association, headquartered in New York, and the World Federation of Advertisers in Brussels are actively trying to harmonize these types of data to achieve cross-border comparability.)

Competitive analysis is usually conducted at both the corporate and local levels. For instance, PepsiCo monitors Coca-Cola's global strategy from its corporate offices in New York, while Coke keeps track of Pepsi from Atlanta. But both companies depend on their foreign subsidiaries to observe each other's overseas marketing strategies and tactics, as well as local share data and advertising and marketing expenditures.

In the soft drinks market, for example, shelf space is of utmost importance to sales. In the absence of a syndicated research report on actual retail sales, an audit by someone on the scene of soft drink shelf space in key retail outlets can provide a quick assessment of brand share and the net effects of each soft drink brand's marketing programmes. However, A.C. Neilsen & Company, a worldwide research firm, monitors many consumer product sales, including those of soft drinks, in many countries. Its reports include dollar sales, unit sales, shelf space, prices, promotional activity and other data.

Alaska Airlines, which has routes in the US, Mexico and has plans to fly to the former Soviet Union, bases its marketing effectiveness evaluations on market share. It compares its share gains and losses to those of its competitors in every market it serves. The airline industry as a whole has a wealth of data produced by online computer reservation systems, such as American Airlines' 'Sabre' system, the Galileo system used by British Airways, United Airlines and others and the Amadeus systems used by Lufthansa, Air France and Iberia. Because of this, competitive analysis is somewhat easier to conduct than in many other industries. As a senior executive of Alaska Airlines noted,

'In any given city, we can measure on a weekly basis precise changes in both our own and our competitors' market shares down to a tenth of a percentage point. In this business there are no secrets between competitors when it comes to market share.'

Alaska Airlines also monitors the effectiveness of its advertising strategies when it alone is promoting a destination and when a competitor is promoting the same destination. According to the senior executive,

'We compare phone inquiries about the destination when there is a promotion competition to when there isn't any competition. The number of inquiries gives us a good sense of how well the promotion campaign is being received. If we are losing ground on a heavily promoted destination, we will reconsider the promotion.'

Clarifying the strategic role of the centre

'We maintain a small staff at the centre in Britain which acts on occasion as traffic policeman, sometimes as an orchestra conductor, infrequently as an auditor, and very often as a cheer leader.'
    Richard Giordano, chairman, BOC, to the London Business School

Companies have to begin to address the central/local relationship as a strategic requirement as soon as they start selling to a foreign country. It needs significant numbers of people to sell, distribute or service its products there. Reliance on an independent distributor is sometimes the answer, but usually only a partial and short-term one. Joint ventures, too, have their uses, but for forceful marketing and sales, a subsidiary company, set up from scratch or acquired, is the only effective vehicle. The basic strategic considerations are as follows:

- Customers making important purchases need to feel the supplier's long-term commitment to their interests, and therefore its local presence can be essential.
- The supplier's product range may need to be supplemented or adapted with software and so on, to suit local needs.
- Local manufacture may be necessary, either for the output or to emphasize 'good citizenship'.
- If government contracts are in prospect, a local presence and tax base are politically advisable, whatever the EC regulations may state.
- Good local business opportunities may exist outside the group's product range; acquisition of, or a joint venture with, a local company may also be desirable.
- Nationalistic purchasers prefer to buy from local companies not obviously controlled by outside interests.

As the product range and the number of customers increase, an expanding local presence is almost inevitable. Cash flow becomes an issue and extensive local finance facilities will be necessary, while closer attention has to be paid to the peculiarities of the market.

One recent attempt to clarify the roles that companies adopt at the centre in relation to their portfolio of businesses has been developed by Andrew Campbell and Michael Goold of the Ashridge Strategic Management Centre, working in conjunction with McKinsey's London office. They distinguished three separate 'parenting' roles; controller, coach and orchestrator:

(1) The controller adds value by picking the right managers and motivating them effectively with financial targets.
(2) The coach uses its knowledge and experience of each business to develop and build strategy, judge and improve operating performance, and share skills and best practice (for example, Unilever).
(3) The orchestrator coordinates a chain of businesses to realize the synergies available from marketing and manufacturing (for example, IBM).

Many companies, taken as wholes, fall into either the coaching or the orchestrating categories. But the range of their activities, the stages of development of each subsidiary, the personalities of the individuals, the state of design and manufacturing technology and the degree of competition in a given market ensure that they have to use all patterns selectively for different markets at different times.

Electrolux, whose products range from refrigerators, through earth-moving equipment to plastic flowers, describes itself openly as 'an impossible organization, but the only one that will work'. Its group president and chief executive Anders Scharp acts as an orchestrator toward white goods, as a coach toward Gränges (the aluminium subsidiary) and as a controller toward agricultural machinery.

Still, if the classification helps to clarify the actual relationship between the centre and its operating units, and to implant in managers' minds the knowledge that there are different modes of operation that the central authority can adopt, and that the present one is not necessarily the most appropriate, it will have performed a valuable service.

Case 3.3 Reynolds

Reynolds Metals, a leading producer of aluminium and other metals, believes that, even apart from the coming economic integration, Europe's economic, political and cultural diversity requires that major multinationals have European-based central management teams. Indeed, Reynolds Chairman and CEO Bill Bourke said that the company's decision to create a headquarters office in Europe would have been made 'with or without 1992.'

Bourke spoke from experience. As one of the first chairmen of Ford Europe in the mid-1960s, he helped shape the car maker's organization and strategy for Europe. 'I believe we can't manage Europe from Richmond, Virginia, just as I believed at Ford we couldn't manage Europe from Dearborn, Michigan,' he said.

continues

continued

The natural inclination of country managers to 'go their own way' was reinforced under Reynold's old organizational structure. Managing directors of each European operation reported to the president of Reynolds International at the home office in Richmond. (The company has wholly owned subsidiaries in Germany, Italy, Spain, the Netherlands and France and majority owned affiliates in Austria and Belgium.) Reynolds's president had to juggle 25 direct reports world-wide.

The result in Europe was chaos, admitted Bourke: 'You had salesmen from four or five different Reynolds companies calling on the same accounts – and selling the same product lines – which was a very unhealthy situation.' On the manufacturing side, Reynolds had duplicate operations in many countries for aluminium, aluminium sheet and extruded products and 'no total plan for Europe to go for the cheapest source and best quality,' said Bourke. A fragmented organization in Europe, managed from the US, also worked against Reynolds *vis-à-vis* competitors. European players, like Pechiney in France, VAW in Germany and Alusuisse in Switzerland, are big, government-owned entities. 'If we were going to be successful in competing against them,' said Bourke, 'we needed the scale of being pan-European.'

A headquarters operation seemed the best way to bring unity to the organization. Hence, in 1987 Reynolds established a small regional headquarters office, Reynolds Europe, in Lausanne to oversee manufacturing, distribution and marketing throughout the continent. Bourke chose Lausanne because it is neither in southern nor northern Europe. Although Switzerland was an expensive site, Bourke said he 'didn't want the Italians or Spaniards to think we were abandoning them by locating in Hamburg.' He clearly recalled the experience of Ford Europe, which lost almost half its managers in Germany because it located its headquarters in 'rival' London. Bourke noted, 'There's a lot of talk about a united Europe, but, believe me, European nations are every bit as economically nationalistic as they were 200 years ago.'

Managing directors of country companies now report to the president of Reynolds Europe, who in turn reports to the head of Reynolds International in Richmond. Other managers based in Lausanne include a CFO, an executive vice president in charge of manufacturing and several vice presidents of major functions, such as marketing.

Reynolds Europe provides a 'single voice' in Western Europe to represent the parent company and an organization to help subsidiaries complement, not compete with, each other. Among the benefits cited by Bourke were: a rational manufacturing and sourcing plan, faster decision making, pan-European marketing and advertising (particularly for consumer products, such as aluminium foil). Overall, the company has achieved more power through size. Said Bourke: 'I think we have more clout today – not only with the EC, but also with individual governments – than we had when we were fragmented.' In particular, Reynolds's voice in the influential European Aluminium Association has been greatly strengthened by the company's designation of the president of Reynolds Europe as its sole representative.

Defining the strategy is one of the most important functions performed by the centre in its marketing stance. The process of leadership starts with a vision of some distant and desirable objective and then communicating the enthusiasm for it to the whole group. For many companies contemplating future global, not just European, competition, this has meant abandoning earlier attempts to be strong in many product and service areas in a few geographical markets, in favour of strength in a few products in the majority of markets, especially the Triad.

The UK-based TI Group moved out of bicycles and domestic appliances, among other activities, and concentrated on industrial seals for machinery and hi-tech tubing, markets in which it was already strong and now has leading world shares. It had only 2.5% of the world market for domestic appliances. TI's chairman and chief executive Chris Lewinton argued, 'We either had to sell everything and go into appliances, or sell appliances.' TI chose the latter, leaving Electrolux and the US Whirlpool as the top two white goods manufacturers in the world.

For many companies, this process of consolidation still has a long way to run. Electrolux itself, for example, is likely to hive off some of its more peripheral activities in the near future. But equally important is the need for the central management to spot the weaknesses in whatever it decides are its core products, as well as to take advantage of any suitable opportunities that arise. Acquisition is a natural way of rectifying the imbalance.

Case 3.4 Nestlé

For Nestlé, one of the largest and most successful food companies in the world, marketing is the basic business function:

> 'All our salaries, indeed, all our business, starts when I hear a cash register in a supermarket go "bing" and I see a Nestlé product being bought. That is the beginning – without that you have nothing,'

declared Camillo Pagano, former general manager and executive vice president, marketing, at Nestlé headquarters in Switzerland.

Underlying that statement lies a complex and deeply considered corporate view on strategic marketing, starting with the role of the brands and moving through to how they are communicated. Under the title 'From Product to Brand Marketing', Pagano had been carrying out a world-wide programme to

continues

continued

tell 300 of the top Nestlé executives, along with the company's agencies, what the company's strategic view of marketing in a changing environment has to be. At Nestlé, Pagano said that the role of the centre is to formulate the strategies:

> 'What we like to say is that we have strategies that are centralized and operations that are decentralized. Decentralized does not mean an anarchical state of 125 companies doing what they want and the people at the centre at whatever level just looking at this and doing nothing.'

That does not mean that he and his team do tactical 'marketing'. What the centre does is push to change attitudes, not run the operations. Acting as the 'ayatollah of marketing' means persuasion, not autocracy.

For companies like Nestlé, the years of mass marketing, enjoyed during the 1950s, are dead. In the 1980s and 1990s they were facing:

- Few technological differences;
- The switch of communication/advertising's role from informing to seducing and enticing the consumers to identify themselves with the brand rather than the product;
- An inflation of both media costs and media vehicles;
- The growing power of the retailers because of trade concentration and own-label, which means that the number three or four brand will probably fail;
- The demand for better products from the consumers, who are no longer so easily divisible into convenient social groups.

As Pagano pointed out, 'There is not an average consumer now. The individual consumer becomes an "I am me" consumer and that has created the need for segmenting. And segmenting means what? It is easy to say, but difficult to do efficiently.' It means staying cost-effective while giving the consumer better quality and a perceived difference: all consumers for example, would not be happy buying the same five pound slab of chocolate.

The equation then becomes even more complex. Once you have a clear message, how do you get it to the consumer? And here is where Pagano saw seminal change: classical advertising is becoming increasingly ineffective and is slowly dying and will have to be replaced by a new way of communicating the message. 'People forget that to have a spot on TV only gives you an opportunity – it does not necessarily mean to communicate,' said Pagano. Is anyone in the room? Are they really watching, or flicking channels? So the notion of cost per thousand as a measurement of effectiveness is becoming obsolete. It really only measures how many TV sets are in use.

So, said Pagano, you have effectiveness going down, you have the rise of segmentation, and, to compound the problem, the consumer him or herself is segmented:

> 'The same consumer is the person who has a quick breakfast in his car, has a Big Mac at lunch, and may enjoy a coq au vin with some Bordeaux at dinner. So how do you pick those consumers and beam

continues

continued

to them communications that are in essence the same, but that have to be different because otherwise you antagonize the consumer in a different cluster or age group?'

It calls for a critical reassessment of media planning to find a way to shoot with a rifle instead of 'carpet bombing'.

One of the main challenges for any company, particularly one of Nestlé's size, Pagano agreed, is speed – speed to change, to take decisions, to get from conception to reality, and flexibility: 'This kind of speed, time and flexible reaction by us against competition can only be done if we have as thin a layer of communication as possible.'

What are the elements of Nestlé's philosophy to deal with all these far-reaching changes? They include:

- Informal communication at the top;
- Quick decision-taking;
- Antipaper, antibureaucratic systems;
- Strong cynicism towards projected figures – 'they are always wrong';
- Pragmatism;
- An emphasis on long-term directional planning (LTP) as the basis for all decisions;
- Avoiding the use of market research as a crutch and the sole basis of decisions.

Keeping central strategic control while encouraging local initiative is probably the major issue facing most large corporations. Pagano admitted the juggling act is never easy: 'it is a daily fight between not giving the impression that you have the "Vatican dogma" but at the same time avoiding losing the periphery energy of the empire.'

Nestlé has both a strong but lean headquarters and devolved, decentralized operations around the world. It operates in Europe with a system of 'market heads', a structure it does not see changing in the foreseeable future. What it does need to do, though, said Pagano, is promote a more positive attitude towards intermarket communication:

'What we are trying to say, wrongly or rightly, is look, we have to work together more but also enhance our individual personalities. The key in Europe is to change the attitude from immediately finding what is different and then settle for some harmony. Today we have got to get them to think in terms of first finding out why we are similar and then discuss if there are any insurmountable differences. These are not just words, but changes of attitude.'

Measuring marketing effectiveness

Many current trends, such as tougher, world-wide competition and shorter product lives, throw more strain on the centre's ability to keep itself informed of market trends and to assess the performance of its operating units. Every budget and target implies a judgement as to what is possible, and therefore knowledge of the local conditions.

The large, centralized head office implies that executives there can make an intelligent assessment of, among other things:

- What growth a business unit should be achieving – 20% a year may sound impressive at the shareholders' meeting, but may be sluggish if the market is growing at 50%;
- The local manager's explanation as to why he has fallen behind budget, his remedial action and the value of his predictions for the rest of the period;
- The strength of local competition (including incidence of predatory pricing);
- How the market differs from others;
- The general economic and social trends.

Large quantities of background data and analysis are therefore frequently required, with a high risk that the centre will nevertheless miss the really significant underlying trends, or that the familiar 'paralysis by analysis' will set in.

The entrepreneur's method of relying on personal judgement, or even the cruder 'squeezing until the pips squeak', can sometimes produce spectacular results, at least in the short term, and is the basis of many conglomerates' success. The implications for the long-term health of the operation or for its wider international strategy may not be so favourable, however.

Whatever the approach, marketing performance must be assessed regularly. Many companies evaluate performance at both the subsidiary or country level and the corporate headquarters level. Multinationals with a regional structure typically review performance at the regional level as well.

Marketing evaluation criteria include a combination of sales, market share, customer satisfaction and profit. Every company weights the various criteria differently, reflecting its current priorities and the demand for its products or services at the time. Some firms consistently put more emphasis on purely financial objectives, such as profitability, return on investment and subsidiary earnings per share. Others stress market-based criteria such as market share, number of new product introductions and customer satisfaction. Regardless of the particular criteria a company emphasizes, the key to the evaluation process is to examine any deviations between objectives and actual results of each operating unit and then assess the unit's contributions to overall corporate goals.

Of course, events outside the control of marketing executives such as political instability, recessions, inflation and other factors may be responsible for failure to meet marketing objectives. In 1989, for example, political turmoil in China upset the marketing efforts of multinationals there, many of which had just begun to do business in that country.

For most companies, performance evaluation becomes increasingly difficult as the number of distinct business or functional units increases. Some companies address this problem by formulating what are known as 'market equivalent measures of performance', or MEMPs. These are equations that attempt to factor in differences in per capita GNP, infrastructure, competition, and so on among distinct markets. MEMPs are used to assess the performance of foreign subsidiaries for which domestic performance measures would be of little use because the markets involved are so dissimilar.

Market share is calculated as a percentage of total units sold or total sales in a given geographic or demographic market. It is an especially good performance indicator for measuring the effectiveness of 'tacit marketing strategies' – that is, strategies aimed at either product introduction or repositioning. However, market share does not accurately gauge a marketing strategy's long-term effectiveness because it does not necessarily reflect customer loyalty, consistent profit margins and other characteristics that are important to the future growth of the business. On the contrary, a penetration pricing strategy, which lowers wholesale and retail prices to gain market share rapidly, usually *reduces* profit margins and does not necessarily win loyal, long-term customers, upon whom successful customer franchises are built.

British Telecom uses market share to measure marketing effectiveness when introducing a new telecommunications service. First, a demographic market is targeted. The company then sets up market share goals based on the per-month growth of that segment's customer base. 'In the initial stages, market share is clearly fundamental,' explained Nicholas Kane, BT's director of marketing. 'We are (less) concerned with profitability or return on asset figures than we are with gaining market share (and growing revenue).' During the growth stage, BT's marketing strategies are monitored almost continuously and are evaluated at least monthly. These updated figures are used to set future objectives.

Matsushita Electric Industry Co. (MEI) gives its overseas sales executives complete freedom in setting marketing objectives. Each of the regional directors formulates a six-month plan, including projections of sales, market shares, profit and the ratio of profit to units sold and costs. Also covered in the six-month contracts are figures for total units moved through the distribution system, the number of employees involved in marketing, plans for advertising and pricing and other marketing strategy components. These plans are submitted by the regional directors to headquarters, where they are reviewed, co-ordinated with MEI's manufacturing divisions, and approved by the president of Matsushita. MEI's president and the regional director sign a contract based on the six-month plan.

At the end of each six-month period, Matsushita's regional directors are summoned individually to Osaka. They are held accountable if their operations are consistently 5% above or below projections. If a region is consistently exceeding its contract projections, its executives are considered to be making poor estimates. If results are consistently below projections, the head office is likely to conclude that the regional director is doing a poor job of managing the operations. The director is allowed to present the rationale for the performance, but if results remain outside the tolerance level of plus or minus 5% for four consecutive six-month periods, MEI takes appropriate action, including reassignment.

Olin uses several effectiveness checks to gauge success. For example, the company ascertains whether the product groups are consistently achieving predetermined annual objectives. If performance against objectives falls short, the company must decide if too much or too little authority has been delegated or if the goals and budgets to which the operating units are committed are unattainable. Comparisons are made between the profitability of the overseas business and the profitability of the domestic business, and, in some cases, between specific overseas units and specific domestic units. If subsidiary profitability is substantially higher or lower than domestic profitability, corporate management delves into the reasons behind the disproportion. In the past, Olin has identified such factors as 'effort per dollar of sales' and 'lower selling price per unit of product' to explain the disproportions.

For the majority of multinationals, formal marketing effectiveness evaluations coincide with annual budget reviews, but the frequency of other reviews varies widely. Some companies monitor continuously (with the help of online systems), while others opt for weekly, monthly or quarterly reviews. The US auto industry has traditionally used 10-day reports.

Grand Metropolitan monitors the effectiveness of its subsidiary marketing programmes annually, but evaluation is conducted at sector level more frequently and at the local sales level marketing activity is often measured on a monthly basis.

At the start of each company year, long-term (that is, four-year) objectives are updated and agreed upon and short-term objectives reviewed. (Long-term overall objectives are set by the individual sectors working in conjunction with representatives from the corporate planning department, but specific marketing tasks remain the exclusive province of the relevant sector managers.) Short-term marketing performance is judged by reference to these short- and long-term goals at regular intervals by local management and by sector management, both of which formally review progress at the end of each quarter.

In the autumn, each sector reviews its strategy and, if necessary, revises it. This review is finalized at the corporate centre in December. Local marketing decisions are then amended in the light of any changes that have been agreed to. The review at this time is concerned with strategic concepts rather than specific quantified business objectives. These issues are settled at the subsequent set of meetings that takes place in the spring, at which quantities objectives are agreed for actions consequent upon previously agreed strategies. The final step in the process is the submission and agreement of annual plans at local, sector and corporate level. This takes place in August/September.

Hewlett-Packard, which brings in about half of its sales from overseas, monitors the profitability of its subsidiaries on a monthly and quarterly basis. Each quarterly report contains only actual figures, with no estimates given. Hewlett-Packard's corporate office has each month's world-wide sales figures from each subsidiary on the first day of the following month. Consolidated profitability results are available for performance evaluation within six days of the end of the month.

Case 3.5 Siemens and Ciba-Geigy

Siemens AG, headquartered in Munich and one of the world's major electrical engineering and electronics companies, calls its marketing decision making system 'highly centralized'. 'But', said a company spokesman, 'there are practical limits to the autonomy you can give to a regional headquarters.' Siemens leaves almost all marketing plan elements to the managing boards of its 14 groups.

The managing board of each group formulates marketing strategies with respect to product offerings, sourcing, distribution and pricing. The boards also lay out marketing objectives for each product division. Finally, the boards formulate local product marketing strategies such as promotion, credit incentives, volume discounts and positioning in conjunction with local product executives and the president of each regional division.

Siemen's executives felt that a decentrally planned strategy for every group was a necessity if the whole company were to be successful. 'Local subsidiaries are supposed to aid in the realization of the groups' goals,' the company spokesman said. 'We help the groups meet company objectives.' Indeed, the corporate executive office is involved in every major investment, most business plans and every acquisition before implementation.

Siemens leaves programme execution up to the product executives. 'We do not intervene in the way the groups' product division presidents carry out the plans. We monitor only the execution of the plan.' Once plans have been implemented, a corporate auditing department under the auspices of the corporate finance division keeps a watchful eye on marketing performance.

If Siemens leans toward centralization, Ciba-Geigy Corp., the large Swiss pharmaceutical company, falls more towards decentralization. Director

continues

continued

Martin Ab Egg called his company's policy of delegating marketing decision making 'guided autonomy.' Ciba-Geigy allows its foreign subsidiaries autonomy within certain predetermined parameters.

Ciba-Geigy's world-wide marketing strategy is based on partner orientation, focusing on existing top products and on R&D of new innovative pharmaceutical products. The company gives direction to its overseas subsidiaries by telling them which new products to promote in their geographic markets. The subsidiaries are encouraged to come up with their own strategic plans, based on a common understanding of corporate objectives and intentions. In the parent company's view, it is the executives on the scene who should be formulating marketing strategies because they know the needs of the local market better than anyone else.

The plans are then approved or challenged by headquarters in Basel. Once plans have been given a green light, the subsidiaries are free to move within the predetermined scope of the strategy, and Basel assumes a support role only. 'We do not interfere; we help them to achieve the goals which we have commonly set. We first challenge them to get the plan, we then approve the plan, and then comes the time where we support [the plan],' said Ab Egg. Most of the corporate support he refers to is financial. Ciba executives estimate that the Basel office's role in international marketing is about 70% support and 30% management.

Many aspects of the marketing strategy are determined at headquarters, although the foreign subsidiaries may alter a large number of them. Strategic components that have been changed at the local level include resource allocation, advertising and promotion.

When a subsidiary's president believes a new product idea or modification has promise, he fills out a report, called a checklist, which is analysed in Basel to see if the change is reasonable and, further, if it should be adopted by other foreign subsidiaries. The only checklists Basel does not approve are those it finds unacceptable from a financial and/or strategic viewpoint.

Ciba-Geigy, like Siemens, limits capital expenditures that can be made by individual operating units. When the expenditure level rises over a certain size, which varies from country to country, approval from headquarters is required. Basel keeps an eye on strategy execution through the use of regional marketing representatives located in Basel, who report to the international head of marketing. Ab Egg considered the liaison people as an important channel of communication between the field and the home office. 'These individuals serve as market strategy consultants,' explained Egg. When significant marketing questions arise in a country, then the consultants inject their own expertise and/or involve other headquarter specialists in making suggestions to executives at the foreign subsidiaries. The executives are not bound by the liaisons' suggestions.

Summary

- Developing the strategic framework: translating the corporate mission into a coherent, strategic framework is more important than ever. What has changed is the style of the plan, a style that has to be far more flexible and dynamic. What is called strategic planning is really becoming more about strategic management. The view that says strategy is a plan and has to be implemented is taking a pounding. Instead, companies are beginning to focus on their 'core competences' and how best to exploit them fully.

- Whatever method a company chooses for setting the strategic plan with the market as the focus, it should be able to ask and answer questions like:
  - What business are we in?
  - What business do we want to be in?
  - What business should we be in?
  - Do our strategic objectives take the dynamics of our markets into account so that we can make the best use of resource allocation?
  - Are we geared to coping with the unexpected and unpredictable?

- A marketing audit should be carried out within the context of the overall strategic investigation. It should be a comprehensive, systematic, independent and periodic examination of a company's – or business unit's – marketing environment, objectives, strategies and activities with a view to determining the effective leverage of core competences and recommending a plan of action to improve the company's marketing performance.

- Competitive analysis should be at the heart of strategic planning, since gaining and keeping competitive advantage over rivals is what ensures survival.

- Monitoring the sales and marketing efforts of competitors is not something to be done only in the context of the long-term plan, but is an essential component of strategic marketing planning and should be done on a regular basis.

- Companies have to begin to address the central/local relationship as a strategic requirement as soon as they start selling to a foreign country since it is a key factor in the successful implementation of strategies and influences the speed and flexibility needed to be proactive in the markets.

- Marketing performance must be assessed regularly. Marketing evaluation criteria include a combination of sales, market share, customer satisfaction and profit.

Checklist

In terms of strategic marketing, does your company:

(1)   Conduct strategic planning as a rigid, formalized exercise, or is strategic planning more flexible and based on careful investigations of the organization's markets and its role within them?

(2)   Carry out regular marketing audits?

(3)   Have a system for evaluating and maintaining competitive advantage?

(4)   Rigorously analyse its competitive position by monitoring the efforts of the competition?

(5)   Address the central/local relationship as a strategic requirement?

(6)   Assess the effectiveness of marketing performance regularly?

References

Day, G. S. and Wensley, R. (1988). Assessing advantage: A framework for diagnosing competitive superiority. *Journal of Marketing*, **52**, April

Drucker P., Ohmae K., Porter M. and Peters T. (1990). *Management Briefings*. Special Report No. 1202. London: The Economist Publications, April

Hamel, G. and Prahalad, C. K. (1989). Strategic intent. *Harvard Business Review*, May/June

Kotler, P., Gregor, W. T. and Rodgers III, W. H. (1989). *The Marketing Audit Comes of Age*. Boston: Sloan Management Review Reprint Series, Winter

4

Organizing for marketing advantage

Introduction

The previous chapter examined the elements critical to formulating marketing strategy. This chapter considers more closely the practicalities of organizing for marketing advantage, particularly in the light of the European Single Market where the demand will be for both unity and diversity of the marketing strategy. It gives examples of companies that are restructuring in order to maintain central control over core issues on both a regional and global basis to leverage ideas, expertise and systems. At the same time it juggles with the need to keep in tune with local market needs. It covers the following topics:

- The need to coordinate
- Developing the country manager's role
- The international coordinator
- Product managers and business marketing
- Product managers and consumer goods
- The lead country approach
- Managing through the matrix
- The Japanese way
- Developing teams and task forces
- Creating a networked approach.

The need to coordinate

Many companies are increasingly becoming convinced of the need to coordinate their marketing across Europe, although the rationale is usually rather
more complex than for manufacturing. National markets cross-subsidize the
effective implementation of marketing plans in a number of complex ways:

- They provide opportunities for learning and feedback to other markets;
- Market networks can be used to maximize good ideas and exploit innovation rapidly;
- Market networks help to fight competitive battles through increasing
  options of attack and defence and also through generating the required
  cash flows;
- The strength of the network itself is a competitive advantage, in many
  service industries, for example, providing a 'halo' effect to a particular brand.

There is general agreement that the strength of the product in a given
market and the long-term profit potential can be assured and developed only if
the product is also strong in neighbouring geographical markets. The difficult
issue is not so much the principle of coordination, but the degree of
coordination and the methods by which it is achieved.

Country managers are therefore faced with the need for their marketing
teams to coordinate their activities with their opposite numbers elsewhere in
Europe, often without producing a corresponding financial return to the subsidiary. A number of companies have found that unless some robust organizational changes are made, they risk receiving mere lip-service from country
managers in terms of regional marketing coordination. But if the changes affect
the country manager's bottom line, they probably affect the manager's bonus
as well.

According to Gerry Alcock of London-based consultants Brand
Positioning Services, 'The big divide is whether the profit is centralized or
local. If the local management is in charge of the profit, it will always win in
any conflict.' In some companies, he has found that more energy and market
research programmes are directed at winning the political battles over coordination than in fighting the competitor. Christopher Bartlett and Sumantra
Ghoshal in *Managing Across Borders* have come to the same conclusion:
'Independent units have feigned compliance while fiercely protecting their
independence. The dependent units have found that the new cooperative spirit
implies little more than the right to agree with those on whom they depend.'
(See Case 4.1.)

To resolve this conflict of interest, the lighting division (the proposed sale
of which to the US group GTE was subsequently cancelled) of the UK-based
Thorn EMI is an example of a company that decided to take profit responsi-

bility away from the country manager. Although the division was UK-centred, lighting had become increasingly international. Before the decision to sell out was made, Thorn EMI management had concluded that to safeguard its strong position in the UK commercial lighting market and to grow further internationally, the division would have to be strengthened by acquisition. Therefore, as a first step, it set up an international division to export its existing ranges of light fittings, to develop new products and to search for possible purchases. Having added Holophane in France to its French interests, it put the French country manager in charge of southern Europe and the Swedish manager in charge of Scandinavia. A chief executive for Europe was appointed, and together with the director of manufacturing he started to plan production on a European scale. Four product divisions were set up, with pan-European profit responsibility. It was decided that sales had to be managed locally, and that country managers would be responsible for volume and margin only.

Other companies have been content to proceed more cautiously, leaving the country managers with sufficient powers to run their operations effectively, but gradually drawing them into a network of varying degrees of formality.

For example, changes made to Colgate–Palmolive's (C–P) structure during 1989–90 have been aimed at making better use of its assets. C–P has a mix of international and local brands, and European president Brian Bergin, while anxious to safeguard the profits from the local brands, considered that 'there is a heritage of too much diversity. We need to stress commonality now.' A programme to rationalize production is going ahead, but 'it is not in our culture to be ruthless.'

On the marketing side at C–P:

- The country managers were initially pulled together through regular European meetings.
- For the European brands, category managers have now been appointed and installed at the Brussels regional head office. The aim is to expand these brands' sales from around 50% of current turnover to 75%. Support staff are mostly located in national offices. All are expected to be out in the field at least once a week.
- Country managers retain profit responsibility, for the time being at least, and the four with the largest markets are now members of a European management board to ensure that they play a full role in strategic developments.

Bergin acknowledged that geographical ties 'are a tough thing to beat. A lot of people see it as a win–lose situation, so we're in the process of giving the product categories an unfair advantage. The aim is a matrix of objectives that mutually support one another.'

In the business-to-business sector, priorities may be different, but similar solutions are emerging, as the following case illustrates.

Compaq Computer has built up a European organization from scratch in six years, becoming the number two in European sales of personal computers with a turnover of over $1 billion in 1989. Starting with German and UK subsidiaries, 'the roll-out was done on the basis of very careful and sound business planning,' said Compaq's international president Eckhard Pfeiffer. The group's success has been based in part on a policy of selling exclusively through dealers, and therefore strong national companies are required. The product range is planned and developed centrally in the US, but with strong input from Munich where the international operations are based. Although the terms of the contracts with dealers are similarly uniform, thereafter heavy reliance is placed on the country managers: they are selected for their experience with large corporations, and are expected to play their part in the management by consensus of a big international group.

'It's a combination of Asian, European and American philosophy,' said one senior executive. The central marketing staff are no more than 30 strong, and not all based in Munich. Their specific roles are:

- To oversee marketing communications in order to ensure correct positioning, but not identical advertising;
- To coordinate marketing programmes for major multinational accounts;
- To conduct market research and develop business strategy;
- To develop product proposals;
- To coordinate training for sales and support staff.

However, the aim is to achieve the 'best thing for the company and to leverage the ideas from each subsidiary' rather than to impose central strategies. Significantly, Compaq claimed that its decentralized structure had allowed it to be more responsive to market needs than its rivals (principally IBM), while still being faster in developing and launching new products.

Another problem that has to be dealt with in terms of coordination is differential growth. Organizational theorists sometimes assume that sales and marketing operations in a number of different countries are all at roughly the same stage of development. This is seldom the case. Even if national operations are set up at the same time with the same product range and capital resources, the response of each market is likely to vary, the strength of competition will almost certainly vary, and the abilities of each management will definitely vary.

The result is differential growth, and thus varying demands on central management time and resources. In practice, most international networks spread outward a country or two at a time, initially often via a local distributor rather than a wholly owned subsidiary. In one country, too, one product may be the big profit earner before all others. In another, the order will be reversed, perhaps for market reasons, perhaps merely because of the personalities of the management. Some of these differences may average out, but they may also be incremental and widen the gap between the most and the least successful product.

Heinz provides a clear example of a company that has grown differentially. As a result the organization reflects four levels of development. Just two European countries, the UK and Italy (respectively, responsible also for Ireland

and for Spain and Portugal), account for 40% of the $2.4 billion sales outside the US. These operations therefore report directly to senior vice president, Europe, Paul Corddry, who divides his time between the US and the European regional office near London. A managing director, headquartered in Brussels and also reporting to Corddry, heads operations in Belgium, the Netherlands, France and Germany. An export general manager handles sales to Scandinavia and Switzerland, as well as the Middle East and Central and South America. A second general manager has recently been appointed to handle Central and Eastern Europe and the former Soviet Union, where a joint venture is being set up.

The effective organization thus has to be versatile enough at the very least to accommodate wide differences without strain, and at the most to assist the central management in its natural urge to bring the least developed markets up to the standard of the best. Companies have developed a number of ways of transmitting local excellence throughout a group. Most would admit that this process, though only just beginning, is being given increasing priority.

Case 4.1 Becton

Becton Dickinson (BD), the US-based manufacturer of medical products and diagnostic systems, has adopted what has come to be known as the 'transnational' approach to organizing and conducting international business.

(The transnational organization, as conceived by Christopher Bartlett and Sumantra Ghoshal, in *Managing Across Borders*, gives a multinational the flexibility to centralize functions in which economies of scale are greatest and to decentralize functions that are best made responsive to local demands.) For BD, this has meant organizing manufacturing and R&D on a global scale, with a good deal of centralized control, and leaving control of sales and distribution to the regional and country offices.

BD President and chief executive officer Raymond V. Gilmartin credited the transnational approach for much of the company's international success in recent years. Indeed, it is expected that the growth of BD's international business will continue to outstrip that of domestic operations.

In the mid-1980s, BD undertook a major restructuring of its operations. It began by divesting non-core businesses, so that it could refocus its efforts on its two principal global businesses, disposable medical devices and diagnostic systems. It ended by streamlining its organizational structure, eliminating the international sector. At the same time, it created channels to foster collective decision making based on input from managers around the globe.

continues

continued

After selling off its peripheral operations, the company decided to focus on its 10 core businesses, a legacy of its long-serving and recently retired CEO, Wesley ('Jack') Howe. Among these are hypodermic products, diabetic care products, intravenous catheters, specimen collection, microbiology and immunodiagnostics. These product lines, particularly in diagnostics, are relatively technology intensive.

Gilmartin, in fact, described BD as a medical technology company whose goal is to identify new product markets and to be a leader, not a follower, in their development. 'Our strategy is to address unmet market needs with unique or differentiated products based on a proprietary technology, product or process that builds on our existing business and distribution strengths,' he said. The company has been able to satisfy those needs by developing a number of pioneering technologies and successfully introducing them into clinical practice. Examples are its Facscan immunocytometry system for use in monitoring the immune system, and the Vacutainer evacuated blood collection tubes.

According to Gilmartin, this particular division of functions is best suited to the healthcare products industry. Applying the transnational philosophy in this way, he noted,

> 'we are able to gain scale economies in R&D and manufacturing and to achieve the economic leverage that derives from the fact that medical practices are similar throughout the world. Thus, the function and the application of the product are the same worldwide. Yet we are also able to market the product differently and [to] recognize that markets are at different stages of development in terms of product acceptance.'

The company's new organizational structure reflects this philosophy. At the corporate level, BD has what Gilmartin termed a flat organization, the most salient features of which are its compactness and the absence of a chief operating officer (COO). Two sector presidents (one for medical products and the other for diagnostic systems), who incorporate what used to be the COO's responsibilities, report directly to the CEO. Also reporting to the CEO are the division managers responsible for corporate R&D, planning and development, human resources, finance and medical, and legal and regulatory affairs.

'In the traditional organization,' said Gilmartin, 'the CEO is supposed to think about the long term and the COO is supposed to worry about operations. We adhere to the theory that there is really no separation between long-range strategy and operations – they are tightly linked.' Another structural innovation: in the spring of 1989, BD eliminated the international sector it had maintained separately from the medical and diagnostic sectors. Gilmartin explained that the international sector had come to interfere with the product-based focus of the company and complicated the task of achieving worldwide coordination. The company decided that such coordination could best be secured by retaining just two self-contained product sectors.

continues

continued

Under the two sector presidents are product divisions for the regions, which in BD's system include both traditional regional groupings (Europe, Asia/Pacific and Latin America) and important individual country markets (the US, Canada, Japan, Brazil and Mexico). R&D is considered a world-wide resource, and thus it ultimately reports to the CEO at the corporate level and to regional presidents within each product sector. The manufacturing function lies within the regional structure, and each regional president has a manufacturing director who reports to him or her. However, the firm's production technologies and processes, as well as its products, are fairly standardized world-wide. Gilmartin observed that 'Given that ours is a technology-based industry and given world-wide communication and cooperation in healthcare practice and education, the same product can often be used anywhere in the world. It looks the same, its function is the same, its application is the same.'

But if its products are standardized, how does the company react to the needs of specific markets? Gilmartin said that BD achieves such flexibility through the breadth of its product lines. While using standard functional designs for its syringes, for example, it can offer a variety of needles to fit local medical practices. The same goes for diagnostic equipment: the instrumentation used throughout the world is the same, but the variety of tests can be tailored to the specific diseases prevalent in a given area.

For BD, the key to identifying and meeting local needs is having in place separate marketing and distribution networks in each region and, in some cases, in individual countries. The US and European markets are mature, Gilmartin pointed out, while others, such as Asia/Pacific and Latin America, are still embryonic. 'There is no single formula for how to do business in each one of these regions,' he said. 'You need to have an organization that is knowledgeable about the market in which it is operating and is sensitive to the needs of that particular country.'

Moreover, BD often introduces an innovation to a standardized product that originated with the identification of a local need. A case in point was the closure on the firm's evacuated blood collection tubes. They sold well everywhere but in West Germany. The reason turned out to be that with the advent of AIDS and other new infections, German laboratory technicians became concerned about the danger of infection from blood that accumulated on the tube's rubber stopper. This concern had never been expressed in the US or other markets. Subsequent market research revealed, however, that although technicians elsewhere approved of the tubes, they, too, harboured concern about the danger of infection. In response to the German marketers' discovery of the new need, BD introduced a redesigned product world-wide – a new closure for the Vacutainer blood collection tube and thus met the newly expressed need for safety.

Keeping marketing local, said Gilmartin, thus 'gives us an advantage over any purely global product-line competitor because of the knowledge our people have of local medical practices and the infrastructure and how healthcare supplies are bought in those markets.'

continues

---

continued

      Becton Dickinson's growth abroad has been impressive. While US sales grew 2.6% in 1989, international sales rose 11.6%. Of the company's $1.8 billion of total sales, 40% was earned overseas. Gilmartin expected that in five years the company's international business will break even with domestic business and soon thereafter overtake it as the primary source of the firm's revenue. This means growth of international sales of 15–20% a year.

      The company's largest overseas market is Europe, but it has targeted Asia/Pacific as the region with the highest growth potential. Gilmartin noted that a large part of the firm's annual $300 million in capital spending over the past two to three years has gone toward building up its international manufacturing and marketing presence. It recently opened a diagnostic equipment facility in Fukushima, Japan, and a plant to manufacture disposable needles and syringes in Singapore. Its largest investment, however, has gone to enlarge its sales and distribution networks throughout the Asia/Pacific region.

      Although BD's strength in the US has been in its needle and syringe business, Gilmartin believed that sales of diagnostic equipment will drive its international growth. Thus, by early in the next century, the firm's long-established profile as a predominantly US-oriented supplier of disposable medical products will give way to that of a truly global company specializing in advanced diagnostic products.

Developing the country manager's role

Increasing centralization, noted in Chapter 2, in line with moves to coordinate European marketing and manufacturing have cut the traditional role of country managers, and their disappearance has been forecast. But there are cogent reasons why they should remain with undiminished, if altered, powers. Country managers' job specifications may be changing radically, but for every company that is reducing the country manager's authority, there is a nother that is increasing it. Among the latter is IBM, whose European director of organization, Agnès Roux-Kiener, pointed out simply that 'geography is the market.'

If Europe does coalesce into a Single Market in fact as well as theory, it might be possible to rationalize the structure so that individual countries become, in effect, sales areas reporting to a European head office, along with service, manufacturing and distribution functions. Small hi-tech companies commonly adopt such a structure already, avoiding unnecessary overheads and bureaucratic layers of control.

In cases where there is little direct competition and a small number of customers with predictable and similar problems that demand highly specialized selling requiring relatively infrequent visits, the absence of a country organization and backup can be only a minor disadvantage. Further, the rapid improvement in data communication simplifies the marketing by allowing designs, specifications and so on, to be transmitted back and forth between the central designers and estimators and the customers.

There are probably five main reasons why companies are concerned to preserve their country managers' position and influence in the marketing and sales spheres (irrespective of any responsibilities they may also have for R&D, procurement or manufacturing):

(1)   Managers are often responsible for a significant share of the company's business. International brands and customers may be increasing, but few companies can afford to neglect profits that are derived only locally. In service companies, the local element may be as high as 90% of the total.

(2)   Sales performance depends heavily on the country manager's motivation and profit responsibility: 'I wouldn't accept a job where I was responsible only for volume and margins,' said one senior manager in a company that has rejected that alternative. The country manager's experience, enthusiasm and judgement in building profitable business are a valuable corporate resource.

(3)   Few companies have enough faith at present in their control and logistic systems to keep inventories down and service to the customer up without local warehousing and administration.

(4)   In many industries, community relations are increasingly important. Environmental and social issues, government relations, PR and sponsorship all require sensitive treatment from managers experienced in the local culture.

(5)   Global trends are leading to greater market fragmentation. Even the trend to globalization for many products will actually increase the number of niches as customers become more discriminating.

Only companies with a local entrepreneurial presence can hope to exploit such opportunities effectively. 'The local touch is what makes you win or lose,' said 3M's regional vice president for the European marketing subsidiaries, Edoardo Pieruzzi, 'We debate a lot in our organization on the role of the country general managers. We think they will remain at the head of profit centres, but with more influence over service standards and the information flow to detect opportunities locally.'

Finding and exploiting differences and individual preferences are fundamental to good marketing, and therefore to the role of the country manager. These skills form one reason for the Japanese multinationals' success in Europe. If globalization is allowed to imply as little discrimination between segments as the study suggests, it becomes a top-down, production-led process at odds with the marketer's instincts. In that form, it could be a short-lived phenomenon. But a growing proportion of the coordination work involves taking local successful ideas and 'best practice' and exploiting them elsewhere. That assumes that there is a coherent local management capable of contributing to the bottom-up/top-down decision-making process.

Rank Xerox is one company that freely admits to having learned some hard lessons in the head office/country manager relationship. 'In the past,' said European marketing director Lyndon Haddon, 'we sent a huge team into a country to develop a strategy to improve profit. People would spend all their time arguing over it, and every time we've tried to do a common system here it's been a disaster. So now we say, "In the end, it's up to you".' At the centre, 'our job is to make a generic product,' explained Haddon, and it is then for the country managers to 'add value locally.' Some general managers source their support products such as software locally.

The marketing and support strategies are tailored to suit each particular market. In the German insurance sector, for example, the big companies usually sell their policies through dedicated sole agents, and the Rank Xerox subsidiary has developed systems specifically for them. But in the UK and the US agents usually sell more than one product (at least for nonlife business), so the systems needed are different. Haddon's role is to develop the segmentation process and coordinate best practices across Europe – and increasingly, with the US and Far East.

The Swiss chemical/pharmaceutical company Roche, still in the process of re-evaluating its structure, considers local flexibility to be all-important. The object of any new organization, it said, will be to promote entrepreneurial thinking down the line and to give the person in the field the most efficient support to back entrepreneurial action. Managers must have the resources to respond rapidly to changing customer demands and tougher competition. Even toy maker Lego, with its policy of retaining at the centre everything that does not need to be in the national subsidiaries, recognized the danger of a demotivated local management, and in practice benefits from the local development of products and ideas.

NCR managed to achieve its now-dominant position in the world market for automatic teller machines (ATMs) by devolving authority to its subsidiary in Scotland. In 1980, NCR's old Dundee factory in Scotland was on the point of closure, a victim of the electronic revolution. Its remaining product line, an early small ATM, depended on the parent plant in the US for most of its technology, and according to Jim Adamson, vice president and managing director of self-service systems, NCR's small share of the market at that time could be attributed to the rather slow and cumbersome committee in the financial services division that then ran the ATM operation. 'It was too far removed from the market,' said Adamson.

NCR decided to give Adamson and the Scottish plant a lifeline in the form of a remit to take over the design, development and international marketing of ATMs. Adamson and a small team in Dundee were at last able to provide the focus on the product and its marketing that it did not receive as an appendage of the computer business. Adamson has a centralized, product management organization, but generally works through the NCR national marketing companies: 'There's no way I could run a selling operation in 88 countries.'

However, there's no obligation on them to supply his ATMs or on him to use NCR computers for self-service systems. 'Fred Newall [senior vice president for NCR Europe] can always tell me to get lost – it's made the development organization very customer oriented.' In fact, in some countries, the ATMs are handled by distributors rather than the national NCR company, and one such, Finland's Nokia, has recently taken its first orders for ATMs in the former Soviet Union.

Adamson's team markets directly to potential customers, but as a matter of policy, the national company's account managers are also closely involved. Commented Newall, 'It works quite well because our objectives are the same.' The enthusiastic Adamson now claims one-third of the world's installed base and nearly two-thirds of new installations, and has taken over responsibility for the US market.

In the service industries, the role of the country manager has never been in any real doubt because of the vital need to be near the customer and to respond to day-to-day needs. For example, all of the major advertising groups aim to provide a full range of services in each European capital, in addition to services in the provincial business centres. The network can then serve multinational clients as well as pulling in local business.

A similar reliance on the country managers to build local business is evident at Chep Europe, part of a joint venture between GKN, the UK engineering group, and the Australian Brambles Enterprises. Chep operates a pallet hire service in a number of European countries, mainly for the food industry supplying the retailers. The business is unevenly developed in that it is well established in the UK and France but only just starting in Germany and Italy. Chep Europe's chief executive Nick Butcher recalled that he did consider setting up one European organization, only to reject the idea because, being a service industry, Chep has to make its decisions as close to the customer as possible. In addition, argued Butcher, 'the markets will be predominantly national as far ahead as we can see.'

Cross-frontier business comes in two forms for Chep: local suppliers of wines and food produce reaching out across mainland Europe, and multinationals developing European manufacture and supply. The latter is still small in extent, and an international marketing and development director is sufficient to represent Chep at the international level on the few occasions when it is necessary. Even then, he works through the profit-responsible country manager. 'I like to try to avoid "coordination",' said Butcher. 'Our intention is to standardize as much as possible – from computer systems to personnel policies.'

'One of the real 1992 challenges,' said Brian Bergin, European president of Colgate–Palmolive (C–P), 'will be "Did you lift your profits well compared to your competitors, and take the opportunity to get ahead of them?"' Apart from rationalizing manufacture and logistics, increasing profitability means building on the brands that are, or have the potential to be, Europe-wide because they tend to be more profitable and have the capacity to grow – a subject covered in more depth in Chapter 5. But Bergin noted, 'The difficulty is to ensure that in focusing on the global products you don't lose profitability on the local ones.' Colgate–Palmolive has always been 'geographically propelled', and chief executive officer Reuben Mark has encouraged a fresh spirit of independence and entrepreneurship.

A regional company, Colgate Europe, is already in place, charged with developing a single manufacturing network, and providing the base for profit-responsible general managers for the four core categories of product. These cut across the country managers' responsibilities, and Bergin admitted to 'a number of healthy arguments – but you've got to go through it.' He is determined not to build a big edifice in Brussels – a staff of 50 at the most – and the category managers' support staff may well be located in one or other of the national companies. 'The category has only one purpose – the transfer of experience.' The speed at which it can do that across frontiers will determine long-term success: 'If a company isn't fast enough, rivals will use its idea somewhere else.' Structural changes throughout the C–P group have helped to give the company seven years of volume growth, and it has already comfortably exceeded its target of a 5% after tax return by 1991, set when Mark became CEO in 1984.

The international coordinator

For many companies, the only practical way to combine central and local authority in such a diverse market as Europe is in some form of matrix organization, loathed by many, but regarded as logically unavoidable by some. In consumer goods industries, country subsidiaries almost inevitably duplicate each other's efforts in the great battle to please the customer and beat off the competition. There is also the worry that competitors may be creeping up in other markets unobserved, exploiting opportunities more quickly and effectively, that precious ideas and resources are being wasted on conflicting product positioning, systems development, advertising and promotion and so on. But how can the use of these assets be improved without restricting the country manager's freedom of manoeuvre and dampening entrepreneurial enthusiasm?

The starting point for companies with a country-based marketing structure that want a more coherent European attack is for central management to appoint coordinators. The coordinator is often a senior executive with valuable experience who has perhaps outgrown a country manager's job, but for whom there is not yet a corporate role. Generally, the coordinator's often ill-defined task is to advise country subsidiaries and ensure that best practice is adopted throughout their region. The strongly centralized Italian oil company Agip has a coordinating system, with a special staff department at corporate level to coordinate marketing among its foreign subsidiaries.

Coordination also seems to suit Scandinavian companies. Lego's co-ordinating structure is relatively straightforward, with a small liaison group helping to smooth the paths between the central European company and the 14 sales companies. Electrolux is naturally a great deal more complicated, even within its white goods 'product line', partly on account of the only half-absorbed acquisitions such as Zanussi. At Electrolux, country managers are responsible for most manufacturing and marketing subsidiaries in their territories, but central product area managers coordinate product development and manufacturing. The 'Marketing Europe' team, formed in 1987, pulls together the many strands (and brands) making up Electrolux's marketing platform. In spite of some moves to further strengthen central control, the Electrolux management insists on leaving real authority in each national market.

Some companies have managed to achieve the desired coordination without adding staff or structures. If a brand concept has been clearly defined and articulated – and understood and accepted by local managements – central management can afford to be pragmatic about the details of its implementation. Thus the need for sometimes costly coordination is reduced. Scott Paper, Heinz and Reckitt & Colman all prefer to bring their executives together rather than rely on central staff to coordinate their European strategy. These companies have corporate cultures that are conducive to cooperation – a local Scott managing director who was not prepared to cooperate was replaced. This approach serves to underline the importance of recognizing that structures are only as good as the people they serve; personalities count for more than charts.

But other companies find that the ambiguities of the Electrolux system, and indeed of coordination methods generally, can defeat their purposes. Most important, the issues raised by effective coordination are often too weighty to be hung from a merely advisory link. Changing the priorities between products, for example, could have a marked effect on a subsidiary's bottom line in a way that could be justified only in the wider group context. As long as country managers remain profit accountable – implying a remit from the centre that the manager should give priority to profit maximization within the territory – the unfortunate coordinators are unlikely to get very far. They will therefore be reduced to details that have little effect on the progress of the group – even if they are good enough diplomats not to arouse local antipathies.

This was Kodak's experience. Kodak began experimenting with a coordinating function in the early 1970s, when a European regional organization was first set up. Then, the national subsidiaries were closely regulated by the US headquarters but in other respects were largely self-sufficient. Intensifying competition in the photographic market, with the battle front switching to processing rather than to film sales, meant that the lumbering giant badly needed both a convincing global strategy and sharp local tactics. For a time, it had neither, and the need raised organizational issues far greater than could be solved by coordination, however effective.

Advertising group J. Walter Thompson (JWT) believes it has solved the problem with a centralized European structure where account directors have profit/loss responsibility for multinational clients across Europe. Local offices handle local clients, but otherwise report to head office in London. Chief operating officer of JWT Europe, Miles Colebrook, stressed that these overlords are not toothless coordinators but line management with all that entails. 'It attracts a hands-on operator as opposed to an old-fashioned staff person,' he claimed. He reckoned it gets rid of the 'twilight zone' where many regional coordinators end up in their role of half helper and half policeman. The difficulty is to ensure that everyone pulls in the same direction while being sensitive to local friction or conflict.

The difficulties involved in attempts to coordinate have prompted many companies, especially in the consumer goods sector, to set up European product/brand managers, giving them varying degrees of authority. At the same time many business-to-business companies have been moving to modify and adapt their normally product-based organizations to get closer to the market, as the next section shows.

Product managers and business marketing

Business marketing usually implies relatively small, specialist groups of customers, and particular customs and techniques to meet their needs. Companies structure their operations to suit. The UK engineering group GKN, for example, found in the late 1970s that desperately needed changes to the old-established group were obstructed by its then predominantly regional structure, which supported a large and interventionist head office. In the automotive industry of the 1950s and 1960s, such an organization might have made sense, but the growing globalization of car manufacture, essentially concentrated in Japan, the US and Continental Europe, demanded that GKN should restructure if its world lead in constant-velocity (CV) joints for front-wheel drive vehicles was to be maintained. The transmission management had to be allowed to focus on, and invest in, that business undistracted by the severe problems elsewhere in the group. Now, it is centred in Germany (where GKN had made a major acquisition), and the group's small UK head office maintains an essentially financial control over its affairs.

The vital need was to maximize returns on the heavy investment required in development and manufacturing the CV joints, and to match the handful of world-wide auto manufacturers. For the group's Chep pallet hire operation (see page 87), on the other hand, a high degree of local autonomy was necessary to satisfy a wide range of local producers and retailers.

Even in a mass market business like copiers, certain equipment may need specialist attention in a small product division, without which it would be in danger of being pushed to one side. Costs and profit need to be shown separately, and appropriate marketing and sales techniques developed.

Rank Xerox relies on its geographical units to market its main copier ranges, but its workstations are much more specialized in terms of application, and are likely to be bought by relatively few, multinational clients. Therefore, a central product-line structure handles the workstations throughout Europe, calling on the services of the national subsidiaries when needed.

Product divisions whether of the macro or micro kind may reassure the central management that the return on investment in the product will be maximized, but they have drawbacks that apply to consumer as well as business markets:

- The management of each product division can be insensitive to the shifting sands of the marketplace because the product defines its area of responsibility.
- It may be difficult to obtain an objective view of the whole company's performance in the market outside the product division's immediate segment, or to formulate a strategy for it, if no one is responsible.
- Innovation that falls outside the division's experience may be missed or allowed to wither for the same reason.
- When the divisions grow large, their managers can become remote from their markets, and coverage of smaller, individual markets may suffer.
- Success in some markets may depend on other divisions, whose different priorities and cultures make cooperation difficult.
- Products from different divisions (as in IBM's old, widely criticized example) may be incompatible, and salesmen calling on the same customer may work to different standards and effectively compete with each other.
- Market share on a country-by-country basis may be sacrificed to product divisional profitability, which is often not analysed according to country. Thus individual markets may be overlooked.

For some or all of these reasons, a number of companies have radically altered their product structures. Some, like American Express, abandoned product divisions in favour of national companies long ago. Others, in the industrial sector, have redefined a division's responsibilities round the market rather than the product, or merely attempted to loosen the straps round their product divisions. While the Swedish engineering company SKF, therefore, supplies the needs of the after-market for bearings all over the world from a single division, Du Pont encourages coordination between product groups through the formation of small marketing groups, which bring together representatives from different product divisions to focus on the needs of particular industries – forcing executives to talk to each other as well as to the customers.

In an attempt to grapple with its centralized culture and make its 15 product divisions more responsive to the market, Hoechst has embarked upon its most extensive reorganization in 20 years. It has decided to split the product divisions into 100 business units, about one-third of them centred outside Germany. The divisional sales and marketing staff will be dispersed to the business units, which will be profit centres enjoying a high degree of autonomy. The business unit managers will be free to organize the units in their own way, and even, apparently, to specify their relationship with the centre.

Case 4.2   *Olin*

Olin Corp, a Connecticut based industrial manufacturing company, is organized into three major product groups – metals (which comprises the metals and electronic materials divisions), chemicals (which comprises performance chemicals, industrial chemicals and water products and services) and defence systems. Olin prefers the term 'division' to 'product group' because many of the departments within the divisions produce products. However, metals, chemicals and defence systems each has its own infrastructure including international marketing departments. In fact, a few of the products within these product-based divisions conduct their own international marketing. The firm's structure therefore fits within the classic definition of a world-wide product group matrix. An executive vice president heads each division, and a general manager is the product group's international director of marketing and its director of strategic planning.

Olin also has a corporate general manager for international business, a staff executive to whom the group international directors of marketing report on a functional basis. 'We want our overseas people to know that there is someone in the home office who is responsive to their needs, without diminishing the ability of the overseas people to make competitive strategic decisions on a timely basis,' said Curtis Collyer, vice president, international development.

Olin's planners chose this pattern of organization mainly because it creates product specialists. Said Collyer, 'We think that it is important for the people who sell chemicals to know chemicals, the people who sell defence equipment to understand those products, and so on.' (See Figure 4.1.)

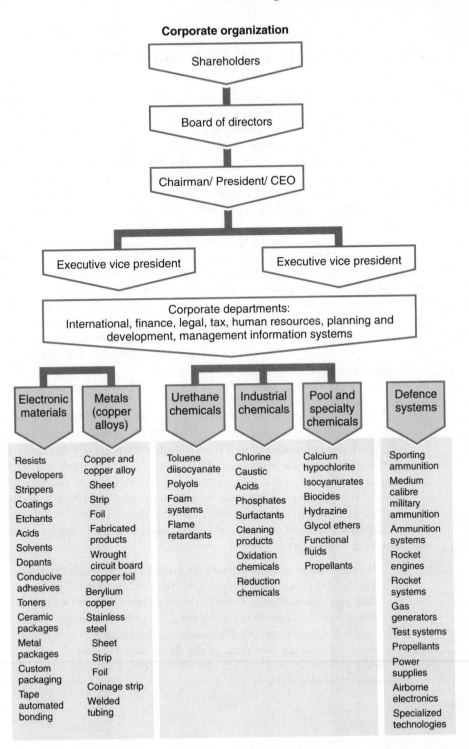

Figure 4.1   Olin world-wide product groups (1990). *Source:* Olin.

Product managers and consumer goods

In consumer marketing, central product/brand managers are gaining popularity as a way of putting additional strength behind coordinated marketing strategies. For different reasons, Moulinex and Bang & Olufsen both deploy international product marketing managers, whose authority *vis-à-vis* the country managers is gradually being increased. Moulinex aims to move its range up-market, and its image accordingly; Bang & Olufsen, the Danish hi-fi manufacturer, needs to guard its world-wide image for sophisticated design and quality very carefully – particularly after its link with the electronics giant Philips.

Few companies are going as far as the highly centralized Gillette, or even Thorn EMI Lighting, which decided to give full profit responsibility to its central managers. Instead, the product managers tend either to share the profit role, or be assigned a more vague remit covering product strategy and development, production control, pricing and so on. Many companies are notably cautious in their handling of the product management issue because of the wide-ranging implications for the status of the country manager. The two exist in constant tension, and the current balance between them is often regarded as a staging point in the move to a more integrated structure, where any increase in the product manager's power has to be matched by a corresponding widening of the country manager's role.

Progress may therefore depend on the speed at which the managers on either axis can be trained or persuaded (or, failing everything, replaced) to accept the new delineation of their roles and adopt the necessary strategic view of the business. Brian Bergin at Colgate–Palmolive warned that 'it requires first-class people to think through the complex, matrix-type decision processes.' If the company is fortunate enough to have plenty of such people, they need to be moved into positions where they can be most effective. According to Klaus Jacobs, chief executive of Jacobs Suchard before he decided to sell control to Philip Morris:

> 'We resolved to concentrate our best management talent in the firing line, making those people responsible for the country-based business units and then ruthlessly stripping away as many as possible of the intervening management layers between them and top management in Zurich. We were determined to encourage business unit heads in this way to think more entrepreneurially about their businesses, and do away with the filtering layers that so often seem to discourage or screen out entrepreneurial ideas.'

Case 4.3   Grand Metropolitan

Grand Metropolitan's organizational approach has been the result of a series of acquisitions and divestitures. The company has organized its international marketing activities by products, of which food, drink and retailing are the main divisions. International marketing strategies are formulated for each brand within the product group's international marketing department. Examples of Grand Metropolitan global brands are Häagen-Dazs ice cream in the food division, Smirnoff vodka in the drink division and Burger King in the retailing division.

Overlaying the product divisions are regionally focused 'advisory committees' (European, North American and Asian–Pacific). The committees work with the product management groups in formulating international marketing strategies on a broad basis. For example, the committees are involved in advising the corporate centre and the individual sectors about industry opportunities, legislative changes and so on, rather than about decisions concerning product introductions and operational issues. The advisory committees help gather information and apply it to the product groups. The committees have an ear to the ground and can advise the product people on potential markets, partnerships and acquisitions.

Grand Metropolitan feels that its organizational hybrid takes advantage of the positive attributes associated with both formations. Those who know the product best work to formulate marketing strategies in conjunction with committees that know and understand the idiosyncrasies of various markets.

The European Advisory Committee has highlighted various opportunities in post-1992 Europe. The specific proposal by Häagen-Dazs to enter the UK market was approved by the International Food sector management. After extensive market research, Häagen-Dazs's international division decided that a premium ice cream like theirs would do well in the UK if positioned and priced correctly. Devising the strategies needed to launch the product successfully was left up to Häagen-Dazs's marketing personnel. The decision that the best way to position a premium ice cream in the UK would be to restrict it initially to selected high-end outlets (in this case, Harrod's) was made by the Häagen-Dazs product executive who was working with the regional marketing committee.

It could be argued that product managers (or 'global product presidents', as Jacobs preferred) represent just such a filtering or coordinating layer. In Jacobs Suchard, they replaced or strengthened a lead brand management system. In early 1990, just before the sale was announced, five regional presidents were added (America, Asia/Pacific, Brussels, Bremen in north Germany, and Paris). Jacobs recognized the contradiction, and located the presidents and other top managers in the centres where the volume of business justified it to ensure that they kept in close touch with their markets. But the effect is largely symbolic: there is no essential difference if the orders come from Zurich or from Brussels. It remains to be seen whether and how Philip Morris attempts to amalgamate Suchard with its own coffee interests such as Maxwell House, Hag and Kenco.

In the airline industry, there is a similar urgency in building a strong international marketing presence ready for the time when the European industry is effectively deregulated. International airlines remain in a peculiar marketing position; they are in effect supplying two products – domestic and outgoing flights, and incoming flights. In these two product ranges, customers, motivations, images and so on, can be quite different. It might be expected that this will eventually be reflected in the airlines' structures. As consultant Gerry Alcock pointed out, 'airlines have got to be much more tactically based' in their marketing programmes.

The Italian state airline Alitalia has responded by abandoning its old functional organization in favour of what are, in effect, product divisions. There are two operational divisions, for passengers and cargo, and two 'complementary' ones, marketing services (including catering and ground services) and leisure. Two route managers are responsible for planning and operating the European passenger services, as well as for marketing them, and the country managers report to them. Alitalia expects the new structure to increase its marketing strength, without going to the extremes of Jan Carlsen at Scandinavian Airline System, who has widely publicized his theory of the 'flattened pyramid' – aimed at giving the staff the authority to act on their own initiative in the cause of good customer service.

The lead country approach

One way of compensating country managers for any job erosion through increased coordination is to install a lead country system, which extends individual responsibilities onto the wider European stage. Many companies regularly nominate certain subsidiaries to be or become expert in a specific product, application, or marketing or sales tactic. It's an old idea which satisfies a number of objectives:

- It helps even out the development of multinational business, discussed earlier; the subsidiaries with long and successful experience with a product or application will be in a good position to pass on their expertise for use in unexploited markets.

- It motivates local staff as well as the country managers by involving them more closely in the wider development of the group.
- It keeps central staff at a minimum, while demonstrating the way forward for cooperation to possibly reluctant subsidiaries in a practical way.
- It keeps development costs on new products and applications in check and avoids duplication of effort.
- It ensures that customers' international needs are adequately provided for.

The system arises naturally in the business-to-business area where the same products are often sold for different applications in different industries. As an executive at TI's John Crane division (making seals for machinery) has found,

> 'As night follows day, one of the companies will have more pump manufacturers on its patch, say, and will become the lead country for that application. Engineers love to design a new product, but the key to making money in this business is to stop them duplicating designs.'

Computer companies also face similar problems in developing applications and software to suit particular industries and market segments. The German subsidiary might therefore be given responsibility for, say, the chemical industry, Scandinavia for paper, France for the food industry, the UK for finance.

Executives who become expert in their field can then be seconded to other countries to build the business there. There are, of course, attendant difficulties, as Alan Stark, managing director of American Express in the UK pointed out. His subsidiary is in the process of being re-integrated into the Europe, Middle East and Africa division after a period outside it. Stark's executives are particularly experienced in database marketing, where computers are used to refine lists of potential clients.

'My people are playing a role across Europe, either on a time-limited or a periodic basis. I'm concerned about my payroll, so if it becomes a working practice, I charge a fee. The danger is if staff get stolen or get distracted by the joys of travel.' In other companies, it has been found that the lead country is not always strong enough and possessed of a broad enough vision to carry the extra responsibilities.

Confused responsibilities can also be a problem. Professor Peter Doyle's research into the behaviour of UK, US and Japanese subsidiaries (see Chapter 2) found one US company operating in Europe where the French were responsible for market segmentation, the British for promotional planning and the Germans for product development: 'None of the Japanese employed this type of international structure, all giving their UK subsidiaries clear responsibility.' This mirrored the traditional organization in Japan where 'every business is a profit centre.'

Doyle found that the problem with the US approach was that no one felt they had clear responsibility for and control of performance in the UK market. 'Headquarters or the regional office was often blamed by local managers for imposing the wrong strategy or for inadequate information – for example "The French are given responsibility for segmentation and they never tell us".'

A more radical development of the lead country idea is to give the marketing management of the lead country specific Europe-wide responsibility, a method Procter & Gamble has long favoured.

Procter & Gamble (P&G) first nominated a lead country as long ago as 1973 when launching its Pampers brand of disposable diaper (nappy) across Europe. The product was developed and launched in Germany, and the senior manager in charge moved on to the European HQ in Brussels to supervise the rollout. The system did not work well because of the friction generated between the Pampers team and the country management, faced with different priorities. For later launches, the system was developed into 'Eurobrand teams', headed by the lead country general manager and consisting of representatives from the main subsidiaries and from manufacturing and so on.

The aim was to exploit local expertise and responsiveness: in fact, the reverse seems to have been the case. Because of all of the parties involved, decision making was pushed up the tree to country manager level, and profitability was easily lost to sight. In consequence, 'category' managers have now been introduced in each country, with profit responsibility over the three main product groups – laundry, personal care and paper products. These category managers report to both the country general manager and the geographical divisional managers in a classic matrix structure.

The traditional P&G brand management system has been downgraded, and the internecine warfare between brands will, observers hope, be replaced by a more mature approach to market segmentation and the optimization of profits from a product category. Meanwhile, the category managers are relieving the country managers of much of their detailed responsibilities, allowing them to spend more time on functions like external relations.

Case 4.4 Procter & Gamble

In order to move faster and more cohesively in Europe, Procter & Gamble (P&G) has introduced senior category managers covering product groups such as detergents, fabric conditioners, beverages and disposables and so on, in major countries, who bring together manufacturing and sales as well as marketing and advertising. These executives, with or without a lead country

continues

continued

role, report in a matrix structure to both the national manager and the geographical divisional managers, who also carry Europe-wide responsibility for a product category. As well as providing a formal European dimension to product management, observers point out that the category managers bring profit responsibility closer to the market, and should prevent the internecine warfare between individual brands that characterized the traditional P&G brand management structure. The structure, excluding personal care and paper products (like Pampers), is illustrated in Figure 4.2 in simplified form.

In one form or another, the lead country system is likely to continue to flourish. The obvious benefits in concentrating expertise in particular offices, and in assigning to one or other of them pioneering roles for the benefit of the group are too strong to be abandoned. Even Nestlé uses subsidiaries to provide 'prime mover markets' to help the central product director convince country managers to launch a newly developed product. The study appears to favour more centralization: Nestlé remains resolutely decentralized, however, and profitable, although as the case study on page 67 shows, it is trying hard to formulate a more centralized approach.

Managing through the matrix

The nature of business involves balancing many incompatible objectives, like maximizing short- and long-term returns, or cutting costs but increasing quality. The European dimension adds a further set, forcing companies to respond to many different local requirements and preferences, while developing new products and services, and cutting costs and overheads through greater volume. That is what makes a matrix inevitable, in the view of some experts, whether the company acknowledges the fact or not, and that is why more companies rely on some kind of matrix structure. As long as one or other axis has dominance, the conflicts and uncertainties may be slight – but the benefits likewise. Hence Colgate–Palmolive, for example, is having to 'tilt the matrix' to ensure that the geographic axis does not have things all its own way.

There is, of course, a variety of kinds of matrix. Functional heads could be on one axis and geographical heads on the other. Lower down the corporate pyramid, the product/market segment matrix is sometimes found (often in the computer industry). But they all have one purpose, which is to rationalize in

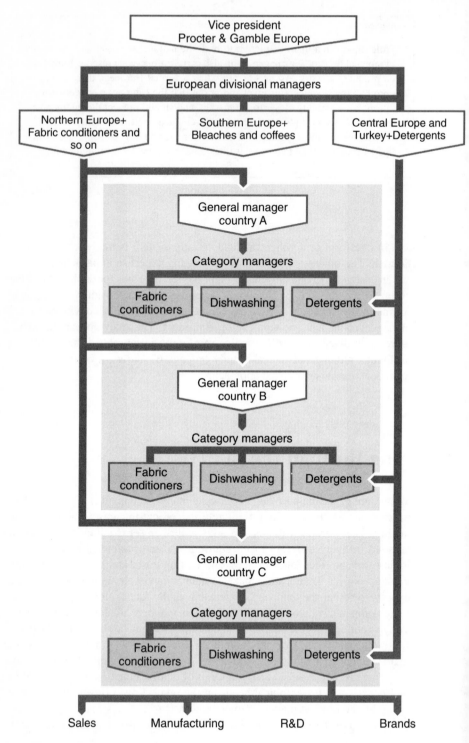

Figure 4.2   Procter & Gamble management structure (1990). *Source:* Procter & Gamble.

organizational terms the inherent conflicts between the two axes, or views of the company's interests:

- The country managers' aim is simply to maximize the profit from their particular territory. They will therefore wish to put most resources behind the opportunities and the products that will achieve that end, some of which may not even be manufactured by the group.
- The product managers, wishing to maximize the global profit for the product group, focus on what they see as the best strategic opportunities and new developments. But across the board, the aim is to reduce unit costs by cutting local variants and raising volumes, which may entail heavier local expenditure on sales and promotion than the country managers are willing or able to afford.

There are, of course, a hundred other potential sources of conflict, all of which lead consultants and others to be very wary of matrix organizations. It is open to debate whether the complexities the matrix introduces, and the management time devoted to resolving the inevitable conflicts and tensions that occur, are rewarded by a better allocation of resources and better corporate performance. One Electrolux executive has likened the matrix to 'leprosy', although the Swedish group probably has more matrices in its organization than most – some, indeed, are three-dimensional. One drawback of the matrix approach to organizational problems was highlighted by Electrolux's white goods head Leif Johansson (1989):

> 'There is too much of a tendency to try to solve organizational problems by designing a structure that quietens conflicts rather than bringing them to the surface.'

Jean-Pierre Rosso, president of Honeywell Europe, believed that people who dismiss the matrix structure are 'escaping reality . . . some sort of balance has to be achieved.'

Until the 1970s, Honeywell operated in Europe through national subsidiaries, but with central product marketing support. The product groups became business units, now five in number, and were gradually strengthened until they shared profit responsibility with the national subsidiaries. Rosso explained, 'The exact balancing point depends on the business – the higher the tech, the more important the business unit.' Subsidiaries and business units report to Rosso, along with pan-European functional heads such as marketing or engineering. 'The sales affiliates [subsidiaries] call the shots when it comes to selling; the business units call the shots on strategic issues, embodied in the marketing or engineering areas etcetera.'

The country managers and the business unit heads meet in a European policy committee, where 'the responsibilities are clear and dependency is a part of life,' said Rosso. In practice, neither business unit nor subsidiary will be responsible for 100% of the profit. The balance is worked out case by case: 'It can happen that optimization at the business level gives one answer, and optimization at the affiliate level gives another.' Rosso has 'a tie-breaking function,' but insisted that 'it doesn't happen very often that I have to decide.'

Rosso argued that the corporate emphasis on partnership overrides the negative aspects of the competition between the business units and the subsidiaries. Outside pressures can also have a constructive effect, particularly where very large projects are involved which could not be handled by a national unit. According to Rosso, 'You don't tolerate nonteaming attitudes in a global business, and when people understand they can't do it alone, it helps a lot.' Even so, Rosso still believed in the benefits of competition:

> 'The conflict is very positive – you need the strongest possible people in the business units and in the affiliates. We must continue to have strong affiliates – some people say they will become cost centres with only sales goals and budgets. I foresee that they will have different sorts of people, but as long as countries exist, the affiliate will continue to be strong.'

Case 4.5 The central think-tank

Smaller companies or companies with simpler structures that are determined to avoid the complications of the matrix still need some central marketing function to act as an intelligence-gathering centre, strategy think-tank or even a new product development unit. In the past, such a function might have been called corporate planning, with a full range of economic forecasting, futurology, scenario planning, market and social research and so on. In the more sceptical 1990s, most of that has been swept away, but the need to keep a corporate eye on world trends and product developments obviously remains. For some companies, the current solution is a small central marketing operation with a handful of executives, whose brief is wide ranging but of limited depth.

At Black & Decker, for example, European chairman Roger Thomas brought product development into a small group marketing organization. 'The best people' were selected from the major subsidiaries but allowed to stay in their national offices rather than move to the headquarters near London. 'I don't believe in planning in an ivory tower,' said Thomas. 'You must know what the European market needs for product development. They have to keep a check on what's going on in the marketplace for power tools, and to develop new product ideas.' The country managers then give their estimates of how many of the new products they expect to sell – 'they're generally not very far out' – and present their marketing plan with any request for more promotional resources.

continues

continued

Glaxo, the UK pharmaceutical group, leaves its national subsidiaries with a high degree of autonomy in the way the group drug portfolio is marketed. It does, however, maintain a small international market development division – part of Glaxo Group Ltd, a central coordinating body headed by a Swiss executive – to act as a repository of experience and to analyse the global market in the broadest sense. It might recommend to subsidiaries how to market a particular product, but, according to one senior executive, 'it would be anathema for central marketing to interfere, and if they tried to tell the MDs how to do it, there would be trouble.'

In IBM's experience, divisional conflict has not always been healthy and changes are now under way to replace it with cooperation and 'interlocking activity'. Some companies, say consultants, have been practically torn apart by conflicts between profit centres: a high price often has to be paid for that elusive quality, synergy. In addition to a clear structure, a favourable corporate culture and careful management are necessary to make a matrix work effectively. As Fred Newall, NCR's senior vice president, Europe, admitted,

'Our matrix breaks down every so often, basically because of personalities. Everyone wants to be a hero and totally responsible for success. As long as there is stability, people can work together with mutual respect. It's when there are changes that conflict occurs.'

Executives at Electrolux stressed that its three-dimensional matrix – country, product line and functional – works only because the people involved want it to and can tolerate the ambiguities. Said Electrolux UK's managing director Jimmy James,

'A lot of the way we organize depends on who you have. You fit the organization to the people. You trust in managers and give them space. If I talk to one of my MDs, we agree on the phone, and that's the end of it. We're able to make, and get, very quick decisions – we're totally unbureaucratic.'

'Kodak has a culture that allows [the matrix] to work,' according to Bob Worden, until recently Kodak's European business research director but now on a US assignment. 'People are used to working in a framework, or a team, to accomplish their ends,' he added. 'They don't get overly frustrated at this type of relationship or the series of checks and balances that are imposed. We try to get people to think of themselves as European members of the Kodak family.'

The company's business units set up in the mid-1980s are now meshed with the national companies (see Figure 4.3). There are business unit managers in each country, for, say, consumer imaging (such as colour film) or business imaging (that is, copiers). They report functionally to the national general manager, but also through the European region business unit manager to the central product groups. The national managers report up through the region to the international group. Individual factories report to the central manufacturing group, and the research laboratories to the international research group. There is thus considerable organizational 'distance' between research, manufacture, business unit and marketing and sales. It is also noteworthy that Kodak is still organized as a US company with some international operations, an issue that the new chief executive, Kay Whitmore, may have to ponder.

At the operating level, both country manager and business unit carry profit responsibility, and these two reporting streams are not even brought together at the European level. 'In some areas it might be difficult, and it probably generates additional work,' Worden conceded.

> 'Some might say that Kodak has not yet shaken off its bureaucratic or paternal ways, and when the push comes to shove, personnel have to examine their career opportunities. A lot is laid down, but a local general manager has a high degree of responsibility for resources. In the development of new products, he will input his needs early on. But his role is changing – now he spends more time thinking about how he can implement corporate global goals.'

In the old days, the country managers would have expected to take on special projects themselves, using their own research and manufacturing facilities where appropriate. Now, the business units have the responsibility and control the research programmes in the group laboratories. But some Europrojects are 'missioned out' to individuals or subsidiaries as appropriate. However, developments outside the business units' sphere of influence are in danger of being neglected, leaving the company flat footed when faced with a competitive challenge in a particular market. New ways are being sought to handle these, and one possibility is the use of 'technical centres of excellence' in national companies.

With or without an effective matrix, the search is still on for more effective ways of achieving the great goal of combining local flexibility and initiative with a central strategy. The informal Japanese style or a range of *ad hoc* solutions can provide answers for some, without committing themselves to the challenge of the network. But the number of alternative structural solutions to the problem of meshing central and local authority is relatively small. Most companies, though not all, depend on variants around the theme of geographical managements, aided or limited in some degree by central, product-based departments.

One company, Unilever, has developed a structure appropriate to its own special circumstances but noteworthy for its originality and apparent

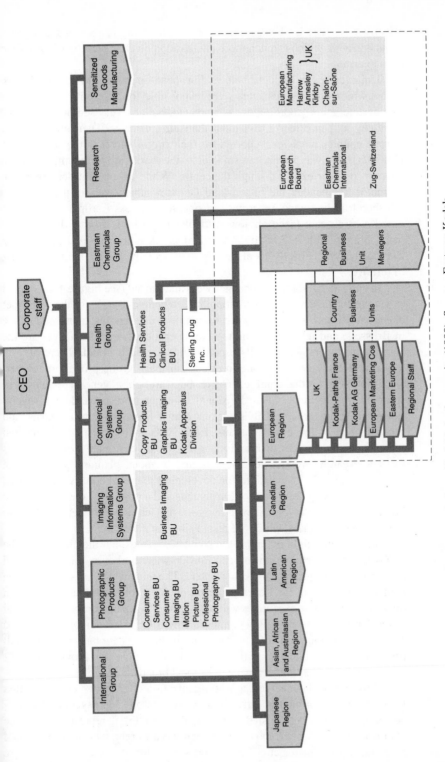

Figure 4.3 Eastman Kodak's business units (1990). *Source* : Eastman Kodak.

effectiveness. The Unilever organization applies only to its soaps and detergents business, which is much more international in character than frozen food or margarine.

Unilever began to coordinate its European operations in the late 1960s, before which country managers were responsible for all profits. In 1968, the role of detergents 'coordinator' was created, but at a very senior level in the hierarchy and in effect a divisional managing director. Thenceforth, Lever Europe country managers reported for their profits direct to the coordinator. However, there was no mechanism to draw the marketing programmes of each country together except through the centre. While the present detergents coordinator has headed the French and German subsidiaries in the past, and has therefore had wide experience of operating across Europe, his London-based central team faced obvious difficulty in pushing, from a distance, the many brands with international potential or 'convergence brands' into the European arena. Strictly local brands now account for no more than 20% of turnover.

In early 1990, some key changes were announced (see Figure 4.4). A chief executive for Lever Europe was appointed to be responsible for the consumer detergents business, including manufacturing. He has his own head office in Brussels, and reporting to him via an operations general manager are the country managers with profit responsibility for each brand. There are six 'divisional managers', who are in effect European group product managers, also reporting to the chief executive but through a general manager of strategic management. Each divisional manager is responsible for several European brand groups (EBGs), teams drawn from different countries and based in one of the major markets. Each EBG will consist of a dedicated manager and a number of brand managers from 'customer' countries, plus market research, product development and financial planning support. The EBGs will now be responsible for developing the marketing strategy, pack design, advertising and so on for Eurobrands and a number of the convergence brands. They will have their own budgets, but will have to 'sell' the mix to the customer countries, which are responsible for execution.

Such a split might not appeal to some companies, but the plan is that the EBGs will be effective in the crucial Europe-wide marketing function as well as reconciling the product and country axes. The fact that the axes are not given formal expression in the Lever organization does not mean that the problem does not exist. Some executives will have split jobs – part European, part local – but that is now increasingly common. It will help, the company hopes, to break down nationalism. Just as important is that the national subsidiary will preserve its role, and will have the freedom to manoeuvre and provide ideas for the common good as well as manage its local brands.

However well conceived, a neat organization chart with solid and dotted lines and names printed in different sizes suffers one big psychological disadvantage: people are misled into thinking that (a) it represents how the company actually works, and (b) if the reality is different, then the chart should be right, not the managers. There is no suggestion that the Lever structure

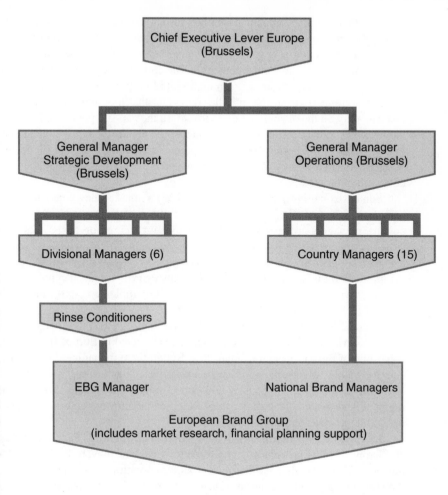

Figure 4.4   Lever Europe management structure (1990). *Source:* Lever Europe.

suffers unduly in this respect, but in any company, the organization chart can
take on a life and a rationale of its own. The managers, conscious that the health
of the business, not the organization chart, is the key issue, sensibly respond
by running it as circumstances and their personalities and inclinations
dictate. Intermediate layers of authority are short-circuited, coordinators are
kept in the dark and informal links are established to secure the desired
outcome.

A more pragmatic policy is to start with the business and the people,
and work back to the simplest structures that will help them to work together
in harmony. This is the principle underlying the Electrolux and Nestlé
structures.

Whether or not a company has built a formal matrix structure, the need to ensure that country and other senior executives feel part of the team remains paramount, particularly in such a diverse market as Europe. The issue is not simply one of motivation and enthusiasm. The company needs all the management expertise it can muster in formulating its European, indeed global strategy. The reduction of the middle ranks in the hierarchy puts greater responsibility on the operational managers to fill the gap and provide a countervailing voice to the central authority. Whether the big decisions are going to be made in Tokyo, Rochester, New York or some European centre, the European markets have to present a coherent opinion, and the structure must facilitate the deliberation process.

Senior executives, in the words of IBM's market development vice president Elio Catania, 'must feel part of the European team.' At IBM, country managers at least 'share the decisions on a common basis.' Catania liked to emphasize that his executives have 'two hats – their own country and a Euro-responsibility.' Evidently, their concerted view would be difficult for the product divisions back in the US to disregard, just as the individual managers would find it difficult to drag their feet in implementing the majority decision.

For smaller companies, the principle is the same, even if the span of control is rather larger. Scott Paper, for example, is directed in Europe by a board consisting of the European president Jack Butler, three managing directors of country groups, plus some world-wide executives. 'Each of us,' said Butler, 'has responsibility for a country plus one important strategic thrust on a regional basis, such as consumer marketing, manufacturing, commercial and industrial, procurement of fibre etcetera.'

In 1989, Glaxo established a new coordinating entity, Glaxo Europe, consisting of the European regional director (resident in Verona, Italy), the directors for the smaller northern and southern countries, and the managing directors of the bigger countries. Glaxo's chairman, Paul Girolami, believed that the formulation of policy should be kept separate from its implementation to ensure that it was not distorted by short-term enthusiasms. As a result, Glaxo Europe acts primarily as a coordinating body between the autonomous national companies and the centre. The particular nature of the pharmaceutical industry has driven this process, according to Girolami:

'It has very high and risky research expenditure, which must be a central responsibility. On the other hand, clinical trials and the marketing requirements and conditions are highly specific to each country, and the local management must have the freedom to manoeuvre as circumstances demand.'

'We run the group as an integrated business,' said Girolami. 'Every company relies on other companies for success. We lay down very strict policy rules on what you can say and on quality.' But within these guidelines, local managements have extensive autonomy: 'The national MD's main job is to lead and monitor performance . . . we can't tell him in London how to do it.' For Girolami, the key to establishing an effective group-wide strategy was to respect the human factor: 'You've got to motivate people – you don't give orders, you influence them. It's a combination of delegated response guided by central strategy.'

In contrast, Honeywell's European policy committee is specifically charged with strategy formulation, although at one stage removed from the US headquarters. Nevertheless, European president Jean-Pierre Rosso was as careful as Girolami about developing local support for corporate decisions: 'We spend a lot of time on "ownership" of strategy. They [the business heads] are buying it in, and if they do, we have a lot less problems.' Heinz, too, relies on a quarterly steering committee consisting of the three European heads, the European head of Weight Watchers, and Paul Corddry, senior vice president, Europe. Its role is to develop the Heinz pan-European strategy, to monitor progress and to 'ensure the left hand knows what the right is doing,' and to examine three or four current issues in detail.

It would be difficult to run a European operation without regular meetings of the country and product managers in one way or another (in addition to the normal round of planning and budget meetings). But everything depends on the use made of the meetings by the central authority and the members. In one company, the country managers normally meet only once a year, but being in the engineering industry, they may have found that this is adequate for the rate of change. In the computer sector, life is more hectic, and quarterly or even monthly sessions are more usual.

The numbers of country and product managers involved in Europe can make such meetings unwieldy and expensive in executive time unless they are layered. A usual distinction is between the big four markets – UK, France, Germany and Italy – and a wider plenum. But not all companies are equally strong across Europe, and markets where they are still building their presence may demand more input and provide less output in the way of experienced advice than the mature ones.

The Japanese way

An emphasis on performance rather than structural neatness appears to characterize Japanese companies. One Japanese electronics company, which prefers to remain inscrutably anonymous, but with a strong world-wide brand name, is notably relaxed about the coordination of its marketing policies in Europe. The European headquarters does not have executive authority, and the national companies work together through committees, one member of which might be placed in charge of a particular project. Although the company as a whole is organized on functional lines within product groups, cooperation between executives from different functions, like sales and manufacturing, at a tactical level is claimed to be widespread and liberal.

At Canon, the European headquarters is given a rather stronger role but it still lacks the clarity which US multinationals, for example, would regard as vital. The simplicity of its structure considering its size – it employs 7000 in Europe alone, 300 of them in the Europa headquarters near Amsterdam – is notable. But Canon prides itself on the level of internal communication. There is a price to pay, however: executives probably spend more time in meetings than their opposite numbers in Western countries. World conferences are held twice a year in Tokyo and last anything up to two weeks. They are attended by the regional executives, the country managers, heads of department and occasionally senior marketing managers. The heads of the big four European countries plus the two factories also meet every two months 'to ensure harmony about policy on pricing, marketing, finance, product development and so on,' explained European president Takeshi Mitarai.

One Canon country manager calculated recently that, in aggregate, he spent nearly two months a year in liaison and other meetings, and if there is conflict – between, say, the business planning division, covering production and sales of each product, and the country managers – 'we compromise in a very Japanese way.' A wider purpose of the meetings is to help Canon's central departments in Tokyo, with little experience of anything outside Japan, comprehend marketing conditions in Europe. They are not always successful, and language remains a much bigger barrier for the Japanese than for any Western nation. It is also a barrier for Westerners working in Canon, some of whom feel disconnected from the Japanese grapevine. Despite this problem, there is little doubt that communication in Canon is better than in many Western multinationals.

Canon has learned to its cost the absence of communication in Western companies. One senior Canon director complained,

> 'We licensed some technology to one Western company, and I had to explain one thing to 100 people separately because there was no communication between them. In Canon, if new technology arrives, the information is passed to everyone involved, even to others in different centres.'

That also applies to its understanding of the market, according to another director, who claimed: 'We try to understand the particular demands of different markets. People's requirements and tastes are not the same so we are flexible; we try to find a compromise between countries, and not to force our views on the markets.'

Case 4.6 Matsushita

The accelerating globalization of the operations of Japanese manufacturers is already leading to substantial changes in their traditional organizational patterns. One example is the giant Matsushita Electric Industry (MEI) group, one of the world's largest makers of electrical consumer and industrial goods.

Until 1 April 1988, as with many other Japanese manufacturers, the Osaka-based group had its own trading company, Matsushita Electric Trading Co. (MET), which enjoyed full responsibility for the Matsushita group's overseas trade. Within the main company, Matsushita Electric Industry Co., domestic production, development and marketing have been and continue to be the responsibility of the presidents of MEI's product divisions.

As the Matsushita group rapidly expanded its international trading and manufacturing operations in the 1980s, coordination between MET and MEI's highly autonomous production divisions became more difficult. Even though most of the shares of MET were held by MEI, the former was independently traded on various stock exchanges. In pursuit of its own benefit, MET sometimes contradicted the interests of its parent: for example, some sales scored by aggressive MET traders may have come at the expense of MEI's manufacturing divisions, which sold products both through MET and through its own sales forces.

MEI President Akio Tanii's prescription was to merge MET into MEI as the main company's overseas business division and assign it the responsibility for coordinating the operations of Matsushita's regional and local subsidiaries. This move enhanced the ability of the Osaka headquarters to exercise effective leadership over the fast-growing global operations of the MEI group on an integrated basis.

However, along with this centralization on the strategic level, MEI placed operational control closer to its major markets by shifting regional management responsibility from the Osaka head office to three newly established corporate management divisions (CMD). The headquarters for these units are sited, respectively, in Singapore (covering Asia, Oceania and the Middle East), London (for Europe and Africa) and Secaucus, New Jersey (for North and South America). The presidents of the regional headquarters have now received the authority to manage product development, production and marketing on a fully integrated basis, subject to the group-wide planning process. This range of responsibility now parallels that of the presidents of MEI's autonomous product divisions. These product divisions retain the primary responsibility, along with the advice of the head office and the regional corporate management divisions, for the management of overseas production facilities.

Tanii's determination further to bolster the power of the regional offices was shown in August 1990 when MEI moved to rationalize its global distribution network by reducing the number of distribution centres from 67 to

continues

continued

about 20 warehouses and put them under the direct management of regional or, in the case of Europe and Asia, country-level management.

Matsushita officials indicated that the reorganization is proceeding smoothly. Among the benefits have been improved intracompany communication, better global customer service and more efficient distribution. For example, MEI is now restructuring local distribution systems in the regions with the aid of new computer-aided information-processing systems and communication links, collectively called the 'Pana-VAN' (for Panasonic value-added network) system. When in place, purchasing, sales and inventory information in any Matsushita operation linked to Pana-VAN will be verifiable by any other Matsushita office world-wide.

Perhaps the major remaining issue is one common to all mergers: combining the two corporate cultures. In the over 50 years of its existence, MET developed an internationalized and aggressive tradition: 'We acted like hunters for opportunities around the globe,' said one former MET executive. While some analysts fear that MET's strong global thrust may be watered down with the merger into the more domestically oriented MEI, others expect that MEI's absorption of MET will lead to a wider diffusion of global awareness in the group as former MET staffers make their mark felt in nontrading functions.

Developing teams and task forces

Differential development of the various markets has encouraged some companies to develop more specialized committees as well as 'task forces' to take on specific projects. These frequently cut across the normal departmental boundaries and are an obvious way of tackling many marketing problems. As the need for closer cooperation between national subsidiaries and central product groups grows, this type of response is likely to become more popular. Currently, examples range from Renault's project teams, which aim to speed the development and launch of new models, to Canon's corporate PR group.

At Heinz, Corddry preferred bridge-building committees to a coordinating marketing group, which he stressed was not in the corporate culture. As a result, 'We've really changed the way we're operating, and you can see the impact elsewhere – the thinking is much less insular.'

In addition to the steering committee, Heinz has utilized a series of major task forces to examine specific 'prongs of our strategy.' Permanent Euroforums have also been established in each function – marketing, personnel, finance and so on – to share information and determine appropriate action. The chairman of each forum is assigned a specific agenda and 'strict marching orders,' according to Corddry. One innovation that has already emerged and proved its worth is the 'product fair', where the marketing executives from Heinz marketing companies were invited first to the UK to study the market conditions and the products Heinz was marketing there, then to Rome and so on. The purpose is to share experiences and hopefully trigger new ideas.

As a result of all of these consultation exercises, claimed Corddry, 'When we have met to discuss strategy, and the pressure is put on to apply a foreign solution, it's amazing how easily companies have embraced it, because the executives are wide open to it.'

In general, the teamwork approach has a number of advantages:

- No extra staff are required, although if these exercises take too much time, the executives' principal duties may be neglected;
- Jobs can be distributed through all the subsidiaries to avoid national bias and involve them in the ultimate solutions;
- Good use is made of available expertise in the group, and individuals are given valuable multinational experience;
- It may be the only effective way of tackling the kind of nebulous, multi-department problems that afflict many large organizations.

There are considerable drawbacks, however:

- Committees, even when given the name task forces or action teams, have an innate tendency to waste executive time – particularly if a lot of travelling is involved – and to get in other people's way;
- Their solutions may be difficult to keep track of and control;
- They may take longer to find the solution than one executive working full time;
- 'Forming a committee' is a well-known excuse for inaction.

Creating a networked approach

As global corporations become ever larger through foreign acquisitions, joint ventures or direct investments overseas, some multinationals have decided that none of the conventional organizational forms work for them. At the same time, these companies want to stay flexible, maintain the ability to respond quickly to fast-changing technology and become product innovators. Companies as diverse as Philips NV and computer group ICL have decided that the only way to accommodate their needs is through a new organizational structure called a corporate network.

A networked company is one in which all employees in all parts of the world create, produce and sell the company's products through a carefully cultivated system of interrelationships. Middle-level managers from R&D,

marketing, distribution and so on, discuss common problems and try to accommodate one another. Information need not travel along inflexible routes or organizational lines. By contrast, traditional corporate organizations, discussed earlier, formally divide marketing on the basis of products, functions or geography, or some combination of these; and information travels according to a set chain of command.

The network approach involves no formal chain of communication. Marketing people in France are encouraged to speak to manufacturing people in Singapore. Lateral relationships spur innovation, new product development and better quality control. Supporters of the network approach perceive it as the only effective way a company can be innovative in today's bureaucratic world. Networking puts greater decision making responsibility in the hands of middle managers, who are not required to clear every detail and event with higher-ups. As Fred Guterl stated in *Business Month* (1989), 'The corporate network is not so much a new organizational structure as a departure from the whole idea of structure. Management control is replaced by co-ordination.'

Corporate networks require that the various groups stay in close contact with each other. Vital to the success of a network is fast, reliable communication. It is no coincidence that networks have become popular at the same time that electronic mail, faxing, teleconferencing and other advanced telecommunications techniques have become steadily more accessible and affordable and increasingly recognized as valuable management tools.

Networking in the management sense has to be distinguished from the IT meaning, although in practice, the one is made possible only by the other. The broad principle is to rely far less on the conventional hierarchical relationships, and more on informal groupings assembled for specific tasks and *ad hoc* relationships between individuals.

Apart from the human and personnel issues of networking, a characteristic of a number of companies is the responsibility placed on the country managers and others to pull out of the centre the resources they need – Girolami at Glaxo and Giordano at BOC (see Case 4.7). The requirement to do this for capital expenditure has long been the practice, and the procedure for justifying capital and other projects is well established. Not so common is the extension of the principle to technical, marketing and sales support, the rationale being:

- Subsidiaries are much more likely to use resources effectively if they can call for the support themselves rather than have it thrust down their throats;
- Poor performance cannot be blamed on inappropriate central policies;
- In order to win individual battles in the global war, small subsidiaries must be encouraged to call on group resources even though their own cash flows could not support the investment.

Once again, much depends on the cultural atmosphere. If blame, recrimination and a paranoic anxiety to be associated only with success are the prevailing executive characteristics, no structural device will have much effect. But networking offers some prospect of making cooperation and the deployment of ideas and expertise more effective because:

- Communication is quicker, less formal and not confined to the 'proper channels';
- A network extends horizontally as well as vertically, across departmental boundaries and national frontiers – junior marketing executives in subsidiary A might talk directly to senior service managers in subsidiary C or D to solve a particular problem, rather than only (and if at all) through the centre;
- These links are not dependent on the limited 'exchange capacity' at the centre, in terms either of the volume of traffic, or imagination and responsiveness to new ideas.

The network idea has been taken up enthusiastically in some academic circles, partly because it does promise some practical means of reconciling central authority with local autonomy – and perhaps also because of a natural academic empathy with its egalitarian, anti-hierarchical characteristics. Nevertheless, the problems that networking poses should not be underestimated:

- The primary purpose of a structure is to facilitate effective action toward a centrally determined objective. In a crisis, a network might well impede that process.
- Drive and commitment in the organization can quickly be lost if there is no obvious centre of authority. The geographical identity of the centre has a powerful psychological impact.
- A network depends on a much better accounting and IT system than even the most advanced companies have yet installed (see Chapter 9). The cost of such a system for a major multinational can run into hundreds of millions of dollars.
- A network depends on a degree of maturity and expertise among executives that may take some time to emerge.
- There is little practical experience to draw on: none of the companies in this book has developed networking to any significant degree, nor has the system had to face periods of radical change or crisis.

Despite these disadvantages and criticisms, networking goes with the grain of current developments in corporate organization. Companies anxious to make the best use of scarce and increasingly expensive talent are likely to experiment with networks in some degree, even if the conventional structure is retained in the background.

Case 4.7 BOC'S global network

BOC, the UK multinational gases group headed by the American Richard
Giordano, is moving toward a global network system of management. The
following is from a talk given at the London Business School:

> 'The technology of gas applications is driven by close contact
> with customers' needs. These applications are often prototyped at
> our expense at customer locations. Moreover, the customer profile
> varies considerably from country to country. … On the other hand,
> any single gas application usually does have value in more than a
> few of the countries in which we do business. Finally, the shelf life
> of these technologies can be as short as one to two years. It is
> absolutely essential that technology moves from country to country
> as quickly as possible.
>
> 'Our organizational solution had to cope with forbidding geog-
> raphy, a wide diversity of technical and operational subject matter,
> and the involvement of technical and functional personnel as well
> as general managers. The scale of our businesses simply could not
> afford local self-sufficiency, nor a traditional managerial pyramid
> over the whole group driven from the centre, nor some form of
> expensive matrix organization.
>
> 'Our solution to the problem carries the unimaginative name of
> "networking". We expect managers and technologists in our group
> companies throughout the world to take on their shoulders the
> responsibility for accessing group technology wherever it resides,
> and to keep appraised of and implement best practices in every
> aspect of their business.
>
> 'Our job at the centre is to facilitate communication, and occa-
> sionally audit. We keep at the centre a road map; a written, up-to-
> date technical inventory, telling us where the technology is and how
> it works, rather than complete specifications for implementation.
> We issue publications, sponsor seminars, and create *ad hoc* short-
> lived committees to draw our managers' attention to what is avail-
> able and what is changing. We appoint "lead houses" for specific
> areas of technology or operational problems. A lead house could be
> in Sydney or Osaka, but it would be identified as the most know-
> ledgeable within our group on that subject. It would have special
> responsibilities for dissemination of that knowledge to other group
> members round the world. We don't expect its work to be duplica-
> ted by other group companies.
>
> 'Networking is fast, efficient, but not so easy to sustain. It
> requires that managers live with more than average ambiguity and
> sometimes conflicting objectives. Networking implies giving and

continues

continued

taking. Individuals are often called upon for contributions that have no immediate benefit to their P&L.

'Networking implies a high degree of cooperation and trust rather than authority. ... Our organization also recognizes that there is no single source of wisdom in the group. Networking values speed and flexibility. Above all else, it recognizes that delay is costly and often fatal. ... The biggest challenge we face in exploiting the full potential of networking is cultural. The forging of an Anglo-American management culture was relatively easy compared to the task we now face in achieving that same result with our Far Eastern associates.'

Summary

- Many companies are increasingly becoming convinced of the need to co-ordinate their marketing across Europe, although the rationale is usually rather more complex than for manufacturing. There is general agreement that the strength of the product in a given market and the long-term profit potential can be assured and developed only if the product is also strong in neighbouring geographical markets. The difficult issue is not so much the principle of coordination, but the degree of coordination and the methods by which it is achieved.

- Country managers are therefore faced with the need for their marketing teams to coordinate their activities with their opposite numbers elsewhere in Europe, often without producing a corresponding financial return to the subsidiary. A number of companies have found that unless some robust organizational changes are made, they risk receiving mere lip-service from country managers in terms of regional marketing coordination.

- The difficulties involved in attempts to coordinate have prompted many companies, especially in the consumer goods sector, to set up European product/brand managers, giving them varying degrees of authority. At the same time many business-to-business companies have been moving to modify and adapt their normally product-based organizations to get closer to the market.

- In consumer marketing, central product/brand managers are gaining pop-ularity as a way of putting additional strength behind coordinated mar-keting strategies.

- One way of compensating country managers for any job erosion through increased coordination is to install a lead country system, which extends individual responsibilities onto the wider European stage. Many companies regularly nominate certain subsidiaries to be or become expert in a specific product, application, or marketing or sales tactic.

- The nature of business involves balancing many incompatible objectives, like maximizing short- and long-term returns, or cutting costs but increasing quality. The European dimension adds a further set, forcing companies to respond to many different local requirements and preferences, while developing new products and services, and cutting costs and overheads through greater volume. That is what makes a matrix inevitable, in the view of some experts.

- An emphasis on performance rather than structural neatness appears to characterize Japanese companies.

- Differential development of the various markets has encouraged some companies to develop more specialized committees as well as 'task forces' to take on specific projects. These frequently cut across the normal departmental boundaries and are an obvious way of tackling many marketing problems.

- As global corporations become ever larger through foreign acquisitions, joint ventures or direct investments overseas, some multinationals have decided that the only way to accommodate their needs is through a new organizational structure called a corporate network.

Checklist

In the light of the increasing complexity of markets, has your company:

(1) Established the need to exploit and leverage ideas, expertise and systems on both a global and regional basis as a firm part of strategic thinking?

(2) Evolved into the sort of organization, particularly in a complex area like Europe, that provides for both central control without stifling local initiative?

(3) Drawn in country managers closer to the organizational centre, regional or headquarters, or are they allowed to act as powerful local fiefdoms?

(4) Created a tier of central coordinators who have both power and responsibility?

(5) Created brand/product managers who cut across borders?

(6) Supported more flexible ways of cooperative working such as task forces, either directly or through the corporate culture?

(7) Drawn key executives across Europe into decisions affecting European business as a whole?

(8) Looked at the scope for designating particular countries as lead countries for different products?

References

Bartlett, C. and Ghoshal, S. (1989). *Managing Across Borders: The Transnational Solution*. Boston: Harvard Business School Press

Guterl, F. (1989). *Business Month*, January

Jacobs, K. (1987). *McKinsey Quarterly*, Winter

Johansson, L. (1989). *Financial Times*, June 21

5

Brand strategies

Introduction

Brand theory is not new. The building of brands which attract a loyal and lucrative consumer following has been a familiar concept and one developed by consumer goods companies over a long period of time. But the increasingly sophisticated concepts are spreading throughout businesses of all types because of several key trends:

- The evolution of Europe from separate national markets into one trading area which nonetheless comprises quite distinct segments and which demands a careful evaluation of the brand portfolio.
- The increased emphasis on getting higher margins from creating the added value attributable to premium brands.
- The success of some niche brands.
- The rise of distributors' own brands which match the quality of manufacturers' brands.
- Corporate branding. Organizations of all sizes and shapes are turning to branding techniques to establish a clear, international corporate identity for audiences which include customers, shareholders, employees and the general public.
- The evolution of brand valuation. A very controversial area, it is being used both to arrive at the financial worth of brands in order to allocate resources more efficiently, and to assign that value to balance sheets – a practice spearheaded by several large UK consumer goods companies.

The issues of branding which face companies differ in degree, rather than substance:

- Consumer goods companies are faced with the need to devise a global brand strategy: a complex process which includes acquisition, rationalization, extension of existing brands and new brand development. They also face aggressive competition from retailers' own brands.
- Service companies like financial organizations and airlines are turning to branding techniques as a means of both ensuring and exploiting consumer loyalty and to foster a service culture.
- Business-to-business organizations, which mainly deal with professional buyers, are trying to move beyond the 'slapping labels on boxes' stage and use branding to stand out in the midst of ever-noisier competition. Branding the company and its products for quality, service and/or innovation is also a powerful tool for prising open new markets.

Corporate minds became wonderfully focused on brands when, in 1988, Nestlé bought British confectionery specialist Rowntree, which was capitalized at about £1 billion, for £2.5 billion in order to get hold of profitable brands like After Eight, Polo Mint and KitKat. That same year the food and tobacco group Philip Morris bought Kraft for four times its tangible asset value. It created a form of brand fever as companies began to search through their own portfolios to see what they had, and what they could buy or sell. Table 5.1 shows why brands have become such an important part of the marketing portfolio since 1950.

Table 5.1   The marketing environment: the brands issue.

	1950	*1990*
Technology	A few leaders with a big R&D advantage over a lot of followers	Speed of technology transfer shortens lead time and narrows gap; many companies share same technology
Markets	Mass markets with moderate competition fuelled growth	Mass markets are stagnant with aggressive competition
Products	Simple single runs: production stable and relatively simple	Segmentation and customization require more complex, flexible, manufacturing capabilities
Trade	Fragmented, weak, dependent on manufacturer	Concentrated, powerful control of manufacturer; retail brands
Media	Simple structures and concentrated usage; beginning of long period of television dominance	Explosion in all forms; individual media use fragmented
People	Mass tastes, stable traditional values, predictable lifestyles	Individualistic tastes, discovered values, eclectic lifestyles
Communication	Inform and persuade of product benefits; rational argument	Emotional expression of brand benefits; metaphor, symbols
Who controls markets	Manufacturers	Consumers

Source: Judie Lannon.

There are a number of strands which comprise brand strategy:

- Coping with cultural differences
- Crossing borders
- Local nuances
- Brands and structure
- Finding niches
- Doing the research
- Auditing the brand portfolio
- Service brands
- Corporate branding
- Brand naming
- Brand valuation

What is a brand?

Brands are at the heart of marketing in the sense that marketing should not only be about meeting needs but also about fulfilling expectations. A brand has come to be seen as far more than a name or a product, but as a mix of both real and perceived added values which are recognized by those who buy goods and services. According to one definition (Interbrand, 1990),

> 'A brand is a simple thing: it is in effect a trademark which, through careful management, skilful promotion and wide use, comes in the mind of consumers to embrace a particular and appealing set of values and attributes, both tangible and intangible. It is therefore much more than the product itself; it is also much more than merely a label.'

The qualities that a brand stands for, often defined as its equity, drive both brand recognition and profitability. The very power of brands is underlined by the fact that most established brands, which make up almost 90% of the universe, have been in existence 20 years or more.

Coping with cultural difference

'National differences are great, cultural differences are there and should be recognized and are not about to go away. You should make opportunities out of them rather than see them as some kind of obstacles to your pan-European strategies or tactics.'

Barrie Staniford, marketing director, The Henley Centre

Cultural differences will be a big issue in the European market. They can be viewed as an insurmountable obstacle to expansion or as a source of competitive advantage if properly exploited. National stereotypes play a greater role in corporate thinking than most companies will admit. It is one of the reasons why so many British companies first dip their toes into continental water in Holland and Belgium – because they are perceived to be 'more like us'. But although those countries might indeed seem closer to the home market, it is crucial to find out in what ways they are not. Exploring attitudes like health awareness and habits like the type of breakfast cereals consumed are the sorts of indicators to use.

At one global distribution company, for example, the marketing director for Europe found that while factors like quality and service tend to apply to European countries across the board, demands differ slightly from one nation to another: 'The differences tend to be typical of what people think. The Germans want efficiency, the Dutch better prices, the Italians are looking for a friendly company, and the British want reliability, speed and quality.'

Will European tastes converge? Some, and slowly. Nestlé, for instance, believes that over time in food, an industry deeply rooted in cultural differences and habits, certain products could become semiglobal/regional. As Nestlé former general manager and vice president Camillo Pagano pointed out,

'There is no doubt that there is a trend toward a certain uniformity of taste among young people, for instance. There are opportunities for products that were not regional to become totally regional – within Europe, perhaps – and there are other products that will remain in their region in one nation, and there are specialities that will remain specialities.'

Case 5.1 Coca-Cola

If you have what is reckoned to be the world's biggest, most successful brand, is the Single Market really that much of an issue? To a certain extent, yes, said Suki Kalirai, divisional marketing manager for Coca-Cola North West Europe: "While the impact of the Single Market is less to us because we are already present in those countries it still has a significant impact to us in that borders that existed before don't any more.'

continues

continued

Distribution is, in fact, the key to the soft drinks group's global/local philosophy: because it owns few of the distributors in the 165 or so countries where it operates and so can combine global guidelines with local adaptations.

Coca-Cola has sharpened its European focus: during a management realignment a few years ago a corporate group based on the EC was set up, with five divisions. Kalirai's division covers the UK, Ireland, Benelux, Denmark, Greece and Cyprus. The split is based on both critical mass and distribution similarities: most of the countries in the North West division have one distributor compared to say, Germany's 60.

At Coca-Cola, the brand *is* the spearhead. But how does a division like his, which spans a number of quite different countries, deal with national differences?

'There are more similarities than dissimilarities. There may be differences in how you execute the concept, because it doesn't translate into a particular country's way of thinking. But the actual broad strategic marketing issues are not that dissimilar.'

And even those differences will modify in the runup to the next century, he predicted: 'You will get people with a perspective that is more akin whereas now – if people have grown up in a country – their perspective tends to be more parochial.' Barriers do still exist, however: in some countries the use of 'diet' is restricted, while there are 45 different designs of vending machines alone in 12 European countries.

The company has made a concerted effort over the last few years to standardize the questions being asked for surveys across borders so it can have comparable information on questions like brand recall, consumption occasions and so on. It is important to pick the right indicators: disposable income, for instance, does not seem to play a large role in soft drinks consumption, as Kalirai pointed out: 'Mexico has the highest per capita consumption of Coke in the world.'

Are there many opportunities left, though, for a pervasive brand like Coke? Kalirai was adamant that there were. Not only are there still 'dry' territories, where the product is not readily available (the beaches in Greece, say), but even in the UK, consumption is a third of that in the US. And the competition is fierce – there are 200 different soft drink makes here. So the push is both into other beverage markets and for market share with existing brands.

Crossing borders

The complexity of dealing with one European market that has been 12 quite separate entities has been the catalyst for many corporations to rethink their brand strategies internationally. Judie Lannon, formerly research and development director at J. Walter Thompson Europe and now an international marketing and communications consultant, believed that one of the main problems facing multinationals confronting Europe as a market was how to find niches in each country which, added together, would produce volume growth. A company operating with only 50–60 million consumers will never be able to build enough share in one market to make the kind of money that they could in the days of mass markets. The route to volume is finding a group of consumers who share similar characteristics in a number of markets. Adding these niches together will produce a substantial niche.

The overriding concern will be the management of brands. Lannon believed that it was possible to see the management of brands across different countries as analogous to managing a brand through time in any one country. The first thing that is noticeable with a strong brand in any one country over time is that it tends to have a distinctive personality. A look at 20 years of advertising history, she noted, shows that with occasional exceptions the type of the advertising, irrespective of the strategy which will emphasize different features of the brand at different points in time, is coherent. Persil commercials have always been different in style from Ariel, for example. Different products such as Kodak and Kellogs have distinctive advertising styles, nuances and assumptions.

Lannon felt that this was because over time the elements that make up the brand's personality have been formally or informally codified and passed down to succeeding brand managers and account executives. This can be a fairly stable process. She concluded that managing the brand's communication in different markets can follow the same model.

Figure 5.1 shows Lannon's model for managing the total communication strategy for global brands:

- What is the product? Is the physical product the same in each market or is it made to country specifications (as can be the case with food products)? Does this matter? What does the product actually do, what are its competitive advantages?
- What is the consumer positioning? How do consumers perceive the brand and its 'territory' (that is, its values and competences) in relation to competitors? How similar are the consumer segments, where are the strengths and weaknesses and how much is product-related and how much is communication-related? Is there a core product positioning that the brand can occupy in several countries? For existing brands, history may require clustering markets around two or three basic positions with overlapping territories gradually able to come closer together.
- What is the brand personality and what advertising metaphor is, or could be, used to express it? What personality characteristics define the advertising style? If the brand were a person how would it be described? This is a critical definition because it will be the criterion against which new creative work will be judged. If human personalities cross borders, as experience of

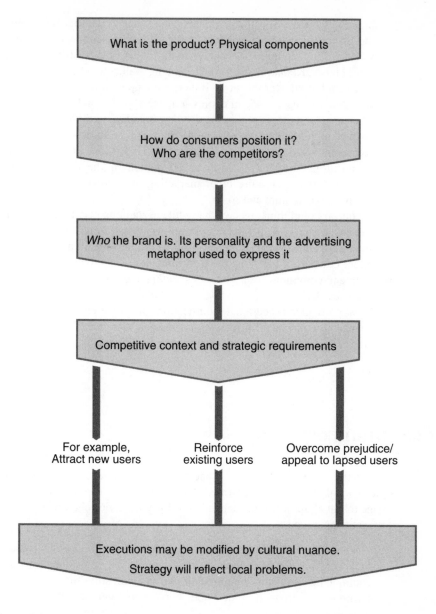

Figure 5.1 Lannon's model for managing total communication strategy for global brands.
Source: Judie Lannon.

life proves they do, so will brand personalities. All successful global brands have a set of rules, codes and conventions that dictate how they are to appear. Some companies write very rigid rule books; others have a more informal set of principles. A vivid visual metaphor helps to define the brand's character. Specific brand metaphors such as the Marlboro cowboy, the Esso tiger, the Levi 501 boy and the Lux film stars travel around the world as they tap universal human myths. Other brands such as Kellogg's Corn Flakes, Kodak, Dunhill, IBM, Johnnie Walker and Bacardi would not look familiar all over the world if there were no guiding principles dealing with colours, logos, style of expression, use of music and so on.

- What are the strategic requirements? Few brands are brand leader in every country in which they are marketed. There will be local strategic requirements that will dictate exactly what the brand needs to do to grow or defend its position. This may require an adaptation of the basic advertising metaphor, it may require other marketing tools, other media, different levels of expenditure and so on.
- European brand thinking says that while executions may require different emphasis, the core personality should stay the same. Think of these situations as different points in time in one culture rather than in different cultures at the same point in time, and the possibility of devising different communication strategies *within* the same brand personality becomes clear.
- What particular executional modifications are required to reflect cultural nuance; for instance, different food recipes to reflect different cultural preferences within a range of slimming or healthy meals.

Local nuances

One of the toughest aspects of brand management is deciding exactly how crucial local/regional nuances are. Does your brand have a strong enough image to travel the world unchanged? As Barry Day, vice chairman of Lintas: International argued,

> 'The global village says that we all have things in common which tend to be very broad, although these things are not necessarily the lowest common denominator. We might all like a certain soft drink, a certain cigarette, a certain training shoe, home computer or whatever. It doesn't really matter.
>
> 'But we are also Europeans. There may be local brands that become European – we all eat pizza, we are more and more eating things like pitta bread, and we use certain toiletries which had a national origin but have become at least European. So there is a refining down from the broad things that we like anywhere in the world to the things that we like mostly here, but not exclusively, to the things we *only* like here.

'I think that the psychology of it goes as follows: the more we are citizens of the world the more we are – however reluctantly – becoming European – because we think we will win as Europeans. But I don't want it forgotten that I am also British/French or whatever. And if you forget I will remind you.'

In some cases ignorance of nuance is bliss. Many US and Japanese companies have regarded Europe as one place for years through sheer insularity. This is not completely fair: the US has often been a world leader in trends that capture the imagination and cut across a broad swathe of the globe like fast food, sportswear and slimming products, while the Japanese have exploited general consumer demand for reliability and miniaturization. The Europeans, on the other hand, shudder at the thought of trying to find similarities between different European nations, and different regions of nations. Like all generalizations, this one is full of holes: but while the Americans and Japanese have to come to terms with finer segmentation, their European counterparts have to find common themes across borders.

Case 5.2   Getting brands to travel

Doing the unthinkable

One of the most high-profile examples of brand realignment to cope with an increasingly borderless world has been carried out by US food giant Mars. It has departed from a strict marketing canon and caused gasps of both disbelief and admiration by simply dropping well-established brand names in local markets and replacing them with international versions. So, for instance, in Europe what was Marathon became Snickers, while the pet food, Mr Dog, from Mars subsidiary Pedigree Petfood, has become Cesar. The American product M&Ms is going global and in the UK that has meant the axeing of the local version, Treets, a chocolate snack.

This is marketing heresy on a grand scale. Kill a name like Marathon? But Mars, a privately owned company run by a paternally autocratic family, has simply ignored the worries that market research might throw up and just done it, risking more than just demotivation. But it seems to be working.

Doing your research first

Jacob Suchard, the Swiss confectionery and coffee company now part of US conglomerate Philip Morris, decided to attack the UK confectionery market initially with its Milka range, which is estimated to be, as Europe's brand

continues

continued

leader, worth about £600 million. The UK market, at about £2.5 billion one of the most sophisticated in Europe is dominated by Rowntree (Nestlé), Mars and Cadbury. But despite Milka's clout in other countries – the Lila Pause bar is number two in Germany – the brands initially made little headway, even with a massive advertising blitz. One of the reasons cited for its relative lack of success was the UK taste for confectionery products like Mars bars instead of block chocolate, which is preferred in Germany.

Prepare properly

German publishers such as Gruner & Jahr and Bauer stormed the UK market with women's magazines like *Prima* and *Bella* when the UK industry had assumed it was safe from attack. But the Germans had carefully identified an new audience segment, came in with deep pockets, a precise plan of attack, and have prospered – at the same time shaking their British counterparts out of their complacency. Not only did several British women's magazines fold, but others had to be dramatically relaunched.

Exploit the right concept

Unilever's now-global brand, Timotei, began life as a small deodorant brand in Finland. The Swedish Unilever counterpart realized that the brand's values of simplicity, purity and naturalness not only reflected the times but was ahead of competitors. In fact, Unilever had picked up on what was a world-wide trend and is now one of the few global brands born in the last 20 years. It is the biggest selling shampoo in Japan, for example, where, by a happy coincidence, its name is adaptable to the Japanese language.

Fill a local niche

Finding a niche for a premium product can work both locally or internationally. Derwent Valley Foods, for example, with its Phileas Fogg range of high quality snacks, came into the crowded UK snack market when the established wisdom said there was not only no room but that their approach was wrong. Their growth has been breathtaking and they are now expanding onto the continent.

Purchase local brands and rationalize them

One of French food company BSN's first moves when it bought a clutch of biscuit brands like Huntley and Palmer, Jacob's and Peek Freans in the UK from RJR Nabisco was to start phasing out the Nabisco name and to axe the 168-year old Huntley and Palmer name in order to put the majority of support behind the Jacob's brand.

continues

continued

Develop an international brand from scratch

One of the few entirely new packaged goods brands launched on an international basis has been the Gillette deodorant Natrel Plus. Started in the UK, Scandinavia and Spain in 1989, it has been created with the global market in mind. It has already gained a small but solid foothold in those markets. One pitfall to be avoided when developing international brands from scratch is to make sure they are not bland and boring.

Brands and structure

Brand management is inextricably linked with the centralization/decentralization debate discussed in previous chapters. Maintaining the quality and positioning of the brand on a regional and global basis – even though the brand might fill slightly different segments in different markets – is essential. The trend is for companies to develop strict central guidelines which allow some leeway for local implementation. United Distillers and Nestlé both follow this line.

Case 5.3   *United Distillers and Nestlé*

United Distillers

The story of United Distillers (UD) is one of how a coherent, central marketing strategy can turn what looks like a marketing nightmare into a marketing dream.

United Distillers, the spirits business side of Guinness, is in the business of brands. Its background is complex and contains an element of high drama following the debacle that was the Ernest Saunders story. Under the steadier hands of Guinness chief executive Anthony Tennant, and UD managing director Tony Greener, it forged a strong, strategic marketing-driven organization from the three disparate elements of the Distillers Company, Arthur Bell (both taken over during the Saunders regime) and Schenley Industries in the US.

continues

continued

The way UD has over time redefined and restructured itself makes it a good candidate for the annals of business case studies, since it acted not only thoroughly but speedily to restore the company's fortunes. Driven from the centre, which housed a strategic marketing unit that functions like a team of strategic marketing consultants, UD has carried out a complete reordering of its brand portfolio internationally.

The marketing strategy revolved around some core issues:

- Reorganizing a confusing and often competing corporate structure world-wide;
- Redefining the marketing strategy towards the brands;
- Restoring the slipping image of what are some of the most powerful spirit brands in the world, and clearing out the weak ones;
- Ensuring that the representation of the brands is coordinated and reflects the core communications strategy, while making consistent the images of the products in each geographical region and hence standardizing pricing.

The first stage in corporate reorganization was to set up a four-cornered regional structure which covered Europe, North America, Asia/Pacific and International (Middle East, Africa and South and Central America). The main purpose was to get the companies closer to their markets. That was a dramatic change from the previous structure, where nine individual companies had existed based around the main brands like Johnnie Walker, Dewar and Haig. That meant that in any one market there could be a lack of coordination which created conflicts of image and pricing.

Since the reorganization in 1988, the total portfolio is managed together in any given market although often there are two distributors. The portfolio is classified on the basis of deluxe, premium and standard according to price and social dimension and generally includes a deluxe whisky, two standard Scotches, a gin and – increasingly – a bourbon, a spirit picked up with the acquisition of Schenley. This grouping of the brands has been based on extensive market research about how the products were perceived in the markets. UD has also increased its control over its brands by buying up its third-party distributors around the world – it now controls up to 80%.

Philip Parnell oversaw the setup of that UD marketing strategy – now being run by his successor, Tim Breene. Parnell was appointed to the new post of marketing director in July 1989 and presided over the central strategic unit at United Distillers headquarters in London. Having been with Guinness in various departments for 11 years, including stints in finance, he was now in charge of the total brand portfolio on a global basis: 'We felt it was essential as we reorganized the business that there needed to be a set of people concerned with the total business and the most profitable long-term way for the business.'

He was aware of the pitfalls a centralized structure can face: 'In the first year or so of owning Distillers, we had central marketing but it didn't function well because it tried to write too many rules and regulations. And you can't run the day-to-day marketing of the brands around the world from London.' So

continues

continued

post-reorganization the central team concentrated on establishing the strategic objectives, while building up a solid working relationship with the regional marketing directors. Parnell wanted to see the development of a 'functional marketing fraternity' within the business. To further that aim he began to hold a world-wide marketing conference – the first was held in autumn 1989.

The central strategic unit is now the repository of brand strategy. This is made concrete with:

(1) Brand strategy books, first done in 1989 and redone in 1990. These are brand bibles and cover historical trends, market analysis, key objectives for the brand, and so on. They incorporate brand maps to show positioning to act as a foundation for the communications strategy. Although the implementation of individual advertising strategies is left, on the whole, to the regions and countries, they must base them on the underlying themes.

(2) Brand reference manuals. These cover the rules that have to be followed for identity, use of colours, and so on in the presentation of the brands. The brands are being revitalized: by the end of 1990, for example, UD will have changed 80% of its packaging to reflect these guidelines.

UD's brand strategy encompasses targeting those brands that will travel, as well as developing both extensions and new products. So Rebel Yell, a new bourbon currently doing well in Australia, is headed for Europe, while a Dutch liqueur is being test marketed in several other countries. Liqueurs are an area ripe for developing new brands since it is a less mature market than spirits like whisky and gin.

UD is a heavy user of market research. Its main objective is to find new pockets of growth by studying the motivational behaviour behind purchasing and matching that up with its brands. The young and affluent in countries like Greece and Spain, for instance, are potentially lucrative targets as increased wealth means they increase their consumption of imported spirits.

Nestlé

Over the last year or so international food group Nestlé has evolved a clearly-defined brand strategy organized into two categories:

(1) The corporate brand. The school of the 1960s said new products do not need to be identified with the company – called the 'Procterization' of brands following the practice of Procter & Gamble. But Nestlé has formulated a basket of 'corporate' brands under the umbrella of Nestlé itself, and others, often acquired, like Findus, Crosse & Blackwell, Friskies and Buitoni. The corporate brands are there to give the image of a company that is a reliable specialist in some area. They are given a 'Nestlé perspective', however, which helps to broaden the perception that Nestlé does not just make chocolate.

(2) The product ranges like Nescafe and individual product brands like KitKat and Crunch.

continues

---

continued

There is tight control from the centre on the policy toward the strategic brands flowing from what the company calls its 'tryptic' of documents:

(1) A branding policy document: this contains the brand's history, what it should stand for, how far it can be used to augment the wardrobe of products under the same brand without overproliferation and so on.

(2) Minimal visual property label sets. These operate as martial law – otherwise, the centre could find itself wasting time and energy enmeshed in detailed pack discussions and 'if you want to control all the details you lose control of the essentials' declared Camillo Pagano, former general manager and executive vice president, marketing.

(3) A seal of guarantee that uses the Nestlé symbol of birds in a nest and which will have been installed on the majority of packs by the end of 1991. Its function will be both to say what Nestlé stands for as a total foods company, but also to act as a subliminal message of quality and assurance to the consumer (see Figure 5.2).

The symbol's use will be strategic. It will not be put on acquired brands, for example, until they meet the defined requirements, or, if for pragmatic reasons, the company feels it should wait until the time is right.

The Nestlé credo says that the brand must reflect:

- the culture of the company that makes it;
- the culture of the category it belongs to;
- the culture of the countries where the products are sold.

Some consultants see a danger in consumer goods companies pursuing international brand harmonization – and organizational structures to match – for benefits that will prove illusory. John Hegarty of London consultants Brand Positioning Services believed managements should be clear what it is they are trying to standardize internationally, and why:

'Is the objective standard production, for example, in one or two factories supplying a whole continent? Or is it rather brand values and their communication in media advertising? It can be important not to confuse the two: major economies may be possible by bringing into line the ingredients/components and formulations/specifications of products manufactured centrally, even though they may be sold under different brand names and with different consumer propositions in different countries. ... Conversely, a single international brand proposition may be delivered successfully in different countries by local formulations produced in local factories to suit local tastes, using a

The Corporate Identity

1. The Nestlé Horizontal Corporate Logotype. Where the first priority is the legibility and the recognition of the Nestlé name, this version, which puts emphasis on the Company name, should be used for stationery, fleet vehicles, annual reports, etc.

2. The Nestlé Vertical Corporate Logotype. Where the Company philosophy or its corporate role needs to be expressed, this version, which puts emphasis on the nest as a Company symbol, should be used on sign-posting, buildings, etc. Preference should be given to this version wherever possible.

NB. *These versions are not to be used on packages (see below).*

The colour for the NESTLE corporate identity is always grey as defined in the NESTLE Corporate Identity Guidelines.

The Brand Logotype

When NESTLE appears as a corporate range or product brand, the solid version should be used. Positive or negative, any colour can be used.

Where NESTLE appears as a corporate brand, it shall, in all applications, be given increased prominence in size, position and colour.

The Nestlé Seal of Guarantee

This version is exclusively for use on packaging, on the side or back panels only of the unit pack, display or shipping carton. It should never appear on any other material.

For exact application, refer to Nestlé Corporate Identity Guidelines.

Any use of the Nestlé logotype and/or the 'nest' device not in line with the above has to be approved by the Trademark owners.

Figure 5.2   General guidelines for the use of the Nestlé logotypes. *Source:* Nestlé.

single international advertising campaign. Too much international marketing seeks standardization for standardization's sake, without a sufficiently clear analysis and definition of the commercial benefits being sought. It is vital to decide why, and therefore what, you want to internationalize.'

This decision process is especially troublesome for large companies with a long list of brands. 'Who decides whether they are different or not?' asked Howard Belton, the senior marketing member of Unilever's Detergent Coordination. Belton was emphatic that 'if you try to impose uniformity, you suboptimize.' The essential issue for an old Unilever detergent brand like Omo, sold in a number of countries, is not one of product specification but one of positioning in each market, different for historical reasons. Making it an effective international brand therefore requires it to be levered slowly into some common position, which will certainly be expensive and could in some instances turn out to be impractical.

Lever Europe, Unilever's soaps and detergents division, has categorized its brands into three groups:

- Established international brands like the modern Jif cleaner and the original, 100-year-old Sunlight soap;
- Local brands;
- Convergence brands – these could become international at some point in the future.

But the predominantly geographical organization that has characterized Unilever's growth is not well adapted to applying the pressure needed to move convergence brands into the international category, and over a decade or more, the European structure has been steadily adapted to meet the new demands in a process of continual evolution.

Companies with a more centralized culture and history may find the harmonization process simpler, but they can still experience problems.

Finding niches

Neither globalization nor regionalization should deter companies from following a niche strategy – unless, of course, that strategy is more about the failure to win market share. US-based Johnson & Johnson is in reality about 150 companies, some of them in big markets and big market leaders, and many of them in small but powerful niches, forming a whole made up of very targeted, energetic operations. In the US, of course, 'niche' brands can claim 1% of a market of 250 million people. Europe will not be so easy.

Doing the research

Globalization/localization demands a far more sophisticated approach to market research. Cross-border studies are still at an early stage and are hindered by the different and often incomparable methodologies used in individual countries. But as companies move towards a more centralized approach to their marketing strategies, they will want a coordinated and consistent approach in gathering information about products, consumers, competitors and tracking the effectiveness of promotional tactics. And they will want this served up not as an indigestible lump of raw data, but as targeted, value-added analysis. That will be accompanied by a desire to know not just who their customers are and where they live, but how they think and act at different times, as well as gaining a better understanding of their buying habits.

International research groups like AGB and Nielsen have come some way in setting up cross-border systems, while other companies involved in areas like advertising tracking have established or are establishing regional and international structures and associations. That the demand by clients for 'commonality' in Europe is growing was highlighted by Richard Piper, director of communication at AGB Market Information UK: 'Until two years ago, you never heard people complain that grocery data is not comparable.'

A number of multinationals, particularly those which keep a tight central grip on promotional strategies around the world, like Coca-Cola, PepsiCo, Rank Xerox and British Airways, already undertake research on a global basis to ensure consistency of message. When he arrived at BA in 1989, former director of marketing and operations Liam Strong began to devise a more disciplined approach to the way research is carried out. He argued that

> 'most companies do quite a lot of research but the discipline is appalling. You should not go into the market just to find out what is going on, but to prove or disprove a hypothesis. That is an old saying. But most companies still do not seem to understand it. What you need is consistency of research over time, a clear understanding of why you are doing it, what your objectives are, and what action will arise from it.'

A notable trend in research is the attempt to devise a European consumer classification system. One example of how some researchers are thinking comes from Europanel, a voluntary association of national research companies which includes AGB in the UK, GfK in Germany, Secodip in France and IHA in Switzerland, which has adopted a socio-economic system called Eurostyles to use in its studies. It was developed by a Sorbonne professor of psycho-sociology called Bernard Cathelat. What his research has done is try to capture groups of Europeans in 15 countries who share certain characteristics. He has mapped out 16 types to help companies planning European marketing strategies which take account of both macro and micro markets:

- The 'withdrawal' mentality. This is made up of four sociotypes (Euro-prudent, -defense, -vigilante, -olvidados) who are older than average (45–60), make up about 23% of European adults, and share to a greater or lesser degree values of relative passivity and the need for social integration in their microsociety where they live and work. They are socially disciplined and earn less than the average income.
- 'Dreamers' consist of Euroromantics and 'squadras'. They are young European couples with children, about 15% of the total. They want to feather their nests, have minimum involvement in the world around them, and like consumer durables.
- Next come the Euroambitious types (Euro-dandy, -business and -rocky), who are between 20 and 25 and are about 25% of the population. They want to succeed, be recognized, and like spending money on leisure, home electronics, clothing, cosmetics and innovative products.
- A smaller number are Euromilitants. At about 10% of the total, they are 'scouts' and 'citizens' and are middle aged, well educated, in comfortable homes and like being involved in the community. They are keen on social and scientific progress with a human face, and spend a large proportion of their high income on their homes.
- The Euronotables (consisting of Euro-moralists, -gentries and -stricts) are ultraconservative and isolationist. Aged 35–64, they make up about 17% of the population, are well-off and educated, prefer traditional values and spend their money on premium products.
- 'Europrotests' and 'Europioneers' are a smaller group, at only 8% of the total, are between 30 and 40 and are the 'greenest' of the lot. They like innovation, nonconformist ideas, and tolerance. They prefer products like quality hi-fi and microwave ovens, while they also spend a lot on cinema, concerts, alcohol and cigarettes.

There has been criticism and scepticism of this system from those who wonder if people can be pigeonholed so neatly. But the desire for some method of pan-European harmonization grows. The European Society of Market Research (ESOMAR) is trying to set standards by looking for comparability in demographics, industrial classifications systems and media research. Bryan Bates, director-general of ESOMAR, believed that 'There is really little sign that people have stopped thinking in purely nationalistic terms. They do not think as Europeans, and they may even argue there is no reason or incentive why they should.'

Companies should keep several aspects of market research in mind:

- They should build up a relationship with a research supplier for the longer-term, rather than just dipping in and out on an *ad hoc*, project-by-project basis;
- They should carry out more research upfront, rather than after the event;
- They should use their common sense when it comes to segmentation studies, calling on their own inhouse data as a guide;

- They should not drown in information overload, and let market research make the decisions. As Ellen Clark (1990), brand manager for Volkswagen in the UK, has been quoted as saying, 'One thing I'm not supplied with is a crystal ball. Lacking all that, all one has to work on is history. But history can only be a guide, just as market research can only represent yesterday's views and opinions. What one must do is consider all these factors, then take a stab.'

Case 5.4 Renault

Creating a new product, or an extension of an existing one, is probably the toughest marketing challenge any company faces. Combine that with a gestation period of up to five years for a product that then has to survive for another ten and it is understandable why Michel Herrard, director of product marketing and commercial development at Renault headquarters in Paris declared that while the marketing techniques he uses can be compared to a counterpart in the cosmetics field, for instance, 'the rhythm is completely different.'

He pointed out that defining the product to hit the target market some years hence means the emphasis has to be on collecting as much information about customers, both existing and potential, as possible.

> 'We have a difficult task, because when you ask people, they don't know what they want in five or six years' time. So you have to try and gain a perspective on what they will want, taking into account the evolution on the environment, consumer habits, ways of life, the economy, technology, and so on.'

And that can lead to a danger any marketer faces: having so much information about that market that it kills what Herrard called 'an element of imagination'. Car companies have been used to dealing in hard, engineering and hence measurable facts. Now they are faced with changing markets with increased customer segmentation, technological similarity and the sheer irrationality of many purchasing decisions – not to mention Japanese competition – which must all play a part in deciding brand strategy. That means they have to avoid the temptation to apply that fact-driven approach to marketing and not let market research smother creative instincts.

Renault had a profit in 1989 of $1.7 billion, while its stream of new and revamped models and ranges over the last few years has won it accolades. It has come a long way from its position in the mid-1980s, when it was losing

continues

continued

money and seemed to have lost its way. Its strategic alliance with Swedish car maker Volvo will both give it more clout, but will also widen its range into a more specialist market. Before its Volvo tie-up, it was fourth in overall European sales.

One of the big issues for car manufacturers, Herrard believed, is to adapt far more quickly to markets: 'Sometimes people in the companies think that when a car leaves the factory it will be sold – no problem. It has been built, it will be sold.' So the emphasis must be on imbuing a market-driven focus throughout the organization because, as Herrard stressed, 'Everybody at the company must make marketing. When you invent a new car, all functions are marketing functions.'

Herrard's department comes in two years before launch in order to make sure the model is optimally adapted to each market, both to ensure it is geared to what customers want, and to avoid costly differentiation. Extensive research is carried out to see how the new product will be perceived by people compared to the older version or model, in terms of price, style, design and how it stacks up against the competition. After launch the car's progress is monitored carefully to decide if any changes are needed. That could include pricing, or creating a more feminine feeling: 'We have to understand why we are not hitting the targets we have chosen and create new versions,' he explained.

The branding issues are complex, since they involve not just the products themselves but the image of the corporate marque. What Renault has been striving for over the last few years is to bring the quality factor more strongly into the equation, like most of its competitors. But it also needs to continue to develop a striking personality since, as Herrard said, 'quality is fundamental in the car market.' The question is 'should we be like Ford and General Motors and make volume products and offer expected quality and equipment to attract a lot of people with the most competitive prices, or do we try and do all that and still be a bit different from them?' Injecting a special flavour has been one reason the company is moving away from its original system of numbering cars. So, the new version of the Renault 5 is called the Clio – after the muse of history. The strategy is to make them more appealing while at the same time not losing sight of the executive, luxury end where the margins are more attractive.

Car manufacturers are, like all industries, having to cope with a changing Europe. Most are still firmly rooted in their home market: French sales account for about half of Renault sales, more than half for Fiat in Italy, and so on. Herrard, however, believed that the more immediate effect of closer integration will be the standardization of technical and fiscal regulations more than a breaking down of cultural differences. But the relentless merging of car makers into huge European operations, and the potential lowering of trade barriers to the Japanese means no company is safe unless it takes both offensive and defensive action.

Brand mapping is one way companies can overcome the problem of devising a centralized strategy for brands without stifling local initiative or finding niches. Brand mapping begins with an indepth analysis of how brands line up according to 'need sets'. According to Gerry Alcock of Brand Positioning Services,

'In determining the feasibility of international brand positioning and advertising it is important to develop a structure and a common vocabulary to identify similarities and differences. To what extent is a brand meeting the same or different consumer needs in different national markets?'

'One way of doing this is by analysing the market in terms of fundamental human needs and then mapping the extent to which a given brand is covering those needs (Table 5.2). And, because we analyse markets by basic customer needs, we are now very confident that fundamental needs are the same around Europe.'

As well as helping to devise the promotional strategy, this form of mapping can also:

- Throw up discrepancies and inconsistencies in the positioning of a company's own bands, or those of the competition;
- Highlight gaps in a new market which could be filled by moving brands in;
- Allow a centralized marketing department to analyse and own the key need sectors while delegating to local subsidiaries issues like the slogans or music use in the advertisements.

As Alcock said, 'Sitting in the centre you should be saying, "I want to own this particular need sector and I require you to come back to me with research to prove that this brand is meeting this particular set of needs".'

Auditing the brand portfolio

This involves taking into account a number of elements concerning the brand portfolio: creating added value, pruning, deciding whether to build or buy brands, and extending or reviving those in the portfolio.

Creating added value

That premium brands command premium prices is not a startlingly original thought. Nor is it any secret that more and more companies, in rethinking their brand portfolios, want to heighten the perception of their

Table 5.2 Comparison of two hypothetical brands of coffee.

Beverages – relevant need set			Brand A UK	Brand A Germany	Brand A France	Brand A Italy	Brand B UK	Brand B Germany	Brand B France	Brand B Italy
Autonomy	Freedom	Independence, freedom, impulsiveness, spirit	•							•
	Self-expression	Individualism, independent-mindedness, self-expression	•						•	•
Inviolacy	Self-respect	Self-respect, self-esteem, self-confidence	•							
Avoidance	Sanctuary	Sanctuary, withdrawal, protection								
	Reverie	Escape, reverie, flight-of-fancy	•							•
	Trust	Anxiety-freedom, confidence, trust		•	•		•	•	•	
	Care-for-self	Basic-goodness, well-being, care-for-self					•	•	•	•
Passivity	Naturalness	Purity, naturalness, cleansing, fitness	•	•	•	•				
	Convenience	Convenience, time-/trouble-saving, ease	•	•	•	•	•	•	•	•
	Calm	Imperturbability, calm, serenity			•	•			•	•
	Pause	Pause, rest				•	•	•	•	
Nurturance	Care	Care, mothering, comfort	•	•		•				
	Consideration	Care, thoughtfulness, consideration, kindness, concern								
Succourance	Thirst-quenching	Basic refreshment, thirst-quenching	•	•	•	•				
	Cleansing	Health, protection, cleansing, fitness	•	•	•	•	•	•	•	•
	Stimulation	Energy, stimulation, vitality	•	•	•	•	•	•	•	•
	Restoration	Unwinding, restoration, transformation	•	•	•	•				
Sentience	Mute-understanding	Support, mute-understanding, empathy								
	Warmth	Smoothness, texture, warmth, glow	•	•	•	•				
	Self-reward	Satisfaction, gratification, self-reward	•	•	•	•				
	Indulgence	Treats, indulgence	•	•	•	•				
	Enjoyment	Expectation, excitement, enjoyment, celebration	•	•	•	•				
	Interest	Variety, choice, interest	•	•						
Cognisance	Discrimination	Discrimination, connoisseurship	•	•	•	•				
	Good sense	Good sense, experience					•	•	•	•
Order	Reliability	Dependability, reliability, predictability	•				•	•	•	•
	Traditions	Routine, ritual, traditions, security								
Acquisition	Possessiveness	Possessiveness, ownership								
	Thrift	Price-consciousness, frugality, thrift, sensibleness			•	•				
Achievement	Success	Achievement, success, luxury, perfection, pride	•							
	Aspirations	Aspirations, prospects, progress	•							
	Joie de vivre	Animation, dynamism, vivaciousness, joie de vivre				•				
Dominance	Self-optimization	Self-optimization, command-of-my-life, fulfilment	•	•						
	Manipulation	Attraction, enticement, seduction, manipulation								
Recognition	Reputation	Reputation, respect, praise, approval, status	•	•						
	Approval	Group-identity, badging, approval	•	•						
Exhibition	Style	Fashionableness, style, impress	•	•			•	•		
Difference	Appreciation	Appreciation, acknowledgement, respect, esteem					•	•		
Affiliation	Involvement	Involvement, loyalty, harmony								
	Responsiveness	Demonstrativeness, responsiveness								
	Group-bonding	Club, clan, group-bonding								
Play	Fun	Amusement, fun, play, smiles, relaxation	•							
Sex	Romance	Romance, fantasy								

brands as consumers get more demanding and more willing to pay for that perceived better quality. But, even if the brand's quality and image are already strong, moving the brand along and up the perception scale is not an easy task. As the Zanussi strategy shows, it demands a coordinated, well-thought-out attack which includes not just customers, but, equally importantly, the retailers.

Case 5.5 Zanussi

Zanussi is part of the Swedish group Electrolux, which has grown rapidly into one of the world's largest white goods manufacturers by a series of acquisitions. It is now structured into three geographical groups: Europe, North America and the Pacific region. Italian-based Zanussi joined the portfolio in 1984. It is now one of the six brands in the UK market; others include Electrolux itself, Moffat, Tricity/Bendix and Parkinson Cowan.

Zanussi UK has its own sales operation and, as marketing director of Zanussi, Francis Huggins was clear about how to run his branding strategy:

'You have to understand the psychology of the marketplace. People do not go to bed at night worrying what brand of washing machine they have in the kitchen. In our marketplace, yes, the brand brings reassurance. But it is not top of the mind, egotistically or status-driven branding. It lies somewhere between a commodity and a luxury.'

There are several stages to the successful implementation of Zanussi's branding strategy:

- Complete the transition to a more marketing-driven culture as part of an overall Electrolux refocusing and refining of the global brand portfolio. Zanussi's engineering base has been strong and noted for its high standards. That has meant the balance has been at times tilted toward production.
- Increase the coordination of the Zanussi brand across Europe. Germany is an example of the problem, where the perception of Italian products is not as favourable as in other European countries. That can complicate matters, as Huggins pointed out: 'I have to bear in mind that if I want to do something, I cannot offer the factory enough volume on my own, so I have to bring colleagues from across Europe in. And they might be in a different position in different marketplaces.'
- Convince the retailers of Zanussi's strategy since they are key to its successful implementation.

continues

continued

The goal is to push the brand into a more premium position in the market and be justified in charging higher prices. White goods have not kept pace with inflation, Huggins argued, lagging considerably behind the Retail Price Index (RPI) over the last 15 years (or would, if the RPI had been around that long). White goods companies have thus been squeezed on two fronts: although they have pushed costs down, prices have not moved up sufficiently to recover inflation from the market, while their distributors and retailers have been suffering from steadily rising rents and logistical costs like fuel, and wages.

Huggins had a three-pronged campaign:

(1) Make the retailers aware that they will not get better margins unless they charge more. This is surprisingly difficult, for traditionally they have measured success on the number of boxes that go out the door, not on sales value per square foot. Retailers must be convinced that volume will not suffer if prices are higher.

(2) Have a product portfolio that the retailer is confident of selling. It is both true and not true, argued Huggins, that a washing machine is a washing machine and a refrigerator is a refrigerator. There are tangible benefits which, if you can convince the retailer and hence the customer, will command a higher price. That means working closely with the retailer to draw customers in with eye-catching promotions.

(3) Branding. Branding for white goods means not just perception, but the way the products are seen in the stores. Zanussi works with the retailers to sharpen up store display and break up the usual monolithic display of appliances which confront potential purchasers. Huggins maintained that Zanussi, with its emphasis on pushing its image through high-profile advertising campaigns has been instrumental in bringing the idea of branding to white goods.

The brands under the Electrolux umbrella do compete with each other, although there is an overall coordinator in each market to ensure really harmful conflicts do not arise. Having six brands is obviously one of the results of growth by acquisition, but having a number of brands is also partly to do with the nature of the white goods market, Huggins believed. However, he said 'I think if we had started with a blank sheet of paper we would not have devised a strategy which said have six brands in each market.'

Pruning

The choice facing a lot of companies is whether what they describe as a niche brand is really a loser, and should be eliminated or sold, or one that, with the right support, could thrive. While there is always room for clever niche brands

– like Ecover, which has picked up quickly on environmental concerns with a range of household cleaners – there will be a massive shakeout of middle, often lacklustre brands as fewer and bigger players begin to dominate the European market.

Food manufacturers have been particularly busy attaining critical mass on a European and global scale, centred around powerful brands which are heavily supported, to counteract the growing clout of food retailers who are not only expanding abroad, but forming cross-border buying alliances (see page 22). The signs of the future can be seen in the sophisticated UK retail market, where own-brands from chains like Sainsbury and Tesco have pushed all but 'The Untouchables' like Nescafe, Whiskas cat food and Heinz canned goods off the shelves.

Build or buy?

Building brands is a risky, lengthy and expensive process. Buying brands, on the other hand, has often seemed like an easier way to market share in new markets. But, according to Peter Doyle, professor of marketing and strategic management at the University of Warwick, acquisitions can be deceptively attractive if companies have not related their branding strategies to primary corporate objectives. He has formulated a theory which categorizes companies as:

- Right-handed, which concentrate on building markets and market share while encouraging a more long-term view;
- Left-handed, which are driven on the whole by financial objectives and are obsessed with short-term results. The acquisition route is more to their taste, although Doyle claimed there is evidence to show that many acquisitions fail to generate long-term value for shareholders.

It is not that clear cut, of course, and, as Doyle said, different companies will apply different techniques at different times. But the distinction is useful when formulating brand strategy. It might save a company from getting embroiled in costly brand building which it doesn't really understand how to do, or, alternatively, being confronted by a confusing muddle of acquired brands which lack any synergy either geographically or with the rest of the portfolio. Doyle has devised a checklist for companies to follow (Figure 5.3).

Extension

Failure rates for new products are staggeringly high – as many as six or seven out of ten, even for companies that have done their marketing homework properly. A study by strategic consultants Goodall Alexander O'Hare in

Market attractiveness	Build	Buy
Market growth	High	Low
Strength of competitors	Weak	Strong
Retailer power	Weak	Strong

Relative cost of acquisitions		
Industry attractiveness	High	Low
Valuation of company	Full	Undervalued
Restructuring potential	Low	High
Brand's potential	Realized	Unrealized

Acquisitions' potential synergy		
Cost reduction potential	Low	High
Marketing competence	Unchanged	Increased
Complementarity	Low	High
Relevant management expertise	Low	Transfers

Brand's strategic opportunity		
Product performance	Breakthrough	Me-too
Positioning concept	New	Mature
Market opportunity	High	Low

Corporate situation		
Growth potential	High	Low
Cash situation	Average	Abundant
Marketing/R&D capability	Strong	Weak

Figure 5.3   Checklist for evaluating brand potential. *Source:* Peter Doyle, University of Warwick.

the UK found that, of new consumer goods products launched between 1982 and 1986, only 29% of the 3458 launches survived in the two-year, post-launch monitoring period. The highest failure rates were in drinks, while the lowest were in household goods. However, almost 50% of line extensions survived.

Consultant Judie Lannon believed that

'The balance is away from new products over the next decade. My guess is that in packaged goods brands probably exist somewhere, and can be moved around elsewhere. The really new brands will probably only come from technology.'

Stretching, or extending a brand, runs the inherent risk of damaging it unless its essence is so well understood by its owners that its core values will stay undiluted and will even be enhanced. Kellogg's shoe polish? No. Kellogg's fruit drink? Perhaps. A Sony range of bed linen? Never.

Lannon called this leveraging brand equity:

'Owners of long established brands own more than the value of the product. The brand's equity can be defined as the latent capacity of a brand to influence the behaviour of the beholder by evoking a specific set of thoughts, feelings and sensations. The stronger these thoughts, feelings and sensations are, the greater the equity – increasingly important as actual physical differences between products in a given category diminish.'

According to Lannon, the view that using an equity built up over time for other products would eventually dilute and destroy the original property was changing. Why?

- Costs. Promotion costs for extensions can be much lower, while their survival rate can be longer than new brands;
- Strengthening the core equity. This contradicts conventional wisdom. But a successful extension can update the image of the original brand, and make the whole bigger than the sum of its parts;
- Successful extensions can be a source of strength against powerful retailers by making the consumer franchise stronger.

One of the more imaginative brand extensions of the last few years which has enhanced and exploited the core brand quality (and one with a high degree of innovation) has been the Mars ice cream bar. There are several notable aspects to this product:

- It used the brand name's authority to attack a market which appeared static and which seemed sewn up by powerful competitors like Allied-Lyons and Unilever's Walls;
- It followed a tried and tested formula allied to the most modern food technology to produce a brand it could put into a premium position and charge accordingly;
- It created a new category which is neither a chocolate bar nor an ice cream but a snack;
- It moved fast, and got in first.

Ray McGhee, of Derwent Valley Foods, makers of Phileas Fogg snacks, had a decided view of extensions: 'You have to juxtapose resources, key marketing principles like "stick to your knitting", and consumer elasticity.' McGhee was 'absolutely convinced that we could brand a non-alcoholic drink, an adult biscuit for instance. But you have to find the property and you don't want to distract yourself from where you are.'

Black & Decker found this to its cost when it moved into small appliances like hair dryers. Consumers could not match up what was a powerful brand name in its own right – and a name that, like Hoover, had almost become the generic for electric drills – with hair dryers, though it had more success with small kitchen appliances in the US. But don't think preoccupation with extensions lies only with consumer goods manufacturers – services corporation like British Airways (BA) think seriously about the issues (see Case 5.6 below), as do technology-oriented companies like Epson, which is combining technological advances with consumer-style brand building techniques to launch itself into the consumer electronics market with a family of high-quality, small screen colour portable televisions.

Lannon suggested four basic principles to follow to avoid mistakes:

(1)   Make sure the parent brand is long established and has achieved 'critical mass' in customers' minds in the first place;
(2)   Understand exactly what the core brand values are, a mix of functional benefits and emotional rewards. The latter are the more important;
(3)   Identify market opportunities that are synergistic with the parent brand's business;
(4)   Beware extensions such as a 'lighter' beer that appeal to the parent brand's core franchise and so reduce the core.

Allan Magrath, director of marketing services at the Canadian subsidiary of a large, diversified US multinational, recently conducted a study of global brands. Writing in *Marketing News*, he recommended that companies wishing to take domestic brands global create a 'family' of brands surrounding the 'mother' brand. This provides more varied uses of the product, which increases its chances of appealing to consumers in a number of countries.

According to Magrath, another brand fortification technique is to extend the brand beyond its original product by finding new uses for it. Two examples of brands that launched successful product extensions are Arm & Hammer and Rubbermaid. Arm & Hammer started with baking soda and then created a laundry detergent, a carpet deodorizer, a toothpaste and cleaning pads. Rubbermaid expanded from rubber and plastic containers and kitchenware to water coolers, closet organizers and casual furniture. However, Magrath warned against extending brands across product categories. He cited Levi Strauss's failure with its 'tailored classics' line, which did not fit in with its traditional rugged denim image. Magrath suggested that Levi's should have created an entirely new brand for the category.

Magrath believed companies should avoid oversegmenting a market with many brands that are indistinct from each other. Brands should also be constantly updated, as new packaging or product variations are vital to a global brand's success.

Case 5.6   British Airways

For Liam Strong, formerly director of marketing and operations at British Airways, branding as such is well understood. In his business the issue is more focused: 'How far can you stretch the brand and change it?'

The concept of 'brands' first took off at BA in 1986. BA has since relaunched both BA itself as a brand, along with all its major services: Club Class in 1987, First in 1989, and Economy late in 1990. And the costs of the three relaunches combined – £115 million – underline the scale on which BA works. Now Strong's next goal is to 'make the application of branding in the business much more vigorous and use it as a specification about what the market needs and what the consumer expects from each segment,' he said.

Strong, who joined BA at the beginning of 1989, added operations to his responsibilities in 1990 and became the third most powerful executive in BA. He comes from a established consumer goods background; his job involved putting together food businesses for Reckitt and Colman in the US. Moving to a service business attracted him, especially one with such promising long-term growth prospects. Also, he was attracted by the relative youth of the industry, where, compared to food, for example, distribution channels are not yet established, while techniques like direct marketing are still in their infancy.

There are some similarities with his previous roles, but the demands of a service business are undoubtedly different. And the *type* of service is far removed from an industry like fast food, where the same process is repeated every day: 'In our case we are dealing with an infinite complexity of inter-reactions between us and the consumer. We use brand as a specification of what the consumer expects, and to educate our people and make them believe it.' That means running brand workshops not just for the product managers, but for front-line people like the cabin crew and ground staff so they can begin to understand the positioning.

BA has been making a huge investment in training over the last few years to make sure its bullish message about itself is backed up by reality. When Strong first joined BA, he found that the positioning had been established in consumers' eyes but it had not been driven far enough through the whole company. Now engineering staff, for example, will be fully briefed on what atmosphere and environment BA wants to create in Club Class. That makes it far easier to explain to them why upgrading audio equipment is important.

BA's latest relaunch hit at the heart of the aircraft – the economy section, in which more than 13 million people travel both short- and long-haul. BA wanted to make more people choose BA positively, particularly for leisure travel, which some estimates say will grow by as much as 40% over the next five years. So, to heighten its visibility in the market, along with trying to rid the section of the stigma that 'economy' can bring, it renamed it the main cabin, upgraded the service, created two categories of Euro Traveller and

continues

continued

World Traveller, and streamlined its leisure products under the name Leisure Traveller, with the BA corporate brand far more visible.

How do you get the enormous numbers of staff – Strong was in charge of some 35,000 people world-wide – to cooperate in fulfilling the image of the brands? It is not easy and even harder when customer expectations have been raised. But they are, asserted Strong, a ready audience for education, and 'soak up information like a sponge. We educate them in the things we expect. We are not simply saying that "on this day you must do these things". In some parts of the operation we do have to tie them down about what they have to do but in other parts there is wide scope in terms of personal interreaction and creating a mood, a relationship with the customer.'

What BA does not do is ask people to go around grinning all the time – the 'have a nice day' approach to customer relationships. Instead, it is a combination of people, training and communications: 'Our marketing department spends a lot of time focusing on the cabin crew, but branding in that sense is an opportunity, not a problem.'

According to Strong, 'The issue for us internationally is what level of branding do you promote? There are only so many countries in the world where you can justify a master brand campaign, along with possible publicity for leisure products and business class, and those are parts of Europe, Japan and the US.' In most of the other countries, BA will promote just the master brand, or business class, alone. The problem is to determine how to deploy funds across the world.

Strong does not believe in 'global' campaigns. BA has an advertisement that is very visual, and designed to run in all countries, but even then shots of different people will be used to reflect certain nationalities, or the backdrop will be slightly altered. This catering to different tastes stretches up as far as the service itself: the food passengers eat coming from Japan to London, for instance, will not be the same as the food from London to Tokyo. After all, Strong argued, 'We can be the biggest airline in the world and could still lose our shirt in Scotland if a local airline offered service more adapted to the passengers' needs.' That need to segment is best exemplified by the US, where the national market has broken down into much smaller parts.

Apart from advertising, branding for BA is all the ways you can influence someone, from putting them in the well-appointed lounge, to giving them a 'privilege card', to speaking at a conference about BA's success: 'You don't regiment it but keep an eye on consistency and be very conscious of the total image BA puts across.'

Revival

According to a survey by Nielsen (1990), Britain's top ten grocery brands have an average age of 42. In the US, of the top 22 brands in 1925, 19 were still leading their product categories in 1985. Some brands will simply click with consumers. A select few will live far beyond their predicted life cycles. Few will survive without careful management.

Take Nivea. Nivea, which means snow white in Greek, first began as a soap in Germany at the beginning of the century and became a creme at the end of the First World War. When German assets were frozen in the UK in the Second World War, a British company picked up Nivea, which finally ended up with Smith & Nephew in the 1950s. It still had the original blue-and-white packaging. The complication was that while the British company sold the brand in the UK and the Commonwealth, the original German company maintained the rights to it elsewhere.

By the end of the 1960s, the brand was ageing and sales were suffering. The first major revamp came in the 1970s, and included an innovative advertising campaign. A return to core values of purity was enhanced by extensions of the cremes for different skin types, hair care, sun care, skin care and, most recently, bath care. More recently, the German and British owners have also co-operated on developing pan-European packaging for the revamped range of lotions.

The moral is that there is nothing wrong with maturity, provided the image is brought up to date and kept fresh. In fact, older brands can stress reliability and reassurance, as well as 'naturalness'. After a desultory time during the 1960s, when it seemed that its days were over, Hovis has now capitalized on its image and moved from being classed as a 'niche' (that is, small) product into a national market brand with Hovis Wholemeal.

Case 5.7 Lea & Perrins

When French food giant BSN bought HP Foods a few years ago from Hanson, one of the little gems it picked up in the brand portfolio was Lea & Perrins Worcestershire sauce. It was the stuff of marketing dreams:

- It had been in existence over 150 years;
- It had 95% of the home market and 40% of the international one;
- Its distribution was spread to 130 countries, with only Coca-Cola and Pepsi having further reach;
- Its bottle and label were instantly recognizable;
- It had a secret recipe which could not be copied;
- It had an image and value that consumers understood.

It would be easy to be complacent. But the company has instead been trying to capitalize on those attributes of tradition, heritage and pedigree and both grow the market, especially in the UK, and boost market share. It is said,

continues

continued

for instance, that there are 8 million bottles lurking in British cupboards. What Lea & Perrins wants to do is get them taken out more often.

Thus it has been promoting new ways to use it, in different recipes, mainly through women's magazines. Last year it ran its first TV campaign in the Central region suggesting new uses like cheese on toast, and stir fry. To test its effectiveness it gave two sets of consumers – one in the region where the commercial ran and one outside – calibrated bottles. Usage among the group who saw the ad went up by 32%. The campaign won the 1990 IPA Award for innovation sponsored by *Marketing* magazine.

The company has also been carefully stretching the brand into other types of liquid spices, and now has a range of 14 extensions. One of the objectives now is to exploit the brand across Europe, in light of the Single Market. The company has a good distribution base on the continent, while it has modernized and standardized its label internationally, so its ambition is to increase the general level of awareness and hence usage.

And that, of course, is easier said than done. Food cultures are still very different and distinct. But there are certain trends at both a macro- and microlevel which the company says enable it to start looking at a more pan-European approach:

- The trend toward more cosmopolitan attitudes to food across different nationalities;
- The move toward 'grazing';
- The rise across Europe of single-person households;
- Slow but definite convergence of taste in both fast food and more up-market dishes.

So the company needs to offer the product in a way relevant to all the countries based on these and other trends, while keeping in mind the specific cooking cultures in each country. In the Mediterranean countries, for example, spices and herbs used in cooking are almost always fresh, whereas liquid spices are used far more heavily in northern parts of Europe as flavour enhancers.

The key is finding clusters of consumers with similar behaviour and tastes, a complex research undertaking which finds those attributes groups have in common and those they do not. Then, after mapping the markets and identifying the clusters, the company can promote both the brand and the liquid spice sector. Its main concern is to ensure that Worcestershire sauce is positioned distinctively against other sauces like Tabasco, soy sauce and others.

The market itself is one of many layers. There are 'on-table' sauces, like ketchup and brown sauce, which will be added to food and in fact take over a dish. Then there are sauces used in cooking which change the whole taste – like Tabasco, soy and pepper sauce. The company wants Worcestershire sauce to be positioned in the European consumer's mind as adding 'piquancy'. But obviously individual market demands will have to be catered for as well. What it does not want to be seen as is either 'old' or 'British' – because heritage can, if not used carefully, make any product seem out of date.

Service brands

Service companies are struggling to come to terms with what branding means for them, particularly since, as the BA case study shows, maintaining a consistent brand positioning demands that every employee is educated into the creed. The dilemma of how to apply branding strategies in the financial services sector, for example, is highlighted by UK clearing banks, which are not only using the word 'brand' to describe their products and services, but are trying to take a short cut along the marketing learning curve by dragooning in hordes of people with classical marketing skills. But changing the banking culture is tough (see Case 9.4).

Midland Bank has come the farthest along the branding route – and, some argue, without the success the energy and money it has poured into it deserves. It has produced a raft of different products with different brand names aimed at different consumer segments – usually advertised without a marked emphasis on the corporate name, a route its competitors are loathe to follow. It also developed a new banking concept called First Direct, which operates like a home shopping service, and which has been heavily promoted with notably quirky advertisements and by emphasizing its convenience and efficiency.

Other banks have, on the whole, not developed new products but thrown a raft of repackaged services under the corporate name at the already confused customer. Critics argue that banks have forgotten why customers go to banks: not to buy a product, but for a service or to get the means to buy another product – a car, a home, insurance, and so on. So this proliferation of products has confused consumers and not given banks the competitive edge against each other they thought it would bring.

And if customers are confused, what about the banking staff? Few have a clear understanding of the corporate policy. Signs are put up in branches extolling the customer-care creed. But that rarely seems to translate into reality. It leads to cynical anecdotes of how the 'Listening Bank' doesn't listen, or how the 'Action Bank' drags its corporate feet.

Corporate branding

'Corporate identity tells the world – whether actively or by default – just what the corporate strategy is.'

Wally Olins (1989)

Issues of corporate branding affect every company. It will be one of the hottest issues of the next decade. As Timothy King, managing director of corporate identity specialists Siegel & Gale in the UK said, companies 'can't hide anymore.' More people are more inquisitive about corporations than they were in the late 1960s/1970s, when companies could get away with being a set of anonymous initials and were only visible through their brands and their products. In the last 15 years, King believed, 'companies have recognized that, whether they want it or not, they have a reputation and an identity.'

Olins (1989) identified several of the factors that are pushing companies to come to terms with their identity:

- External change
  - technological revolution;
  - new competition;
  - social, moral, environmental issues identified by customers/a wider audience;
  - privatization, deregulation.
- Internal change
  - mergers, acquisitions, and so on;
  - expansion into other countries;
  - changes in strategic direction;
  - increased centralization;
  - need to communicate a new focus – service initiatives, repositioning in terms of quality perception.

Interest in business activities has grown astronomically over the last decade. And, unless the image is consistent all the way down the line, there will be areas of weakness open to attack. There was a sobering survey carried out a few years ago in the US which suggested that companies were seen as winners or losers depending on how professional they had been at communications, not just performance.

The sudden discovery of high profile, corporate advertising over the last five years has been no coincidence: the relentless pace of unfriendly takeovers and life-saving mergers which characterized the 1980s has produced a cat's cradle of interlocking names and brands which confuse customers, employees and shareholders. Corporations have rushed to the airwaves to trumpet their identity and virtues, although not always successfully.

Images have to reflect corporate reality. But there is a lurking danger with corporate identity programmes: they become so design-driven that the logo is seen as the strategy, and not the symbol which *reflects* the underlying change. It might sound obvious, but is worth repeating: corporate identity programmes do not change a corporate culture. Commented Siegel & Gale's King: 'It has to be put into a proper perspective. It cannot be bought like a suit.'

The following two examples, BP and Courtaulds, highlight some of the reasons why companies embark on projects which can involve management, from the top down, in several years of time-consuming effort.

BP

BP carried out a year-long corporate image study to answer the following questions:

- How do we see ourselves?
- How do others see us?
- What image should we adopt for the 1990s?

BP had changed radically over the years and the top management decided that only a massive new identity programme would serve to focus attention, both from within and without the company, on the main themes. These included:

- The restructuring of the business to concentrate on core activities of oil, gas and chemicals.
- BP had taken on a more international hue. As a major presence in the US, it wanted to move away from the image of 'British Petroleum'.
- It wanted to show a more dynamic face with the virtual ending of the government stake allied with the takeover of oil company Britoil.
- It needed to take account of the growing concern about the environment and the oil majors' role in it.

The logo was revamped, using the BP colours of green and yellow (in what was perhaps a fortunate coincidence, the colour 'green' had been part of the BP stable long before the environmental question reared its head). Companies were renamed with 'BP' as the corporate brand, while corporate advertising was used to strengthen public perception of the company as a big international and responsible presence.

But the understandable decision to emphasize the colour 'green' turned out to have a sting in its tail. In the summer of 1989 *The Sunday Times* carried its lead story under the following headline; ' "Green" BP fells rain forest'. A company in which BP had a majority stake was, the paper accused, contributing to the destruction of the Brazilian rain forest. While the company has since recovered from the bad publicity, it was a telling lesson in how a change in image has to be reflected in reality.

Courtaulds

This major British company, known for its fibres and textiles interests, had struggled back from near collapse to emerge as a profitable industrial group with interests in a number of other sectors, including coatings, films and speciality materials. The chairman, Sir Christopher Hogg, was determined to show:

- That Courtaulds was no longer just in fibres and textiles;
- That the company had wrenched itself from being production led to customer driven;

- That although the company was still financially prudent, it was now more outward-looking, receptive to new ideas, more design and quality conscious and innovative.

After two years the company emerged with a new coordinated image – which included a new logo using the letter 'c' – that extended to every part of the group. The logo was to be incorporated over two years by the different businesses, which had to ensure that the way they operated matched the promise of the image.

The Courtaulds programme attracted an avalanche of – mainly favourable – publicity and was one of the first to put corporate identity onto the British industrial map. And whether the corporate identity programme was the catalyst or not, since then Hogg has demerged the textiles business altogether into a separate company.

Over the last few years more companies have climbed onto the corporate identity bandwagon. New logos are often treated with a degree of scorn as a superficial exercise. Only time shows if they have been created as more than a cosmetic exercise.

Young & Rubicam survey

Corporate image can play a crucial role in attracting the cream of the graduate crop from Europe's business schools. A study done in 1990 for Young & Rubicam might provide a salutary shock for a few well-known names. The study, which has been carried out in France since 1985, has been extended throughout Europe. Some 1300 engineering and business graduates of Europe's top schools were asked to rate companies according to awareness, dynamism and which they rated as 'the best' in each country, admired and respected for overall excellence. These figures then went to make up the 'best in Europe'. The best ten corporate brands:

		%
1.	IBM	20.9
2.	Mercedes-Benz	12.0
3.	Sony	9.4
4.	BMW	8.3
5.	Unilever	5.8
6.	Siemens	5.7
7.	Hewlett-Packard	5.2
8.	Arthur Andersen	5.1
9.	ICI	5.0
10.	Nestlé	4.9

continues

continued

For the UK:	%	For Italy:	%
1. ICI	23.0	1. IBM	21.2
2. IBM	22.5	1. Sony	21.2
3. Unilever	15.7	3. Group Fiat	18.7
4. BP	10.8	4. Benetton	13.3
5. Procter & Gamble	9.3	5. Mercedes-Benz	11.8
6. Shell	8.3	6. BMW	10.8
7. Arthur Andersen	7.8	7. American Express	6.9
8. Sony	6.4	7. Lloyd	6.9
9. BMW	5.9	7. Hewlett-Packard	6.9
10. Mercedes-Benz	4.9	10. P&G	5.4

For Germany:	%	For Spain:	%
1. Mercedes-Benz	35.6	1. IBM	27.0
2. IBM	26.7	2. Nestlé	17.0
3. Siemens	20.8	3. Hewlett-Packard	12.0
4. BMW	11.9	4. BMW	11.0
4. Bayer	11.9	5. Sony	9.0
6. Airbus Industrie	7.9	6. Arthur Andersen	8.0
7. VAG	6.4	7. Bayer	7.5
8. Sony	5.4	8. Alcatel NV	6.0
9. Bertelsmann	4.5	8. Benetton	6.0
9. Unilever	4.5	10. Mercedes-Benz	5.5
9. Apple	4.5	11. American Express	4.5

For France:	%
1. BSN	8.6
1. Canal +	8.6
3. Aerospatiale	8.2
4. IBM	6.8
5. Airbus Industrie	6.0
6. L'Oréal	5.4
7. Sony	5.0
7. Rhône Poulenc	5.0
7. Apple	5.0
10. Arthur Andersen	4.6

Brand naming

This aspect of branding can often be treated too haphazardly. Creating names, whether of new products or brands underneath an existing umbrella, is a complex process combining not only creativity, but also a systematic approach and hard slog. As well as the difficult task of coming up with names that click, the process involves language testing, consumer research on names, and – an often forgotten chore – the legal search which has to be carried out on an increasingly more international basis. After all, what is the point of pouring huge amounts of resources into new brands or brand extensions and picking a name someone has already snapped up for the Far East? Trade mark registration is one of the most critical ways to protect brand names.

Take Apple Computers. It has been having on–off tussles with Apple Corps, the company set up by the Beatles in 1963, since it was set up in 1977. The two sides came to an agreement in 1981 about the computer company's rights in relation to the Apple trademark, which precluded Apple Computers from entering the music sphere. But the computer company has, logically enough, developed equipment for synthesizing music so the two have found themselves back in court.

As John Murphy (1990), chairman of international branding consultancy Interbrand noted, it is very surprising how little attention is given to product naming. While a lot of attention is given to the design of the pack, the media selection, distribution, and so on, the name can be left to the 'chairman's wife' syndrome as in 'My wife thought this sounded nice for our new brand of ice cream.' But that can be fatal:

- A new, innovative product can end up with a banal name;
- It is unsuitable for overseas which proscribes its fortunes from inception;
- Legal problems arise which have not been foreseen;
- The name focuses on one attribute which loses its significance over time;
- The new name is too easy to imitate and causes confusion;
- It translates badly when travelling; the Fiat 127, for example, was originally called Rustica, which would sound fine in Italy but, with the image of Italian cars as prone to rust, would not fare well in the UK;
- It can be out of tune with the times –for example, macho in a more 'caring' environment.

The personality with which the name endows the product will often play a key role in long-term success. What companies must evolve, argued Murphy, is a *system* of names.

The following examples show that as companies prepare to expand their brands regionally and globally they often have to rename their products:

- One M&M/Mars candy bar brand had the brand name Marathon in the UK, but was called Snickers in the US (see page 129). Faced with the imminent completion of the Common Market, Mars began gradually to phase out the Marathon name in the UK several years ago and introduce the Snickers name. Initially, a banner under the Marathon name on the package and in the advertising indicated that the bar was known internationally as Snickers. More recently, the Snickers name is prominent on the package and the banner says that it was previously named Marathon.

- The Colgate–Palmolive Company has systematically tried to harmonize the naming of its products from country to country. In general, it uses the Colgate name for oral care products, such as toothpaste, and the Palmolive name for body care products, such as shampoos and conditioners.

- Taiwan-based Acer, which was established in 1976, found that a name change was a prerequisite for its entry into non-Asian markets. The original name – Multitech – reflected the firm's initial mission under its founder Stan Shih: to introduce and popularize the use of microprocessor-related technologies in Taiwan. The first product offerings of very basic 'Microprocessor' personal computers and the slogan of 'Gardeners of Microprocessors!' almost exclusively targeted the home market. By the mid-1980s, Multitech had consolidated its base in Taiwan and begun to explore overseas markets for an increasingly sophisticated line of IBM-compatible PCs. Shih realized that a new brand name – less technical, short, easy to remember and distinctive – was essential if the firm was to break successfully into North American and European markets. In 1987, after months of study, 'Acer' was introduced first as the chief brand name for the firm's personal computers, and then, in 1988, as the new English-language name of the company. (The Chinese name was not altered.) Along with the name, Shih coined a new slogan – 'Acer is the word for value!' – to convey a more customer-oriented, systems approach and to associate the concept of excellence with the firm in its rapidly expanding international markets. By 1989, almost 80% of the firm's global sales came from outside Taiwan. Shih expected the new name to help Acer become one of the first Taiwan-based firms to establish its own brand name abroad and not just depend – as most Taiwan manufacturers do – on OEM (original equipment manufacturer) relationships.

- When Nissan Motor Co. introduced its cars into the US, its management did not have total confidence in the quality of their cars, so the name Datsun was used for fear of losing face. However, after 20 years of promoting the Datsun name and building a quality image, the company decided to phase out the Datsun name and substitute the corporate name, Nissan. For a time, the company's cars carried both names, until the Nissan name was firmly established in consumers' minds.

Of course, product names do not always work in every country. The classic story of misnaming a product was General Motors' introduction of the Chevy Nova in Mexico some years ago. It was embarrassed to find out that 'no va' in Spanish meant 'does not go'. More recently, toiletry manufacturer Helene Curtis changed the name of Every Night Shampoo to Every Day Shampoo in Sweden, because most Swedes wash their hair in the morning.

Brand valuation

There are probably more companies which do not know the value of their brands than ones that do – brands are valued by an almost 'seat of the pants' approach. The goodwill which sits on top of a company's physical assets has been usually unlocked only when it is taken over.

However, the realization of the importance of brands has been followed by the highly publicized steps taken by some large British brand owners to put the value of their brands onto the balance sheet. Rupert Murdoch did it to his newspaper brands as long ago as 1984, followed by Reckitt and Colman and Grand Metropolitan when they acquired Airwick industries and Heublein (Smirnoff), respectively. What really set the controversy alight, however, was when Rank Hovis McDougall decided to put all its brands on the balance sheet using a formula developed by Interbrand. The debate about the validity of the practice rages on among financial analysts and the accountancy profession. But some of the UK's biggest companies have voted with their feet and gone ahead, such as Guinness, United Biscuits and Cadbury Schweppes.

It should be noted, however, that when Cadbury Schweppes announced its intention to put brands worth millions on its balance sheet in spring of 1990, it had spent some £700 million on acquisitions the previous year and wanted the brands on the balance sheet. It disagreed with a draft directive from the UK accountancy standards body that, like goodwill, brand valuations should be written off against profits over a number of years. Cadbury's argued that this should not be the case unless there was a permanent and demonstrable decrease in the value. The company's finance director was reported as saying that it made no sense to write down the value of intangible assets when the value would probably be boosted by expenditure on promotion. Some companies supported his stance. Others called it creative accounting and pointed out that the same argument used to be applied to human resources.

Putting brands on the balance sheet has been fuelled by the whole issue of brand assessment and marketing costs. As Interbrand's Murphy argued,

> 'the reason why the interest in brands and branding has become so prominent in my view is that it brings a discipline into the area that has largely been uncontrolled. Marketing for many companies has been a "Eureka" process. There is a need to tighten it up. How can you decide which brands to spend money on if you don't know their value?'

Murphy believed that the debate about the balance sheet had obscured the real value of techniques of assessing the worth of brands. Valuation can:

- Show the brand portfolio on a comparative basis;
- Help in planning strategies for brands;
- Be a deciding factor in the allocation of scarce resources;

- Start a dialogue going between marketing and finance, and alleviate what has been a notorious source of friction;
- Highlight brand weaknesses.

The Interbrand method of brand valuation

The Interbrand method of brand valuation is attracting increasing attention from as far afield as Japan and the US. It works by:

- Assessing the strength of a brand or brands, scoring them against the following factors:
  - Leadership – brand leaders are more stable and hence valuable
  - Stability
  - Market – some markets are less vulnerable to technological or fashion changes
  - Internationality
  - Trend
  - Support – where quality is as important as quantity
  - Protection – including trademark registration.
- Evaluating a brand's profitability. It is often the case that companies will know market share, and promotional spend, for example, but will not have added in all the factors that go into the brand performance.

The strength of the brand gives it a rating which is then applied to post-tax brand profits as a multiplier that, when used with post-tax brand profits, arrives at a valuation. This can be useful when dealing with:

- Disposals and acquisitions
- Putting promotional spending under the microscope
- Finding gaps which might be filled by brand extension
- Repositioning
- Performance tracking: of brand, of management, of agencies.

The world's top brands

The world's top ten brands based on an Interbrand evaluation:

1. Coca-Cola
2. Kellogg's
3. McDonald's
4. Kodak
5. Marlboro

6. IBM
7. American Express
8. Sony
9. Mercedes-Benz
10. Nescafe

continues

continued

The following 40 brands, arranged in alphabetical order, constitute those which should be added to the top 10 brands to arrive at the world's top 50 brands:

Apple
Bacardi
Black & Decker
BMW
Boeing
Campbell's
Chanel No.5
Colgate
Del Monte
Der Spiegel
Dom Perignon
Dunhill
Duracell
Esso/Exxon
Estee Lauder
Gillette
Green Giant
Guinness
Heineken
Heinz
Hertz
Johnson & Johnson
Levi's
Lotus (software)
Marks & Spencer
Mars
Pampers
Pepsi-Cola
Perrier
Porsche
Quaker
Rolex
Rolls-Royce
Schweppes
Smirnoff
Tampax
Toyota
Visa
Walt Disney
Wrigley's

Source: Interbrand

Summary

- The building of brands which attract a loyal and lucrative consumer following has been a familiar concept and one developed by consumer goods companies over a long period of time. But the increasingly sophisticated concepts are spreading throughout businesses of all types.

- The issues of branding which face companies differ in degree, rather than substance:
  - Consumer goods companies are faced with the need to devise a global brand strategy: a complex process which includes acquisition, rationalization, extension of existing brands and new brand development. They also face aggressive competition from retailers' own brands.
  - Service companies like financial organizations and airlines are turning to branding techniques as a means of both ensuring and exploiting consumer loyalty and to foster a service culture.
  - Business-to-business organizations, which mainly deal with professional buyers, are trying to move beyond the 'slapping labels on boxes' stage and use branding to stand out in the midst of ever-noisier competition. Branding the company and its products for quality, service and/or innovation is also a powerful tool for prising open new markets.

- Cultural differences will be a big issue in the European market. They can be viewed as an insurmountable obstacle to expansion or as a source of competitive advantage if properly exploited.

- The complexity of dealing with one European market that has been twelve quite separate entities has been the catalyst for many corporations to rethink their brand strategies internationally.

- Brand management is inextricably linked with the centralization/decentralization debate. Maintaining the quality and positioning of the brand on a regional and global basis – even though the brand might fill slightly different segments in different markets – is essential.

- Neither globalization nor regionalization should deter companies from following a niche strategy – unless, of course, that strategy is more about the failure to win market share.

- Globalization/localization demands a far more sophisticated approach to market research. Cross-border studies are still at an early stage and are hindered by the different and often incomparable methodologies used in individual countries. But as companies move towards a more centralized approach to their marketing strategies, they will want a coordinated and consistent approach in gathering information about products, consumers, competitors and tracking the effectiveness of promotional tactics.

- Brand audits can determine:
  - which brands can travel
  - which should be killed or sold
  - a strategy for the portfolio, including building brands, buying them, extending them or reviving them.
- Corporate branding is set to be one of the biggest issues of the next decade – but it will be more than just a pretty new logo.
- Brand names should be developed systematically, and with a good understanding of trademark legislation and with the international market in mind.
- Brand valuation could play an ever-more important role in corporate strategic thinking.

Checklist

As brand development becomes more costly and more sophisticated, does your company:

(1) Have a strategy for developing global brands if and where it is appropriate?

(2) Analyse the implications of cultural differences for brands across Europe?

(3) Assess the brand portfolio to decide the best approach in terms of brand harmonization in different markets?

(4) Carry out these discussions of brand strategy in light of the organizational structure and culture?

(5) Have a coordinated and consistent approach to gathering research about products, markets and competitors to help both position and promote brands?

(6) Undertake a corporate branding programme in line with brand strategy?

(7) Do name research to ensure protection of name assets internationally?

(8) Discuss whether it is appropriate to consider putting brands onto the balance sheet?

References

Clark, E. (1990). *The Independent*, December 22
Interbrand (1990). *Brands, An International Review*. London: Mercury Business Books
Magrath, A. *Marketing News*
Murphy, J. (1990). *Brand Strategy*. Cambridge: Director Books
Nielson. (1990). Brand-stretching can be fun – and dangerous. *The Economist*, 5 May, p.105
Olins, W. (1989). *Corporate Identity*. London: Thames and Hudson
Young & Rubicam France (1990). *Company Image Today: The View of Tomorrow's Leaders*

Marketing programmes

6

The sharp end of promotion and sales

Introduction

The preceding chapters have considered the broader issues and concepts which are at the heart of strategic marketing planning and organization. The best-laid strategic plans and organizational charts, however, will prove of little use if not translated into the sharp end of promotion and sales. The problem of the global/local divide applies just as much to how companies actually reach their customers. This chapter will thus consider the issues of communication involved, examining:

- Advertising
- Corporate advertising
- Sales promotion and direct marketing
- Sponsorship
- Exhibitions
- Public relations
- Recipes for sales success
- Selling services

Two appendices will also consider two further factors which are relevant to these areas:

- Using outside consultants
- Global advertising regulations and barriers

Advertising

Advertising as a component of global marketing strategy has undergone significant change over the past decade in the face of intensifying competition and the transformation of many countries and regions by external events. Many developments, among them the sweeping shift from communism to various degrees of capitalism in Eastern Europe, the EC Single Market, the unification of West and East Germany, the democratization of much of Latin America – along with the severe economic problems in some Latin American nations – are causing companies to rethink the way they promote and sell their products outside their home countries. Advertising is available today in media such as radio and TV in almost every country in the world.

In recent years some well-known consumer products companies, like McDonald's, Coca-Cola, PepsiCo, Levi Strauss and Sony, have done well with 'global brands' advertised in much the same manner around the world. Their successes have prompted renewed interest in centralized advertising campaigns among other multinationals, although many products are not well suited to a global branding strategy. Some that are include:

(1) Gillette, whose 'Sensor Shaver' global advertisement programme was designed to introduce this new product simultaneously in 19 countries throughout North America and Europe. Its commercial in every country uses the theme, 'Gillette, the best a man can get', which is accompanied by highly charged images of strong, energetic men, along with a whisker-clipping diagram. Commercials are adjusted to fit local circumstances by the headquarters' advertising people and the company's ad agency.

Some of Gillette's required copy changes are quite subtle. For instance, the French theme uses the phrase, 'La perfection au masculine' – which roughly translates into 'perfection, male-style'. This particular phrasing was necessary, according to the company, because the French word for perfection takes the feminine pronoun ('la'). Other differences in the commercials include the use of American football in the US commercial and soccer in all the others. With the help of dubbing, the actors in Gillette's commercials will give the same sales message (not too macho, not too soft) in 26 languages.

(2) PepsiCo, which develops most of its global brand advertisements at its corporate headquarters in Purchase, New York. PepsiCo's strategy of promoting its flagship brand Pepsi-Cola as contemporary, forward-looking and all-American is used in every market where the soft drink is sold. The ads usually show active young people enjoying the beverage in an outdoor setting and prominently feature its red and blue packaging.

Case 6.1 Gillette

Gillette is a diversified global consumer products company based in Boston, Massachusetts. Many of its products are household names world-wide. The best known of the lines it manufactures and markets internationally are razors and other shaving items (sold under such names as Gillette and Sensor), stationery supplies (Paper Mate and Waterman), small appliances (Braun), and toiletry and personal care items (Oral-B, Right Guard).

The company markets its goods in over 130 countries and has manufacturing plants in every region in which it operates. Gillette's global organizational structure can best be categorized as a 'hybrid' – a form in which some of a company's operations use one organizational approach, while other operations employ another. In Gillette's case, the mixture actually involves the use of three organizational patterns – regional entities, an international division and product groups.

For the past two years Gillette's global operations have been divided into two broad geographic regions, Gillette International and Gillette North Atlantic. Both are headed by corporate vice chairmen who report directly to the chief executive officer, but organizationally they differ significantly. They also make different strategic decisions in some important areas, such as the choice of ad agencies.

Gillette's global decision making is mostly centralized. The recommendations of executives based overseas are sought and considered, but major marketing decisions, including those that concern strategic goals, the price structure and global advertising, are made in Boston. However, both International and North Atlantic are responsible for operational decision making in their own regions.

Within Gillette International, key marketing decisions are generally made at the headquarters level in Boston, and management of the three component regions is based there, too. Implementation decisions, such as advertising placement and local distribution, are made at country level.

Advertising campaigns are sometimes fine-tuned at the local level. Promotion campaigns, although developed locally, must also support marketing goals established by headquarters.

Most of Gillette North Atlantic's significant marketing decisions are made in Boston by the product division at the general manager's level. Like International, most strategic decisions are centralized there, too. Overseas executives are mainly involved in moving products through the distribution systems to the final consumer and designing and implementing local store promotions, coupon campaigns and so on.

Gillette International's advertising strategy is formulated at the regional level, and Gillette North Atlantic's at the product group level. Both North Atlantic and International centralize virtually all aspects of advertising. This

continues

continued

usually means simply dubbing foreign languages into ads created by head-quarters, which typically are made with only music on the basic soundtrack. Then the various messages used in different countries are dubbed in with voice-overs. This approach is designed to make ads easily transferable from one market to the next.

In rare instances, when mandated by official regulation, overseas opera-tions use local actors in locally shot commercials. Even then, however, the creative aspects, including the dialogue, theme and slogan, are developed in Boston.

These images strike a universal chord in people from Tampa to Tuscany. Local subsidiaries are permitted only to make language changes. By using commercials that rely heavily on images to convey a message, it is able to introduce commercials globally: for example, the commercial featuring Michael Jackson appeared in 60 countries. This had a dual beneficial effect in that not only was it instrumental in boosting sales of Pepsi but also of Jackson's world tour sponsored by the company.

(3) Philip Morris, which also successfully employed this type of global creative strategy for its Marlboro brand cigarettes. The Marlboro cowboy rides his horse through rugged mountains and deserts on billboards all around the globe. He appears in every Marlboro ad, even in countries where one would not think the local people would identify with or appre-ciate the image of a cowboy. The image of the Marlboro Man is so pow-erful and enduring that it has transcended political, social, cultural and ethnic boundaries.

Instead of a global orientation, some multinationals are opting for regional advertising strategies. The most obvious manifestation of this approach is in Europe, where many companies that previously used a country-by-country approach are planning and implementing pan-European advertising programmes to take advantage of the EC's increasing integration, although a survey by advertising group Alliance International in 1989 showed that many companies are still trying to decide if the advertising as well as brands can travel across borders (see box, page 173).

A further complication to devising advertising strategies is the still-strong persistence of the 'local is best' view, which runs counter to the trend of adopting more uniform advertising messages globally or regionally. Companies with that viewpoint localize their ad strategies even more than in the past, leaving country subsidiaries to run major campaigns with very little input from parent head-quarters.

Alliance International survey

In 1989 advertising group Alliance International commissioned Research Services Ltd to survey 250 marketing directors and marketing decisions makers across nine European countries to discover whether 1992 would have a major impact on how they use advertising and agencies. The survey reached these general conclusions:

- It did not appear that 1992 would have a major impact on marketing strategies and, in particular, how companies deal with their agencies;
- Europe was still, and would be likely to remain for the foreseeable future, a collection of national markets.

The survey's authors gave two possible conflicting reasons for this: that on the one hand many major companies were already advertising on a pan-European scale, while, on the other, 1992 might still have seemed a long way off when it came to budget-setting.

The following two tables show the breakdown country by country:

Descriptions of major advertising campaigns (%)

	Total	UK	France	West Germany	Spain	Italy	Nether-lands	Belgium	Portugal	Eire
Worldwide/ International	12	11	21	21	5	8	15	5	—	10
Pan-European	11	13	11	26	3	3	25	5	—	—
National	74	76	68	53	87	84	55	80	90	90
Other	2	—	—	—	3	—	—	—	1	—
Don't know	1	—	—	—	3	—	—	—	10	—

Changes in advertising campaigns after 1990 (%)

	Total	UK	France	West Germany	Spain	Italy	Nether-lands	Belgium	Portugal	Eire
Your campaign will extend to countries outside the existing one	18	26	8	5	24	26	20	15	20	10
You will run more national ads	8	11	—	—	16	13	5	15	10	—
You will be administering campaigns originating from colleagues in Europe	4	5	3	—	—	3	5	5	—	30
No difference to present situation	49	53	47	89	32	29	55	45	10	60
More coordination between countries Intensify/reinforce present coverage	2	—	3	3	—	5	—	—	—	—
	2	—	3	3	—	5	—	—	—	—
Other	3	—	8	—	—	11	—	5	—	—
Don't know	15	5	21	3	29	11	15	15	60	—

continues

continued

> Almost half thought there would be no changes to their campaigns, although the more export-minded countries like Germany and the Netherlands were running cross-border campaigns already. The UK, Spain and Italy, however, were starting from a small base. What was more significant, perhaps, were the respondents who didn't know what the changes would be. A case of keeping their options open?

As a group, industrial goods manufacturers centralize advertising decisions to a greater degree than consumer-oriented companies. Industrial advertising lends itself to centralized decision making because the specifications and uses of many industrial products are essentially the same around the world. Thus, a single industrial advertising message usually appeals to intended buyers on a global basis. Frequently, industrial advertising strategies are built around the placement of ads in international and local trade journals and business publications, and focus on price and features only. There is generally little if any adaptation to local customs and trends beyond translating the ads into the local language.

Companies that market directly to consumers face a much more heterogeneous market. Although world-wide tastes and preferences are converging, consumer goods makers often *must* localize the content of their advertising to win market acceptance because consumer perceptions still vary greatly throughout the world, reflecting the persistence of country-specific characteristics (see Case 6.2).

Exceptions to the preceding generalizations do exist. There are industrial goods corporations that decentralize advertising decisions, and there are consumer goods manufacturers that centralize all advertising matters at corporate headquarters.

Case 6.2 Acer

Acer, a fast-growing personal computer multinational based in Taiwan, makes most advertising decisions at its central office in Taipei. The corporate office defines the overall strategy, including company-wide slogan or tag-line

continues

continued

and the basic content of the ads. Examples of 'common themes' for advertising campaigns set by corporate headquarters have included 'Bridging the gap for a better tomorrow' and – after the firm changed its English-langauge name to Acer from the colourless 'Multitech' in 1988 – 'Acer is the word for value'. As for content, the company might insist that all ads for a new personal computer model highlight its size or built-in memory capacity. Occasionally, the corporate promotion office even produces prototype advertisements (print or video) as guidelines for its regional subsidiaries' local promotion efforts.

Within these parameters, however, the regional subsidiaries have the authority to create their own ads. Max Wu, Acer's vice president for marketing promotion, preferred this arrangement because of the differences among the markets Acer serves. Noted Wu: 'In Europe, people want advertisements to talk more specifically about the product and prices, even though you are not allowed to make direct comparisons with your competitors in most European countries.' Wu also noted that colourful ads work well in the US, while very stylish or innovative ads hold consumers' attention best in Japan.

Acer's regional divisions plan the local media placement strategies in conjunction with the home office. In its initial entry into new markets, Acer has placed ads in professional computer publications and high-tech journals, such as *Computerworld* or *PC World* magazines in the US or *Nikkei Personal Computing* in Japan. These early product-introduction ads usually focus on specific products and their attributes. Once Acer products are somewhat established in the local high-tech community, ad placement switches to widely circulated general business and trade publications, such as *Fortune* and *Business Week* in the US. The last stage is to run advertisements in newspapers highlighting Acer's corporate image and its ability to provide solutions to corporate information needs.

Local product advertising lends itself to decentralized decision making. For consumer goods especially, brand names can be powerful sales tools in overseas markets. A local brand name, signifying that the product is part of the local scene, may be all that is needed to give the product the acceptance it needs and to position it properly. In the case of luxury items, however, a foreign name may provide the desired upscale image and help the product to command a premium price. If the item is imported, rather than made locally, a foreign name may be essential to communicate the proper image.

What some companies are trying to do is balance the benefits of having strong centralized messages which nonetheless do not arouse fierce local resistance to having ads imposed from the centre. Companies like United Distillers (UD) which have central strategic marketing units (see Case 5.3, page 131) are very careful to plan campaigns with the full cooperation and involvement of the region concerned. At UD both Dewars, its leading US whisky brand, and Black & White, a European brand, have been successfully extended into other regions as far apart as Thailand, Australia, the Caribbean and South America by gaining regional support and adaptation of central campaigns.

Besides the impact on local initiative and motivation, there are a number of reasons for decentralizing advertising decisions or at least modifying ad campaigns to suit local market conditions. Language differences are the most obvious, although simply translating the same message can work for a product with universal appeal. National, cultural and ethnic preferences are more important. In Europe, for example, the same brand or type of cheese may be served mainly as an hors d'oeuvre in Sweden, a breakfast food in Italy and a sandwich filling in England. The cheese maker who tries to use a single 'neutral' image – say, simply a piece of the cheese on a cutting board – risks forfeiting sales in all three markets. But the maker who picks only one of the three uses and advertises the cheese in that way in all three markets may lose sales in two of the three. Toothpaste is also perceived differently from country to country, according to research by Colgate–Palmolive. Toothpaste is viewed more as a cosmetic product in Spain and Greece, while in the Netherlands it is seen more as a treatment to prevent cavities. Similarly, Spaniards treat soap as a cosmetic item, while Britons consider it more of a functional commodity.

Another reason why local adaptations of advertising are necessary is that media standards and practices differ from market to market. Many countries around the world do not allow television commercials or allow them only for certain types of products. In the US, cigarette and liquor commercials are no longer permitted to run on broadcast media, but are still perfectly acceptable in many other countries (Table 6.1).

Several factors should be taken into account in planning advertising in different markets, including:

- How the company is set up. Is it centralized/decentralized and are the lines of management clear to both the company and outside agencies? Does the balance reflect the strategic and market requirements?
- What about the advertising agency? Does it have a true network, wholly owned subsidiaries, or one person with a fax in Paris?
- What about the agency's media expertise? The media mix in each country can vary a lot. Does it use independent media buying agencies?

Table 6.1   Selected countries with restrictions on advertising.

Private TV	Private radio	Govt TV and radio	Billboards	General magazines	Daily newspapers	Direct mail
Sanitary napkins and tampons						
Indonesia	Ireland	Argentina	Argentina		Argentina	Germany
Trinidad and		Ireland	Bahrain			Mexico
Tobago		Korea	Ireland			
UK		Lebanon	Kenya			
		Trinidad and	Korea			
		Tobago	Mexico			
		Turkey	Trinidad and			
		Venezuela	Tobago			
Male contraceptives as birth control devices						
Argentina	Chile	Argentina	Argentina	Argentina	Argentina	Bahrain
Chile	France	Austria	Bahrain	Bahrain	Bahrain	Denmark
France	Greece	Bahrain	Canada	France	France	France
Greece	Ireland	Canada	Chile	Ireland	FR Germany	FR Germany
Lebanon	Japan	Chile	Denmark	Lebanon	Greece	Japan
Malaysia	Lebanon	France	France	Mexico	Japan	Lebanon
Mexico	Malaysia	Greece	Greece	Paraguay	Lebanon	Mexico
Paraguay	Mexico	Ireland	Ireland	Peru	Mexico	Paraguay
Peru	Paraguay	Italy	Japan	PR China	Paraguay	Peru
South Africa	Peru	Kenya	Korea	South Africa	Peru	South Africa
	South Africa	Korea	Lebanon	Taiwan	PR China	Sri Lanka
	Taiwan	Lebanon	Malaysia	Trinidad and	South Africa	Taiwan
	Trinidad and	Malaysia	Mexico	Tobago	Trinidad and	Trinidad and
	Tobago	Mexico	Paraguay		Tobago	Tobago
	Venezuela	Paraguay	Peru			
		Peru	PR China			
		PR China	South Africa			
		South Africa	Taiwan			
		Switzerland	Thailand			
		Taiwan	Trinidad and			
		Thailand	Tobago			
		Trinidad and	Turkey			
		Tobago	Venezuela			
		Turkey				
		Venezuela				
Toilet paper						
Belgium	Belgium	Argentina	Argentina	Bahrain	Bahrain	Bahrain
Brazil	Brazil	Bahrain	Bahrain	Brazil	Brazil	Brazil
Japan	Japan	Mexico	Belgium	Japan	Japan	Japan
			Brazil	Trinidad and	Trinidad and	Trinidad and
			Japan	Tobago	Tobago	Tobago
			Mexico			
Sauna, suntanning machines						
Argentina	Malaysia	Argentina	Argentina	Thailand		Argentina
Malaysia	Thailand	Malaysia	Thailand	Trinidad and		Thailand
Thailand	Trinidad and	Thailand		Tobago		Trinidad and
	Tobago	Trinidad and				Tobago
		Tobago				

(continues)

Table 6.1   *(continued)*

Body, foot, mouth deodorants

Private TV	Private radio	Govt TV and radio	Billboards	General magazines	Daily newspapers	Direct mail
			Argentina			
			Denmark			

Feminine douches

Private TV	Private radio	Govt TV and radio	Billboards	General magazines	Daily newspapers	Direct mail
Australia	Australia	Argentina	Argentina	Argentina	Argentina	Bahrain
Chile	Chile	Bahrain	Australia	Bahrain	Bahrain	Hong Kong
Hong Kong	Hong Kong	Chile	Bahrain	Hong Kong	Hong Kong	Japan
Japan	Ireland	Ireland	Canada	Kenya	Ireland	Kenya
Lebanon	Japan	Kenya	Chile	Malaysia	Japan	Mexico
Malaysia	Malaysia	Korea	Denmark	Mexico	Kenya	New Zealand
Mexico	Mexico	Malaysia	Hong Kong	Singapore	Malaysia	Norway
Philippines	New Zealand	Mexico	Ireland	South Africa	Mexico	Peru
Singapore	Philippines	New Zealand	Japan	Sri Lanka	New Zealand	Philippines
South Africa	South Africa	Peru	Kenya	Taiwan	Philippines	Singapore
Sri Lanka	Taiwan	Philippines	Korea	Thailand	Singapore	Sri Lanka
Taiwan	Thailand	Singapore	Malaysia	Trinidad and Tobago	South Africa	Taiwan
Thailand	Trinidad and Tobago	South Africa	Mexico	UK	Sri Lanka	Thailand
Trinidad and Tobago	UK	Sri Lanka	New Zealand		Taiwan	Trinidad and Tobago
UK		Thailand	Norway		Thailand	UK
		Trinidad and Tobago	Philippines		Trinidad and Tobago	
		Turkey	Singapore		UK	
			South Africa			
			Sri Lanka			
			Taiwan			
			Thailand			
			Trinidad and Tobago			
			UK			
			Venezuela			

Home pregnancy test

Private TV	Private radio	Govt TV and radio	Billboards	General magazines	Daily newspapers	Direct mail
Argentina	Brazil	Argentina	Argentina	Argentina	Argentina	Bahrain
Brazil	Canada	Austria	Australia	Bahrain	Bahrain	Brazil
Canada	Denmark	Bahrain	Bahrain	Brazil	Brazil	Hong Kong
Lebanon	Ireland	Canada	Brazil	Canada	Canada	Lebanon
Malaysia	Lebanon	FR Germany	Canada	Denmark	Hong Kong	Malaysia
Mexico	Malaysia	Ireland	Denmark	Lebanon	Lebanon	Mexico
South Africa	Mexico	Kenya	Kenya	Malaysia	Mexico	PR China
Taiwan	South Africa	Lebanon	Lebanon	Mexico	PR China	Singapore
Venezuela	Switzerland	Malaysia	Malaysia	PR China	Singapore	
UK	Taiwan	Mexico	Mexico	Singapore		
	Venezuela	Peru	Peru			
	UK	PR China	PR China			
		Singapore	Singapore			
		South Africa	South Africa			
		Sri Lanka	Sri Lanka			
		Venezuela				

(continues)

Table 6.1   *(continued)*

Private TV	Private radio	Govt TV and radio	Billboards	General magazines	Daily newspapers	Direct mail

Haemorrhoid remedies

Private TV	Private radio	Govt TV and radio	Billboards	General magazines	Daily newspapers	Direct mail
Argentina	Australia	Argentina	Argentina		Argentina	Argentina
Australia	Belgium	Austria	Australia		Brazil	Brazil
Belgium	Brazil	Bahrain	Bahrain		Denmark	Denmark
Brazil	France	France	Belgium		France	France
France	Greece	Greece	Brazil		Greece	Greece
Greece	Iceland	Iceland	France		Iceland	Iceland
Iceland	Lebanon	Lebanon	FR Germany		Singapore	Mexico
Lebanon	Malaysia	Malaysia	Greece		Trinidad and	PR China
Malaysia	New Zealand	Mexico	Iceland		Tobago	Singapore
Mexico	Switzerland	PR China	Lebanon			Trinidad and
UK	Trinidad and	Singapore	Malaysia			Tobago
	Tobago	Switzerland	Mexico			
	UK	Trinidad and	Peru			
		Tobago	PR China			
		Turkey	Singapore			
			Trinidad and			
			Tobago			
			UK			

Male undergarments

Private TV	Private radio	Govt TV and radio	Billboards	General magazines	Daily newspapers	Direct mail
Argentina	Lebanon	Argentina	Argentina			Argentina
Chile	Malaysia	Lebanon	Lebanon			PR China
Malaysia	Mexico	Malaysia				
Mexico						

Adult protection (incontinence diapers, panty shields, and so on)

Private TV	Private radio	Govt TV and radio	Billboards	General magazines	Daily newspapers	Direct mail
Australia	Australia	Argentina	Argentina	Argentina	Argentina	Bahrain
Canada	Canada	Austria	Australia	Austria	Austria	Canada
Finland	Finland	Bahrain	Austria	Bahrain	Bahrain	FR Germany
FR Germany	FR Germany	Canada	Bahrain	Canada	Canada	Japan
Hong Kong	Japan	FR Germany	Canada	Finland	Finland	Kenya
Indonesia	Lebanon	Kenya	Finland	Japan	FR Germany	Korea
Japan	Malaysia	Korea	FR Germany	Kenya	Japan	Nigeria
Lebanon	Portugal	Lebanon	Japan	Nigeria	Kenya	Portugal
Malaysia	South Africa	Mexico	Kenya	Portugal	Korea	Thailand
South Africa	Thailand	Nigeria	Korea	Thailand	Nigeria	Turkey
Thailand	Venezuela	Portugal	Lebanon	Turkey	Portugal	
Turkey		South Africa	Mexico		Thailand	
Venezuela		Thailand	Nigeria		Trinidad and	
		Turkey	Portugal		Tobago	
		Venezuela	South Africa		Turkey	
			Thailand			
			Turkey			
			Venezuela			

Female undergarments (bras, and so on)

Private TV	Private radio	Govt TV and radio	Billboards	General magazines	Daily newspapers	Direct mail
Chile	Malaysia	Bahrain	Bahrain	FR Germany	Bahrain	FR Germany
Malaysia		Malaysia	Kenya		PR China	Trinidad and
		Mexico	Mexico		Trinidad and	Tobago
		PR China			Tobago	

(continues)

Table 6.1   *(continued)*

Private TV	Private radio	Govt TV and radio	Billboards	General magazines	Daily newspapers	Direct mail
Laxatives						
Belgium	Belgium	Argentina	Argentina	Brazil	Brazil	Brazil
Brazil	Brazil	France	Australia	France	France	France
France	France	FR Germany	Belgium	FR Germany	FR Germany	FR Germany
FR Germany	FR Germany	Greece	Brazil	Greece	Greece	Greece
Greece	Greece	Iceland	France	Iceland	Iceland	Iceland
Iceland	Iceland	Lebanon	FR Germany	Singapore	PR China	Singapore
Lebanon	Lebanon	Malaysia	Greece	Turkey	Singapore	Turkey
Malaysia	Malaysia	Singapore	Iceland		Turkey	
	Switzerland	Switzerland	Lebanon			
		Turkey	Malaysia			
			PR China			
			Singapore			
			Turkey			
Over-the-counter female contraceptives						
Argentina	Brazil	Argentina	Argentina	Argentina	Argentina	Austria
Brazil	Canada	Austria	Bahrain	Bahrain	Austria	Bahrain
Chile	Chile	Bahrain	Brazil	Brazil	Bahrain	Denmark
France	France	Canada	Canada	France	Brazil	France
Greece	Greece	Chile	Chile	Kenya	France	Greece
Japan	Japan	France	France	Malaysia	Greece	Japan
Malaysia	Malaysia	Greece	Greece	Mexico	Ireland	Kenya
Mexico	Mexico	Ireland	Ireland	Portugal	Japan	Mexico
Philippines	New Zealand	Japan	Japan	Singapore	Kenya	New Zealand
South Africa	Philippines	Kenya	Kenya	South Africa	Malaysia	Norway
Taiwan	Portugal	Korea	Korea	Thailand	Mexico	Philippines
Thailand	South Africa	Malaysia	Malaysia	Trinidad and	New Zealand	Portugal
UK	Thailand	Mexico	Mexico	Tobago	Philippines	Singapore
	Trinidad and	New Zealand	New Zealand	UK	Portugal	South Africa
	Tobago	Peru	Norway		PR China	Thailand
	UK	Philippines	Philippines		Singapore	Trinidad and
		Portugal	Portugal		South Africa	Tobago
		PR China	PR China		Thailand	UK
		Singapore	Singapore		Trinidad and	
		South Africa	South Africa		Tobago	
		Thailand	Thailand		UK	
		Trinidad and	Trinidad and			
		Tobago	Tobago			
		Turkey	UK			
Over-the-counter acne medication						
Argentina	Belgium	Argentina	Argentina	Argentina	Argentina	Brazil
Belgium	Brazil	France	Brazil	Brazil	Brazil	Denmark
Brazil	France	Ireland	Denmark	Denmark	Denmark	France
France	Ireland	Lebanon	France	France	France	Singapore
Mexico	Lebanon	Mexico	Ireland	Singapore	Singapore	Trinidad and
		PR China	Lebanon			Tobago
		Singapore	Mexico			

(continues)

Table 6.1   *(continued)*

Private TV	Private radio	Govt TV and radio	Billboards	General magazines	Daily newspapers	Direct mail
Male hygiene products (anti-itching powder, and so on)						
Argentina	Argentina	Argentina	Argentina	Argentina	Argentina	Bahrain
Hong Kong	Hong Kong	Austria	Australia	Austria	Bahrain	FR Germany
Indonesia	Indonesia	Bahrain	Austria	Bahrain	FR Germany	Hong Kong
	Trinidad and	Indonesia	Bahrain	Hong Kong	Hong Kong	Indonesia
	Tobago	Ireland	FR Germany	Indonesia	Indonesia	Philippines
		Peru	Hong Kong	Sri Lanka	Sri Lanka	Sri Lanka
		Sri Lanka	Indonesia	Trinidad and	Trinidad and	Trinidad and
		Trinidad and	Ireland	Tobago	Tobago	Tobago
		Tobago	Peru			
		Turkey	Sri Lanka			
			Trinidad and			
			Tobago			
			UK			
Swimsuits						
Malaysia	Malaysia	Malaysia				

Source: Boddewyn, Dr J. (1989). *Sexism and Decency in Advertising: Government Regulation and Industry Self-Regulation in 47 Countries.* New York: International Advertising Association

Case 6.3   Advertising – the acid test

Whatever the theory behind a company's European structure, clues to the real balance of power between the centre and its outposts often have to be sought elsewhere, and advertising policy provides one revealing test. The freedom allowed over the selection of a local advertising agency, and the brief given to the agency as to the advertising expected from it, do not always correspond to the company's professed organizational policy.

Heineken beer and Volvo auto advertising demonstrate a sharp contrast between local campaigns and centrally sourced ads, reflecting differences in distribution rights and management strategies. The evidence suggests that, at least in the consumer goods industries, the advertising process is being made to conform more closely to the corporate structure and systems.

This is not to imply that international campaigns, or even themes for campaigns, are on the increase. Rather, as multinationals' European structures evolve toward a balance between central and local forces, so the advertising agencies serving them must:

● Be ready to adapt their own methods of working, and assist with the liaison and coordination process as and when required;

continues

continued

- Provide a channel for international marketing spending – on market research, advertising production, and the small but growing international TV and press media;
- Act as guardians of the 'values' that a brand stands for, to ensure that they are not devalued as they are interpreted and applied in different markets. One Spanish agency, for example, when called upon to produce a local version of the famous Johnnie Walker image, turned him into a kind of ghost – far removed from the warm and friendly image that proprietors United Distillers wished to convey;
- Provide ideas suitable for multinational application when required. This can be achieved by maintaining an international outlook, if not a network of offices.

It has long been a matter for debate in the advertising world as to whether companies are better advised to look for the best agency available in each market they are addressing and then aim to coordinate the results, or to put their faith in an international chain, calculating that uniformity will make up for the lack of individual flair and that the agency will carry the overheads associated with coordination. In practice, most companies use a combination of international and local agencies to cover their European markets, partly out of necessity (client conflict and so on) and partly, perhaps, because of the need for quality and diversity. Coca-Cola's well-known monogamous association with the US agency McCann Erickson (which expanded across Europe originally to serve its US clients' international aspirations) is unusual.

The single-agency policy may be tidy, but it can bring problems in its wake, and these have deterred Levi Strauss from pursuing a similar strategy to Coca-Cola. Apart from Coke, it would be difficult to find a more universally American image than that of jeans. But whereas a US agency has handled its advertising in the US, a London-based agency Bartle, Bogle Hegarty (BBH) has produced the TV commercials for use throughout Europe through a string of local agencies. Although it has no network of its own outside the UK, BBH said, 'We invest a lot of time in researching the market and talking to the Levi Strauss subsidiaries and retailers.'

Colgate–Palmolive (C–P) is representative of the companies that use their agencies as an integral part of their marketing resources. 'They are partners in the total process,' said European president Brian Bergin. 'Their first role is to support local initiatives.' But the agencies also have the brief to align C–P's advertising with global assignments, and 'we meet regularly as a group on European issues. The agency is a good outreach and input for things we might overlook. With our tradition of employment from within, it's important we don't fall into the trap of navel examination.'

But Bergin was adamant that 'we wouldn't use an agency as an intelligence source,' referring to the criticism that some US companies rely on their US agencies to act at best as marketing auditor and at worst as an internal CIA, to check that their national subsidiaries follow instructions.

continues

continued

'Multinationals shouldn't use their agencies as Trojan horses for greater standardization,' advised Harvard academics John Quelch and Edward Hoff. 'An undercover operation is likely to jeopardize agency–client relations at the country level.'

At the opposite extreme from the single- or dual-agency policy stands Nestlé, which at one time was alleged to use no less than 137 agencies to advertise its products in Europe, itself a reaction to the practice in the 1960s when a central, 60-strong department vetted all subsidiaries' advertising. Now, the centre is working toward a more rationalized advertising process which is orchestrated if not devised from the centre.

3M recently decided to concentrate its international business through three agencies with European networks rather than the 40 it once employed. It chose a US agency, one that is Brussels-based and another in the UK.

Advertising is a much less significant part of the policy mix in industrial and business-to-business marketing, but even there, differences are indicative of wider policies. Digital Equipment, for example, aims at a global marketplace and maintains central control over its advertising in all countries, not just Europe, explaining that 'when it was left to the countries, it was a mess and we lost synergy, so now we're back to a world-wide image and advertising.' It does, however, place great emphasis at a national level on sponsoring arts and other events.

Canon, by contrast, allows its national subsidiaries a very free hand in their advertising, relying on an agreed common marketing strategy to ensure coherence. Local interpretation is coordinated only through regular marketing committee meetings. It does, however, sponsor international sports events such as football and motor racing, which naturally require more careful coordination. In the past, Rank Xerox attempted to apply a central advertising strategy and even provide centrally sourced advertising material. But now, the European headquarters merely asks its national subsidiaries to project a strong, common image and message. Execution is a local responsibility, and although 'people do use each other's ads and promotions, there is no intention to make it mandatory.' Coordination is secured through a European advertising council.

Corporate advertising

Many executives feel that with political and economic barriers coming down in Europe and elsewhere, companies must become as well-known globally as their products are in order to compete successfully in the decades to come. This does not mean simply gaining a foothold in a market, but also making sure the company name is instantly recognizable. Last year companies from the US ran more corporate advertising throughout the world than businesses from other countries; AT&T, IBM and Ford topped the list.

Global corporate campaigns are very common among high-tech companies. General Electric uses its 'We are GE, we bring good things to life' slogan world-wide. And Hewlett-Packard has corporate image advertising that was developed by the corporate 'MARCOM' (marketing communications) department in conjunction with the international division's staff.

Globally focused corporate ads are generally shown in one form all over the world, with voice-overs in the local languages. As with global brand advertising, companies sometimes delegate the production of these corporate image ads to foreign subsidiaries while retaining control over the content.

For some companies, corporate image advertising is increasingly being used for more specific purposes than just for general image enhancement. In the US, where concern over long-term trade deficits and the impact of foreign investment is mounting, many companies, especially from Japan, have launched massive corporate ad programmes.

Toshiba America Inc. recently created a TV commercial humorously likening the company president, Ken Hiyama, to rock star Bruce Springsteen. In the ad, Hiyama, carrying a red, white and blue guitar, explains that although he was not 'born in the USA' (the title of one of Springsteen's biggest hit songs), he still loves New Jersey, the home of the company's new North American headquarters. In one of its recent ads, Mitsubishi Electric America Inc. declared that it employs more than 3000 Americans in facilities located in Ohio, Georgia, North Carolina and California.

Corporate image advertising often has another benefit. Promoting the corporate name behind a brand can strongly reinforce a global brand's success (see Case 5.3). Companies like Coca-Cola, IBM, Levi Strauss, Minolta and Canon pay a great deal of attention to corporate image advertising around the world. Enhancing the corporate brand can also pay dividends in terms of recruitment and community relations (see Chapter 5, corporate branding).

Obviously, corporate ad programmes lend themselves to centralized decision making. Indeed, such campaigns cannot really be run from anywhere else because the strategies are designed to benefit all operations and products world-wide. For example, Seiko Epson, the high-tech Japanese computer and peripherals manufacturer, maintains an extensive global corporate advertising programme planned and developed centrally at its headquarters in Nagano. According to N. Niwa, deputy general manager for the marketing and sales division, corporate advertisements are devised for regions, not individual countries, and aim to highlight Epson's technological prowess or its corporate culture. For example, a corporate ad recently designed for the Asian region featured local Epson employees in an attempt to indicate the firm's belief in localization. Responsibility for product advertisements, however, is borne by country-level affiliates, with guidance from Nagano. Approximately 10–15% of Epson's annual advertising budget is consumed by its corporate programme; the remainder is spent by affiliates on product or image promotional efforts.

Corporate advertising is not used by every globally oriented company. Some companies simply do not wish to promote their names in foreign markets because they want to position their products as indigenous to each local market. Usually this entails renaming the product so that it will not be perceived as coming from a foreign-based company. Other companies simply do not believe in enhancing the corporate image when the funds could be used to promote a specific product instead. In addition, positioning a company as a multinational without having a broad product line in many markets can be dangerous. The customer's reaction could be 'What are they selling me?', rather than simply establishing or enhancing a positive corporate image.

Changing roles of the promotional mix

Classical advertising has traditionally been the dominant player in the overall promotional mix. It is indeed a powerful tool. But the next decade could see the final disappearance of the 'above and below the line' distinctions that have divided advertising from the other, perceived as less glamorous, activities like sales promotion, direct marketing, sponsorship, exhibitions and public relations. For example, if a catalogue is being designed for a car manufacturer, is that design, sales promotion, direct marketing, advertising or all of them to a certain extent?

The move is toward the formation of a total marketing communications package. Why?

- Soaring media costs have placed a premium on conventional media advertising;
- New techniques enable companies to define much smaller segments of existing and potential customers which can be better reached using a 'shotgun' method like direct marketing rather than a 'scatter gun' approach like advertising;
- Complex markets demand a more imaginative combination of promotional strategies;
- The growing concentration of retailers, and the increasing success of own-brands, means that the old formula of classical advertising to pull customers into stores to buy branded goods is no longer as effective as it was;
- It is easy for an ad to get lost in the bombardment of messages engendered by the proliferation of media vehicles;
- There is a growing threat of legislation to reduce the amount of advertising some companies can do, including sectors like tobacco, drinks and pharmaceuticals (see Appendix B, page 201).

Table 6.2   Advertising expenditure per head at current prices and exchange rates, 1980–88 ($).

	1980	1981	1982	1983	1984	1985	1986	1987	1988
Austria	48.0	37.6	38.9	42.4	42.5	44.9	66.2	86.1	100.5
Belgium	57.6	45.3	40.1	41.9	41.2	43.6	62.9	87.4	97.2
Denmark	99.0	85.1	78.5	77.5	75.6	80.3	113.6	142.7	154.1
Finland	118.6	124.0	127.2	132.2	142.7	153.1	202.8	254.3	305.6
France	58.7	51.6	50.2	51.9	49.9	54.4	80.3	107.0	124.2
Germany	99.1	80.4	80.0	80.3	77.0	80.5	112.7	142.8	153.6
Greece	10.6	12.5	13.8	12.3	11.5	11.7	16.6	22.3	29.9
Ireland	37.5	31.0	28.8	25.1	25.2	28.1	43.9	58.8	66.0
Italy	25.5	25.1	27.2	31.3	32.7	36.1	57.3	72.7	88.0
Netherlands	121.1	94.3	90.3	85.7	81.7	83.5	123.4	156.8	173.6
Norway	108.4	104.0	106.8	98.6	104.2	111.2	150.7	181.5	181.0
Portugal	5.4	5.8	5.5	5.9	4.9	5.8	9.5	16.5	23.4
Spain	31.1	29.6	34.0	30.5	32.3	36.7	58.4	86.2	115.0
Sweden	95.2	84.7	77.8	72.5	78.0	83.9	114.8	147.1	177.1
Switzerland	162.7	148.6	139.5	143.8	135.0	143.0	209.3	277.5	296.4
UK	105.5	101.4	96.9	96.2	95.6	100.3	131.9	166.0	211.3
Europe	69.1	61.4	60.5	60.8	60.0	63.9	91.1	118.0	139.1
EC	65.7	58.1	57.4	57.6	56.6	60.3	86.2	111.8	132.7
Japan	66.1	72.2	67.5	74.7	77.7	94.2	136.8	172.1	218.1
USA	155.9	172.8	186.9	211.8	242.4	256.4	271.9	286.2	302.9

Note: These figures have not been adjusted to account for different methods of compilation and are therefore not fully comparable.

Source: UK Advertising Association.

Nevertheless, advertising has been a very important big industry throughout the world (Table 6.2), particularly as companies from sectors that have not advertised traditionally come on stream. In the UK, for example, retailers, companies warding off hostile takeovers with bursts of corporate advertising extolling their own virtues, privatizing organizations and the financial services had all begun to pump far more resources into TV and press advertising until the impact of the worsening recession began to hit expenditure. While advertising itself may fail to return to the halcyon days of the big spending 1980s, the 1990s will see new entrants from the heavier end of industry and from the professions like accountancy and law as they flex their promotional muscle and start using tools like public relations, sponsorship and product placement.

Integrating the communications package and deciding the weight to be given to each part of the mix should revolve around the answers to two simple questions:

(1)   Do I know whom I want to communicate with?
(2)   Do I know what I want to say to them?

As Chris Morris, manager of campaign marketing for IBM Europe, at last year's European Direct Marketing Association conference in Brussels said,

'Looking at the developments from the sixties and seventies, we used to work on image advertising separately in one group. There was another group on sales promotion and events, who worked separately, and then there were our face-to-face sales forces. That was the way we delivered the messages to the market. Then in the eighties people started to try and communicate specific solutions. We used to call direct marketing "mass marketing" but in the nineties there is an immense opportunity. The move from "advertising" into "relationship-building", the move of mass marketing into "response generation", the application of the database to drive all this, and the importance of dialogue is a clear message for the future. The competitive edge will go to those who can manage to deliver all that.'

One major problem is that too many companies still eye their promotional efforts as *ad hoc* and add-on, rather than as an extension of a well-thought-out strategic marketing plan. One of the first decisions companies tend to make at times of slump is to chop the promotional budget, an expenditure, they complain, where they cannot see an immediate payback or are unable to judge effectiveness. This can be very unwise: if companies cut down drastically on promotions in the short term to give a fillip to the bottom line, it could harm their long-term marketing strategy.

This has been the argument used by Grand Metropolitan, the international food, drink and retailing group. In 1990, for example, it boosted its marketing budget by £175 million compared to the previous year, spending £833 million compared to profits of £919 million. Chairman and chief executive Sir Allen Sheppard claimed that the increase helped the company deal with adverse economic conditions.

In general, the danger is that the marketing budget can be pruned easily without affecting the company next year. So even blue-chip companies, when they have pressures on the bottom line, will raid the marketing budget. But that can undermine the bedrock of the company. It means that the company has not thought through the link between marketing strategy and the marketing mix.

Sales promotion and direct marketing

Both of these activities still tend to be run on a country-by country basis not only because of the varied rules and regulations, but because tastes are still so different. Moves are being made to standardize the approach across Europe by both the sales promotion and direct marketing industries, but it will take the next decade at least for truly pan-European campaigns to be established (Table 6.3).

Table 6.3 What can be done and what can't, across Europe.

Technique	UK	Eire	Spain	Germany	France	Denmark	Belgium	Netherlands	Portugal	Italy	Greece	Luxembourg	Austria	Finland	Norway	Sweden	Switzerland
On-pack price cuts	Yes	Yes	Yes	Yes	Yes	Yes	Yes	Yes	Yes	Yes	Yes	Yes	Yes	Yes	Yes	Yes	Yes
Banded offers	Yes	Yes	Yes	Poss	Yes	Poss	Poss	Yes	Yes	Yes	Yes	No	Poss	Poss	Poss	Poss	No
In-pack premiums	Yes	Yes	Yes	Poss	Poss	Poss	Poss	Poss	Yes	Yes	Yes	No	Poss	Yes	Poss	Poss	No
Multiple-purchase offers	Yes	Yes	Yes	Poss	Yes	Poss	Poss	Yes	Yes	Yes	Yes	No	Poss	Poss	Poss	Poss	No
Extra product	Yes	Yes	Yes	Poss	Yes	Yes	Poss	Poss	Yes	Yes	Yes	Yes	Poss	Yes	Yes	Yes	Poss
Free product	Yes	Yes	Yes	Yes	Yes	Yes	Poss	Yes	Yes	Yes	Yes	Yes	Yes	Yes	Yes	Yes	Yes
Reusable/alternative use pack	Yes	Yes	Yes	Yes	Yes	Yes	Yes	Yes	Yes	Yes	Yes	Yes	Poss	Yes	Yes	Yes	Yes
Free mail-ins	Yes	Yes	Yes	No	Yes	Poss	Poss	Yes	Yes	Yes	Yes	Poss	No	Yes	Poss	No	No
With-purchase premiums	Yes	Yes	Yes	Poss	Yes	Poss	Poss	Poss	Yes	Yes	Yes	No	Poss	Yes	Poss	Poss	No
Cross-product offers	Yes	Yes	Yes	No	Yes	Poss	No	Poss	Yes	Yes	Yes	No	Poss	Poss	Poss	No	No
Collector devices	Yes	Yes	Yes	No	Poss	Poss	Poss	Poss	Yes	Yes	Yes	No	No	Poss	No	No	No
Competitions	Yes	Yes	Yes	Poss	Poss	Poss	Poss	Poss	Yes	Yes	Yes	Poss	Poss	Yes	Yes	Yes	Yes
Self-liquidating premiums	Yes	Yes	Yes	Yes	Yes	Yes	Yes	Poss	Yes	Yes	Poss	No	Yes	Yes	No	Yes	No
Free draws	Yes	Yes	Yes	No	Yes	No	No	No	Yes	Yes	Yes	No	No	Yes	No	No	No
Share-outs	Yes	Yes	Yes	No	Poss	No	No	No	Poss	Poss	Yes	No	No	Poss	Poss	No	No
Sweepstake/lottery	Poss	Poss	Poss	Poss	Poss	No	Poss	Poss	Poss	Poss	Yes	No	Poss	Yes	No	No	No
Money-off vouchers	Yes	Yes	Yes	No	Yes	Poss	Yes	Yes	Yes	Poss	Yes	Poss	Poss	Poss	No	Poss	No
Money-off next purchase	Yes	Yes	Yes	No	Yes	No	Yes	Yes	Yes	Poss	Yes	No	No	Poss	No	No	No
Cash backs	Yes	Yes	Yes	Poss	Yes	Yes	Yes	Yes	Yes	No	Yes	No	Poss	Poss	Poss	Yes	No
In-store demos	Yes	Yes	Yes	Yes	Yes	Yes	Yes	Yes	Yes	Yes	Yes	Yes	Yes	Yes	Yes	Yes	Yes

Source: IMP Europe Marketing

There are notable exceptions, of course, like Readers' Digest and American Express, who operate on a global scale but tweak the message for different regions.

The potential for these industries is vast. Direct mail already plays a substantial role in transnational communication. According to the Direct Mail Sales Bureau in the UK, 27% of European companies active in other countries use direct mail, although figures vary between countries. Switzerland, for instance, uses direct mail for 59% of cross-border advertising, while the figure in the UK is 32% and in the Netherlands about 27%.

But direct marketing has to tackle some tough problems – not least, its very image – along with the vexed issue of lack of infrastructure, communication blockages and language differences (Table 6.4).

But if trends in the US are any indication, the omens are favourable: according to figures from the US Direct Marketing Association television shopping is already worth about $2 billion, consumer catalogues about $25 billion, inbound consumer telemarketing about $170 billion and outbound business telemarketing about $200 billion. There are over 10,000 mailing lists alone.

Sponsorship

Sponsorship is one of the fastest growing techniques. It is estimated that the sponsorship market could have risen to $2 billion by 1992 in Europe. Some of the attractions of sponsorship in a pan-European/global drive are as follows:

- It can act as a bridge into a new, untested market;
- It can enhance the corporate image either for its own sake or to provide a base from which to boost brands in new markets;
- It can travel across a number of different cultures;
- It can make an impact in markets where traditional advertising is restricted in some way, either because of lack of availability or legislation;
- It spreads the company name among both opinion formers and potential employees.

The Japanese and Americans have been quickest to latch onto the benefits of sponsorship in Europe – not surprisingly, since they, unlike their European counterparts, have always, for the right or wrong reasons, considered Europe as a whole anyway. US computer maker Compaq, for example, has signed a five-year, multimillion pound deal with the International Tennis Federation which will involve setting up a new grand slam event. Compaq wants to extend

Table 6.4 Main trends affecting consumer direct marketing to 1995.

Factors	Belgium	Denmark	France	Germany	Greece	Ireland	Italy	Netherlands	Portugal	Spain	UK
Demographic	More (macro) economically active old	Fewer children	More working women	Ageing of the population	–	Later marriage, fewer children	More older people with money	More smaller households	–	Drop in birth rate	More working women
Economic	Increasing consumer spending power	Poorer economic conditions	–	Higher disposable income	–	Rising incomes	–	–	–	–	–
Population movement (micro)	–	–	–	–	Population moving from big towns (pollution)	Emigration and migration of young	–	–	–	Population moving to outskirts of big towns	–
Media/electronic	Use of EFTPOS technology	–	Use of telephone and Mintel for shopping	New media developing	–	–	Mail order and clubs very acceptable	Acceptance of new media	–	–	Use of telephone inbound is acceptable
Lifestyle	–	–	More people weekend in countryside	Convenience is key to working women	New shopping habits	–	Concern moves from welfare to well being: greater demands	More niches/ new trends	Consumer revolution under way affecting all aspects of demand	–	Lifestyle changes: convenience is important
Other	–	Regulations against data storage	–	–	Lack of experience of direct marketing	–	North/south differences are considerable	–	–	–	–

Source: Ogilvy & Mather Direct Survey.

perception of its products outside its high-technology audience and make its brand seem more 'user-friendly'.

Exhibitions

An underrated tool for companies to get a foothold in other markets is attendance at exhibitions. In the UK the image of exhibitions has on the whole been low-grade and tacky – not helped by unwelcoming exhibition halls. That is in sharp contrast to a country like Germany, where exhibitions are seen as a draw for whole families, as well as being an excellent showcase for both company and products. Exhibitions command almost one-fifth of the promotions budget in Germany, compared to less than a tenth in the UK, although that is changing. According to figures from the Exhibition Industry Federation, UK expenditure rose in 1989 to £1.34 billion from £1.26 billion the year before.

International exhibitions, used properly and taken seriously, will be invaluable for:

- Testing new markets on a cost-effective basis;
- Demonstrating new producers/services;
- Meeting existing/new customers;
- Assessing reactions face to face;
- Finding interested agents/distributors.

Public relations

Public relations is probably the least understood part of the marketing mix, and yet it is undoubtedly one of the most powerful. There is the strategic strand, which is how a company positions itself with all its audiences, and the publicity element, which can be used to enhance the profile of a product or service. Although the global worth of 'PR' is estimated to be well above £3 billion, few companies have yet to develop an overall strategy that embraces both corporate positioning and product publicity. But those companies that can see beyond the presentational role of public relations, and use it as a tool to show that corporate image is matched by corporate reality, will over time see those efforts rewarded at the bottom line.

Recipes for sales success

Whatever companies conclude about the proper location and structure of their marketing operations, and how to operate the promotional strategy, there is no such controversy over sales. The need to keep close to the customers, and to put as much decision-making power as possible into the hands of the executives in contact with them, ensures that sales will remain a fundamentally local operation. That does not necessarily mean that local salesmen deal only with local business, or that the bulk of the business will remain local; only that whereas marketing in its truest sense as apart from promotion is primarily about strategy, and therefore needs to be in a position to scan distant horizons, selling is essentially tactical and always depends on local, practical contact however and wherever the customer is organized. The sales structure must therefore reflect that fact.

Yet selling in the European context evidently presents multinational companies with a problem similar to marketing. With a growing proportion of cross-border and international business, how should the sales force be organized to:

- Provide the close attention to local customers that they demand?
- Coordinate its actions with company sales teams in other countries to provide a coherent service to cross-border customers?
- Utilize its reputation with a customer in one country to assist the development of sales to that customer elsewhere?
- Concentrate, develop and deploy corporate expertise in solving customers' problems?
- Service effectively the small but growing volume of essentially international business, whether from retailers' buying groups or international services like credit card operators and airline booking systems?
- Mount an effective 'instant response' to unexpected business opportunities that do not fit the company's existing organization?
- Set prices that meet the demands of the local market while relating to the wider European context?

Few companies claim to be satisfied with the organization that they so far have in place to meet these objectives, and admit to having made mistakes in the past when they tried to tackle the issues too enthusiastically. Ten years ago, the Swedish paper and packaging company ASSI experimented with cross-border selling to its carton manufacturers in an attempt to cut costs, but quickly found that 'it didn't work very well', and ever since has maintained national sales forces. That appears to be the pattern for many companies, and looks likely to continue at least for the next five years, although some executives foresee possible adjustments of boundaries. This could mean, for example, Bavaria and Austria being treated as one administrative unit, and Belgium being divided according to language. Generally, however, customer sensitivity is going to be accorded a higher priority than bureaucratic convenience.

The situation changes when customers themselves spread across borders and demand a similar service on both sides. At Kodak, for example, 'we all think the general corporate structure [which includes national sales forces controlled ultimately by the country managers] is now about right.' But there is a tacit acknowledgement that the multinational client problem, although still small in relation to the total business, has not yet been solved. Canon, however, is relaxed about its solution. It found that

> 'some customers want a special relationship worldwide, even a worldwide contract but with local distribution and service, and so we need more coordination. And if countries really come together after 1992, we shall need some new structures – but we can do it at any time.'

Being locally based, most salesforces have been the direct line responsibility of the country managers, and have in effect provided their power base in the organization (unless they have manufacturing responsibilities as well). Nothing happens, as sales people are fond of saying, until somebody sells something, and the vital importance of maintaining sales volume is what makes many companies cautious in tinkering with the organization. But as they have been placing more emphasis on planning and coordinating their marketing across Europe, the sales force as well as the marketing staff are faced with more ambiguous reporting relationships.

At a minimum, Danish toy company Lego has adopted a central sales liaison group to coordinate its operations. Headed by a senior European sales vice president, it consists of a number of junior liaison officers representing the centre in each country, and the countries at the centre. Generally, the country manager is still the boss on matters to do with sales targets and their achievement, but the way these are achieved and the direction of the sales team to target customers and market segments are increasingly the concern of business units, product directors and so on, taking a Europe-wide view.

Bringing the two together is not always easy. Union Carbide, for one, has found in its gases division that communication between the field and the central marketing operation in Geneva has not been good enough. Apparently, its sales people can see marketing as a diversion. In consequence, a marketing manager 'with sales experience' is being appointed in each sales subsidiary to act as an intelligence officer, gathering information about the market and feeding it back to Geneva.

Where companies already have critical mass in a country, with sufficient cash flow to cover the overheads, they can afford a more detailed coverage of the market. In the major reorganization of SKF, for example, the old functional structure with domestic sales, international sales, manufacturing, finance and so on, was replaced by global product divisions within a 'business area'. Thus Bearing Industries is divided into the automotive division (the biggest, but with very few, very large customers), machinery and some smaller divisions, all with a lot of smaller customers. In the major national markets, each division maintains profit-responsible business units within the national company. Sales, however, remains a local responsibility, with budgets and targets set locally but agreed with the product divisions.

Explained marketing director Anders Braennstroem, 'We have the resources here centrally to initiate and lead the work, and to follow it up. We do not have the resources to undertake the task in the field.' Braennstroem explained that issues such as product specification and design are developed for customers in particular market segments. The system is in a state of constant evolution: 'We're always fine-tuning it', said Braennstroem. 'The reasons why it works or doesn't are in many cases a question of fine-tuning. Where are the resources, where is the knowledge; are those with the knowledge really doing the work?'

In the rather static light bulb industry, the Siemens-owned Osram has enjoyed a unified product range across Europe ever since the establishment in 1927 of the Phoenix cartel, which set price and product standards among other things. That has long since been abolished, but the standardization largely endures. Even so, per capita consumption of light bulbs varies by a factor of more than five from one end of Europe to another, and distribution conditions are equally diverse. Because inflation in one country is much higher than in another, wholesalers' priorities in holding stock are widely different, and in some countries, retailers' brands account for a large share of the market. The sales operation remains highly localized, therefore, whereas product management is highly centralized in Munich, and the Osram brand identity is heavily promoted internationally.

There is an obvious distinction to be drawn between the consumer goods sales executive calling on wholesale and retail buyers to offer standard products like light bulbs or detergents, and the industrial equipment representative hoping to apply corporate expertise and technology to a customer's problem. What the sales executives offer in both cases will generally be a mix of international and local products. But success in modern markets demands that they and their companies draw on marketing and technical expertise stored either at the centre or somewhere else in the network, and rigorously apply it according to a centrally agreed strategy.

Roche, for example, saw that the big food groups, customers for its vitamins, flavours and fragrances, will eventually have one central buying unit for the whole of Europe. Roche will therefore have to build 'Eurosales teams' to deal with one central organization. It will place bigger orders and make more sophisticated demands which the teams will have to develop the expertise to meet. The company structure becomes the delivery mechanism. If the plans of Associated Marketing Services (see Chapter 1) for the food industry become a reality, food manufacturers will have to act sooner rather than later to take a European view of their business. AMS members already account for 12,000 stores supplying an average of 11% of total grocery sales in nine EC and EFTA countries. The costs and the benefits of doing business with AMS are therefore a prime corporate issue.

The growing number of multinational customers is likely to exacerbate the inherent conflict between the need to satisfy local customers and the need to take a global view. Most companies still buy locally, but as Canon has foreseen, there may be a need to coordinate sales operations across several countries – with the inevitable penalty to pay in a restriction of the local freedom to do a deal. The volume or other discounts offered, special terms, credit allowed and service levels may all be affected, and demand not only some degree of uniformity but a great deal of communication between subsidiaries to put together a viable package and work out how the costs will be shared.

The advantage, of course, is that the company can use its existing business with a company in one country as a means of developing opportunities in another. However, it is a tactic likely to be effective only if communication between the two subsidiaries is at least as good as communication inside the potential customer. Bad news can travel faster than good, and if the customer is dissatisfied in Munich, it is unlikely to be very receptive in Manchester or Madrid. In these circumstances, greater responsibility is placed on the sales and other staff handling the business in one country, both to do a good job and to pass along useful information to help colleagues elsewhere do the same. The problem arises as to how this process should be managed, without merely adding to central staffing levels.

The simple solution is to nominate as lead country the national subsidiary with the biggest stake in the business, the most knowledge of it, or just the one in whose territory the customer's head office is located. The country manager of the lead country is made ultimately responsible for the development of the world-wide business with a particular customer. The other subsidiaries then have to liaise with the manager before making a significant move. One well-established example is TI John Crane, the Dutch subsidiary of which has Shell as its international customer. Thanks to Crane's information system, it can keep a running check on the business the account is yielding. Companies that still cannot aggregate their sales and profit data across countries by product, market segment or customer are at a clear disadvantage.

Crane was satisfied with its system, but in other sorts of business and corporate cultures the familiar problems of conflicting loyalties and motivation may arise. If the company is not prepared for them, internal turf battles may be fought more strenuously than those with its competitors:

- Will the lead country be successful in persuading its fellows to put as much urgency behind satisfying its own customer's foreign offshoots as they would their major accounts?
- If a lot of effort is involved to win the business, should the subsidiaries spend their time on that rather than on their own, perhaps hotter prospects?
- If money is involved, who pays, and who receives the ultimate commission or bonus?

As the volume of cross-border business grows, therefore, a more formal procedure for dealing with these problems may be necessary. Rank Xerox designates account managers in lead countries who are paid a small commission on sales to their accounts made outside their territory. Such business is still relatively rare, said a Rank Xerox executive. It has only 30 or 40 such accounts at the moment, 'but we're now adding 20 or so a year. We can't go faster than the customers want us to.' Some want a consistent price across the world, while others want to transfer special systems to other centres. American Express, for one example, uses Xerox technology to produce reduced copies of all its transaction chits, which it wanted to bring to Europe. It talked to its US account manager, who passed the matter on to a small coordination team in the European headquarters, which passed it on to the UK account manager. It may be long-winded, but if American Express is satisfied – as will be seen, it has its own coordination problems, possibly over companies like Rank Xerox – the process is worth it.

At Honeywell, some 50 account managers are deployed world-wide to deal with its big multinational customers. They are essentially an extension of the subsidiary and are based near the customer's head office. The account manager for Shell happens to be Finnish, and lives in Brussels. The local subsidiary takes responsibility for building the business, but, explained European president Jean-Pierre Rosso, 'if the affiliate wants to cut 15% to get the business, the account manager may say no because of the worldwide implications. The business unit has to be linked in, and the account manager gets at least as much guidance from there as from the affiliate.' If it turns out that a small subsidiary has to shoulder heavy costs to support account managers, a cost-sharing system comes into effect.

Compaq makes use of its small, Munich-based central marketing department to perform a similar function. Many of its 20–30 staff are in fact based in the subsidiaries, and their role is to support rather than lead. Once again, Shell is one of their targets, particularly after Shell's US operation 'bought thousands' of Compaq PCs early in the computer company's development, according to one senior executive. Compaq in the Netherlands therefore had to make certain that its credentials were known and understood at Shell's Dutch headquarters in the Hague, and that the Dutch subsidiary could offer the same (or a better) level of service as its US counterpart.

'You can't operate in one market without having a potential effect on the others', said a senior executive. 'Each market has its own qualities and distinctions which we must utilize but still remain consistent in our message, terms and conditions etcetera. Hopefully, we achieve the right balance.' One new development Compaq is now encountering is the growing number of its dealers, including the US chain Businessland but also some from the UK, that are building networks in other European countries – underlining the virtue of Compaq's original insistence on standard terms and conditions for its dealers world-wide.

L'Oréal, the French hair care and cosmetics house and one of the leaders in the world market, controls its product development, packaging and advertising programmes centrally, but devolves other aspects of marketing and sales to national subsidiaries. Sales targets are not set centrally. Said Giles Roger, assistant director for consumer products,

'The desire to sell more is not handed down from the president telling his employers to do so; it comes from wanting to make and sell performance products – that's really company consensus. From the moment a product is ready for launch, there is a will to sell and sell more. But we develop products to be excellent, not to satisfy figures – everyone in the company agrees. Always trying to fulfil targets could even hamper our performance.'

Selling services

The service industries often represent a more complex problem in that standards are less easily defined and interconnections more important. Advertising agencies, for example, have developed international chains of offices to serve their multinational and other clients, some of which rely on them to provide a coordinated service to subsidiaries in a number of countries – as is the case with J. Walter Thompson (see Chapter 4, page 90). Others work differently.

Satisfying a client in each country, whether in the interpretation of the advertising ideas or in other aspects of account servicing such as media buying, billing and so on, is not easy, and most of the big agencies suffer from a wide variation in the standard of service they can offer in their international networks. Some, like WPP, owner of the J. Walter Thompson and Ogilvy & Mather chains (and a host of smaller marketing services firms), reckons to find at least 15% of its new business from 'cross referrals', that is inquiries fielded elsewhere in the group. However, there is a continuing debate among advertisers – a variation, in fact, of the global/local theme – about whether they benefit more from a coordinated service from an international agency, or from selecting the best agency for their purpose in each market.

More detailed integration is required for services like charge cards, which are used increasingly internationally by their holders. One part of American Express's sales programme is directed toward its 'service establishments' (SEs), the retailers, hotels, oil companies' gas station chains and so on, that accept the card; the other part to major employers that issue the cards to their staff. (Selling to the consumer is carried out largely by advertising and direct marketing, handled round the world by Ogilvy & Mather and McCann–Erickson.) But both the SEs and employers have cross-border operations which Amex takes into account when calculating charges.

The implication, explained UK managing director Alan Stark, was that 'there need to be a lot of lines of communication. You have to define exactly who does what.' The national subsidiaries look after all SEs based in their territories and employers issuing fewer than 10,000 cards. The London-based European headquarters handles the large employers and the international marketing for the SEs. Employers are given a discount based on the total number of cards they issue but paid in local currency, although some may be offered a dollar price. The sales forces therefore have to network information on companies with foreign offshoots promptly and accurately, and groups specializing in, say, hotels or airlines meet regularly to coordinate sales programmes and conditions, and unravel the problems.

Appendix A   Using outside consultants

There are an awful lot of consultants. The Single Market alone has proved an exceptional breeding ground for advice-givers, who spring from a bewildering variety of backgrounds. As one highly respected, but somewhat cynical, consultant said, 'Consultants have only one thing in common – they say yes.'

That is probably much too hard on consultants. After all, what they do is reflect client need. And clients can too often be unsure, unclear and uncertain about what they want from outside advisors. But with the realization by companies that marketing has to be the core of the business, there is confusion about who is best for what. It used to be easy: chief executives called in high-powered management consultants like McKinsey or Bain to deal with 'strategic' issues, while the marketing director might deal with – or oversee others doing so – a mix of lower-level strategic and/or tactical problems: advertising, brand doctoring, new product development, direct marketing, process consultancy (to give a bit of 'bolt-on' resource). Either his/her minions, or people quite outside the marketing department's scope, trafficked in sales promotion, design, exhibitions and so on. With corporate identity the chairman usually picked the pretty new logo. Too many companies still operate this way.

But clients are changing their structures as their needs change. Their growing obsession with their image and/or brands will entail a shakeout in how consultants operate and what they have to offer. Companies are beginning to take back responsibility for the overall strategy as they develop more centralized objectives. Successful consultants will sense these trends and play on their strengths while broadening their skills.

At the top, the big international management consultants – both the independents and those allied to accountancy firms – still hold the high ground, but there are signs that even large multinationals are also turning to less structured 'thinkers' for a more lateral and less orthodox approach.

There is also a wide middle ground of consultants who can advise on marketing strategy and/or tactics; the best have probably worked in companies before, have proven knowledge of other markets and can exploit their strengths in both branding and positioning. They are usually found by word of mouth. Another added advantage they offer is to act as temporary marketing muscle for companies with skill shortages, or those who have pruned back their marketing departments too hard.

The role that advertising agencies play is set to change substantially. They are currently grappling with what is for many of them the unhappy novelty of recession, while trying to work out their approach to European/international expansion to meet their clients' needs. But the heart of the matter is the shift in the balance of power back to the client as marketing strategy gets decided at the highest level. Do agencies then get involved in a more strategic way? After all, all consultants ache to reach the top decision makers.

Clients want promotional strategies coordinated across disciplines. They do not want to spend a fortune on media advertising if a more cost-effective way can be found. What is happening with consumer goods companies will spread right across the board: agencies will have to juggle an understanding of clients' needs for coordination and orchestration of all the instruments that have to play the same music to different clusters of population, with a renewed focus on creativity to make their campaigns stand out in the media circus. Clients will also want a more sophisticated approach to media planning. But the most swingeing impact on agencies' culture will be changes in the way they are paid.

Henkel, the German chemicals to detergents group, started paying agencies on a fee-based system in 1989, calculated (among other criteria) according to a brand's market share and how well known it is to consumers. The company believes it motivates agencies to perform to the highest standard. Other companies are following this route – the method by which all other consultants are paid. That is allied with the move by the big multinationals to 'align' agencies internationally as a way of ensuring consistency and loyalty.

There are some encouraging signs that the big international advertising agencies have been successful in getting clients to approach them for more strategic advice about pan-European expansion. A recent (1990) survey for *The Director* magazine asked marketing directors in over 250 major European companies what sort of consultants they were turning to as they faced the Single Market. While 35% said they were using management consultants, the largest percentage, 57%, said international advertising agencies. The comparative British figures were 59% management consultants and 78% for advertising agencies.

In general, the demand by companies for coordination and creativity runs right across the marketing mix. That means agencies in advertising, sales promotion, direct marketing, public relations and design are in the midst of trying to decide how to cater for their clients' pan-European and global needs.

There is no pat solution for the agencies. After a decade of over-hasty expansion within both Europe and the US chastened agencies have retrenched (see Case 6.4 below). One design consultant believes that the answer for creative consultancies is to maintain a strong, central core of talent which operates as a hotshop of ideas and can travel to clients on a world-wide basis. While having local offices will probably be necessary to ensure that cultural nuances are taken into account and for market research, the centralization of clients' strategies will be echoed in the consultancies.

In addition, if trends in the US are followed here, there will probably be a rise in 'marketing communications' consultants who try to straddle across the disciplines. But these will not be megagroupings of different services: one-stop shopping has yet to prove itself.

Although clients will always dictate the service they require, they could help agencies perform better by reviewing their agency management policy. One important step they need to make is to further long-term relationships with agencies of all types. *Ad hoc* research, design or sales promotion helps neither an agency's security nor its ability to understand the problems. It is hard to believe that even in this day and age there are companies who keep 15 different design agencies on their roster and ask them to pitch for each new job.

Case 6.4　Global ad agencies: a trend or a fad?

Although the mergers and acquisition activity in the advertising industry over the past decade resulted in the disappearance of some of the best-known agency names in the US and other countries into huge mega-agencies, the jury is still out as to how well these advertising conglomerates actually serve their clients' needs.

The British advertising agency Saatchi and Saatchi led the trend of buying well-established American agencies such as Ted Bates & Co., Backer Spielvogel, Compton, Dancer–Fitzgerald–Sample and Campbell Mithun. The WPP Group plc, another British agency, bought the J. Walter Thompson and Ogilvy & Mather agencies.

Product conflicts abounded and many clients shifted their business to other agencies. Warner Lambert ended a 30-year relationship with the Ted Bates agency and moved $68 million in billings to J. Walter Thompson and Young & Rubicam. Colgate–Palmolive, a long-time client of Ted Bates, left that agency and reallocated $100 million worth of billings to Young & Rubicam and Foote, Cone & Belding.

Theoretically, the use of such agencies makes sense for large multinationals that have global brands and/or those that wish to standardize their appeal and message. Giant ad agencies with offices in countries around the globe make a persuasive case that they can best handle the diverse needs of global companies in a creative, yet cost-efficient, manner.

Despite their global reach, a number of mega-agencies are experiencing managerial or financial problems, as they try to assimilate and integrate the many new additions to their core agencies. Whether they have taken over

continues

continued

other agencies entirely, purchased equity holdings in overseas agencies, established wholly owned subsidiaries or simply contracted with local agencies to represent them, the practical difficulties of coordinating a world-wide agency network have generally proved to be considerable.

Still, the rise of global agencies has made it possible for some large companies to consolidate their world-wide advertising work at one or two agencies. In the early 1980s, for example, Colgate–Palmolive had 13 ad agencies and within three years narrowed its list to three agencies and now uses only two. Gillette also uses only two agencies to coordinate global advertising campaigns of its brands.

AT&T's International Communication Services group is represented around the world by Young & Rubicam, which assigns an account manager to coordinate the global campaigns. The agency designates a 'lead contact' in each local market, and these individuals work with the global account manager and AT&T's advertising and product managers to arrive at strategic advertising plans. Y&R's overseas offices make creative recommendations through their lead contacts to the global account manager, and locally based Y&R managers handle media purchases and placement in each market. The global account manager at Y&R serves as a communications link between AT&T's executives and the agency's people abroad.

Appendix B   Global advertising regulations and barriers

Advertising across national borders – including the free movement of actual materials and services needed to create and distribute advertisements – has become slightly easier to accomplish in the past five years. This trend is the key finding of a new report from the New York-based International Advertising Association, entitled *Barriers to Trade and Investment in Advertising: Government Regulation and Industry Self-Regulation in 53 Countries*.

However, the study's author, Dr Jean Boddewyn, professor of marketing and international business at Baruch College, City University of New York, also found that for every country that had made headway toward deregulation, another had moved in the opposite direction. The important distinction, in his view, was more qualitative than quantitative. 'The specific types of restrictions some countries have added are not necessarily the most significant ones from the advertiser's perspective,' he said, 'while on the more critical issues, like the ability to own a local agency, there has been clear progress.' (See Table 6.1.) Although it is now easier to import foreign tools-of-trade materials (non-saleable items such as filmstrips, artwork and manuals for employee education) without having to pay duties on them, there has been a small increase in the total number of countries restricting the importation of foreign-produced advertisements (mainly commercials) through high customs duties, import quotas and total bans. (The number of countries with total bans has not increased, however.) Indeed, the use of foreign-produced advertisements in local media remains the most heavily regulated aspect of international advertising.

Governments are typically motivated to adopt policies and regulations favouring local producers, writers, actors and others by the desire to generate jobs, strengthen national identity and limit the drain on foreign exchange. In addition, unions may play an important role as well in trying to preserve jobs for their members. Usually, exceptions are made only when foreign locations or talent are absolutely necessary.

Nevertheless, multinational advertising agencies that wish to expand their foreign networks have begun to find the door to foreign investment wide open in most countries. Of the countries surveyed, 68% now allow full foreign ownership of a local agency; three countries allow majority foreign ownership; one permits 50% foreign ownership; and 10% allow a foreign owner only a minority position. Only three countries ban totally foreign ownership: Indonesia, Nigeria and Pakistan. Their rationale for restricting foreign ownership is that otherwise the development of local agencies would be constrained.

Tolerance of the use of foreign languages in local advertising is quite high in most countries, probably because it is not a widespread practice. Foreign copy is sometimes used in special situations where the advertiser wants to target foreign-speaking ethnic groups or expatriates, or the use of foreign expressions adds credibility or prestige to a product, or a standardized advertisement in a particular language will be understood by a large number of people in different countries. Foreign product names are generally unrestricted except in Quebec, Taiwan, India, and in some Arab nations that boycott Israeli products. Television and radio, two media often under government control, tend to carry tougher restrictions than others.

Boddewyn expected that in the years ahead, regulation will continue its pendulum swing. Local political and economic circumstances will probably bring a more relaxed regulatory climate to several countries. Contributing factors will include more imports (Korea, Nigeria and Taiwan), fewer labour restrictions (Thailand and the UK), economic liberalization (Hungary) and the US–Canada Free Trade Agreement. At the same time, however, increased limitations are expected in 10 other nations, mostly due to nationalist and protectionist motivations. These countries are Costa Rica, El Salvador, Greece, Guatemala, Mexico, the Netherlands, the Philippines, Portugal, South Africa and Spain.

New technologies will also generate concerns in the near future. For instance, satellite broadcasts purposely or inadvertently reaching foreign countries represent an area ripe for regulation although such broadcasts currently are confined mostly to Europe. On the other hand, cable retransmission of foreign programmes and commercials is growing steadily, raising the question of which standards to apply.

The push by advertisers and advertising agencies for deregulation will continue, with the EC, the OECD and General Agreement on Tariffs and Trade (GATT) all playing an important part in the outcome. Some governments, such as the US and the UK, are already using these forums to press for further liberalization, and the US is exerting pressure on countries, such as South Korea and Taiwan, that are eager to retain broad access to the US market. At the same time, developing nations are likely to remain protective of their new industries, including service industries like advertising.

There is also concern at some of the directives coming from the EC which could affect promotional strategies. Companies, either through their own offices or industry associations, should keep well abreast of EC thinking on these topics in order to be able to make sure their voices are heard at the early stages.

Summary

- The best-laid strategic plans and organizational charts will prove of little use if not translated into the sharp end of promotion and sales. The problem of the global/local divide applies just as much to how companies actually reach their customers.

- Advertising as a component of global marketing strategy has undergone significant change over the past decade in the face of intensifying competition and the transformation of many countries and regions by external events. Many developments, among them the sweeping shift from communism to various degrees of capitalism in Eastern Europe, the EC Single Market, the unification of West and East Germany, the democratization of much of Latin America – along with the severe economic problems in some Latin American nations – are causing companies to rethink the way they promote and sell their products outside their home countries.

- In recent years some well-known consumer products companies, like McDonald's, Coca-Cola, PepsiCo, Levi Strauss and Sony, have done well with 'global brands' advertised in much the same manner around the world. Their successes have prompted renewed interest in centralized advertising campaigns among other multinationals, although many products are not well suited to a global branding strategy.

- Instead of a global orientation, some multinationals are opting for regional advertising strategies. The most obvious manifestation of this approach is in Europe, where many companies that previously used a country-by-country

approach are planning and implementing pan-European advertising programmes to take advantage of the EC's increasing integration.

- A further complication to devising advertising strategies is the still-strong
persistence of the 'local is best' view, which runs counter to the trend of
adopting more uniform advertising messages globally or regionally.
Companies with that viewpoint localize their ad strategies even more than
in the past, leaving country subsidiaries to run major campaigns with very
little input from parent headquarters.

- Classical advertising has traditionally been the dominant player in the promotional mix. It is indeed a powerful tool. But the next decade could see the
final disappearance of the 'above and below the line' distinctions that have
divided advertising from the other, perceived as less glamorous, activities like
sales promotion, direct marketing, sponsorship, exhibitions and public relations
as companies move toward a more integrated communications package.

- Whatever companies conclude about the proper location and structure of
their marketing operations, the need to keep close to the customers, and to
put as much decision-making power as possible into the hands of the executives in contact with them, ensures that sales will remain a fundamentally
local operation.

- In terms of using external consultants, companies are beginning to take
back responsibility for the overall strategy as they develop more centralized objectives. Successful consultants will sense these trends and play on
their strengths while broadening their skills.

- Advertising across national borders – including the free movement of
actual materials and services needed to create and distribute advertisements
– has become slightly easier to accomplish in the past five years.

Checklist

In terms of establishing consistent marketing programmes, has your company:

(1) Developed a position on advertising in terms of crossing borders?

(2) Found ways to overcome coordinating promotional strategies in different
countries not just because of different brand positioning but because of
local resistance?

(3) Ensured that the entire promotional package is well orchestrated –
for example, coordinating the advertising, sales promotion and public
relations advisors to make sure the messages are consistent?

(4) Evolved a promotional strategy that reflects the balance adequately in
terms of centralized/decentralized decisions making?

(5) Used corporate advertising in new markets to help boost the position of the products/services that are being or will be offered?

(6) Formed a clear understanding of just how the rules and regulations of advertising and other promotional techniques affect the company's stance in different markets?

(7) Organized and coordinated the sales teams both to reflect the tactical needs of each market but also in light of longer-term market developments in customers and distribution systems?

References

Advertising: leading the great consultancy race. *The Director*, pp 48-53, July 1990

Boddewyn, Dr J. (1989). *Barriers to Trade and Investment in Advertising: Government Regulation and Industry Self-Regulation in 53 Countries*. New York: International Advertising Association

7

Setting the price

Introduction

The globalization of marketing has put tremendous pressure on multinational pricing systems. Over the past few decades, as companies moved from purely domestic operations to exporting and then to overseas manufacturing and marketing, they had to transform their pricing structures. Those structures, originally set up to function in a single-market setting, had to be adapted to the much greater heterogeneity of the international environment.

Today, perhaps for the first time, the operating environment that international companies face is replete with complexities, including competition, an increasing number of global players, rapid technological change and high-speed communication among markets.

Executives of internationally oriented firms must now grapple with many questions to which there are no simple or precise answers; for example,

- What is the best approach for setting prices world-wide?
- Which variables should be considered in arriving at prices for foreign customers?
- What level of importance should be attached to each variable?
- Where in the global company should pricing decisions be made?
- Should prices vary across markets? by customer types? over time?
- Should price play an active or passive role in a company's international competitive strategy?

Most executives are quick to recognize that pricing decisions cannot be made in isolation, since pricing interacts with and affects all other marketing policy variables. Among other things, prices do the following:

- Influence customers' perception of value;
- Determine the level of intermediaries' motivation;
- Have an impact on promotional spending and strategy;
- Compensate for weaknesses in other elements of the marketing mix.

This chapter considers the following aspects of pricing policy which confront many companies:

- The factors affecting global pricing
- Centralized pricing decisions
- Decentralized pricing decisions
- Resolving centralization/decentralization conflicts
- Different approaches to price setting
- Options in export pricing
- Transfer pricing policies
- Factors affecting transfer pricing policies
- Facing the European market.

The factors affecting global pricing

Global managers readily acknowledge the critical role of prices in overseas marketing success. After all, prices do have a measurable impact on sales and directly affect profitability. They often invite competitive reaction and, indeed, can be driven down by determined competitors. Conversely, they can escalate to unreasonable levels because of tariffs, taxes, necessary increases in markups to cover rising costs and so on. They can complicate a firm's marketing strategy in unforeseen ways when price variations among different markets lead to grey-market imports. Finally, prices are one of the most flexible elements of the marketing mix, because they can usually be changed relatively quickly.

Consequently, multinationals take great time and care in establishing pricing policies and setting prices for international customers. In addition to the basic factors of production cost, demand and competition that must be considered, pricing decisions for the global market must take into account such variables as exchange rate fluctuations and duties as well as external costs, for example documentation, freight and insurance.

Within the large constellation of factors that influence pricing for international markets, the five discussed below stand out as most important.

Nature of product or industry

A specialized product, or one with a technological edge, gives a company price flexibility. In many markets there is no local production of the item, government-imposed import barriers are minimal and importing firms all face similar price escalation factors. Under such circumstances, producers are able to remain competitive with little adjustment in price strategy.

A relatively low level of price competition usually leads to administered prices and a static role for pricing in the marketing mix. In such instances a 'skimming' price strategy is often used. (Skimming involves the introduction of a product at a high price. Eventually, however, as price competition develops and technological advantages shrink, specialized and highly technical firms must make more and more market-based exceptions to their previously uniform pricing strategies.)

Pricing strategies are also influenced by industry-specific factors, such as fluctuations in the price and availability of raw materials. In order to reduce uncertainty, a growing practice of companies is to negotiate fixed-price agreements with suppliers before making their own bids for major contracts.

Another problem for corporations in some industries is predatory pricing by particularly aggressive competitors. Recently, that strategy has been pursued mainly by market-share-hungry new players, most notably those from newly industrialized countries (NICs) in Asia.

Location of production facility

Despite the proliferation of foreign-owned manufacturing facilities around the world, many companies' only participation in the global market is by exporting products they make in their home countries. The usual reason is that the volume of their sales abroad is simply not large enough to justify foreign sourcing and manufacturing.

When production is kept at home, a company is tied to conditions prevailing in that market, a circumstance that reduces its pricing flexibility in its export markets. Economic and political developments at home – and even natural disasters – can force export prices up at a time when local producers in the overseas market or exporters from third countries are not similarly affected and can keep prices low.

One example might be a trade embargo observed by only a few governments. Because of the boycott, the supply of certain needed raw materials would be reduced, driving up the cost of making some products. Competitive products made in nonboycotting countries would obviously enjoy a clear price advantage in export markets.

In contrast, companies that manufacture abroad often enjoy greater pricing flexibility both in the countries in which they are located and in export markets. In addition to being better able to calibrate production to local demand and competitive conditions, those multinationals find it easier to respond to foreign exchange fluctuations.

Distribution system

The channels of distribution a company uses dictate much in international pricing, particularly export pricing. When a company is able to distribute its products through its own overseas subsidiaries, it has greater control over final prices, including the ability to adjust prices rapidly, as well as first-hand knowledge of market conditions.

An exporter working with independent distributors, however, usually finds that it can control only the landed price (the exporter's price to the distributor). As one might expect, many exporters are concerned about the difficulty of maintaining price levels. Some firms report that distributors mark up prices substantially – up to 200% in some countries. Using manufacturers' representatives gives a company greater price control, but this method is used less frequently by international companies, which usually require the services of a 'full-service' intermediary in the export market.

Direct selling to end users is required in many industries, especially those involving large systems or technical equipment. In the case of sales to government agencies, a protracted bidding process and negotiations preclude the use of list or other standard prices.

Firms often attempt to establish more direct channels of distribution for reaching their customers in overseas markets. Indeed, that is sometimes a motivation for establishing a company-owned subsidiary. By reducing the number of intermediaries between the manufacturer and the customer, the adverse effects of successive markups can be avoided.

Location and environment of the foreign market

Pricing is affected by factors not always immediately perceived as price related. For instance, climatic conditions in foreign markets may necessitate costly product or distribution modifications, and prices must be adjusted to cover those extra or special expenses. A maker of soft drink equipment must treat its machines intended for tropical markets to prevent rust corrosion, while an agribusiness must take into account climate, soil conditions and the country's infrastructure before making any bid.

Foreign currency differentials

Economic factors, such as inflation, exchange rate fluctuations and price controls, may hinder market entry and effectiveness. These factors are a major concern to most firms. The dollar's unusual strength in the first half of the 1980s, in fact, led a number of companies to introduce compensating adjustments as part of their pricing strategies.

Since currency fluctuations are cyclical, exporting companies that find themselves blessed with a price advantage when their currency is undervalued must carry an extra burden when their currency is overvalued. Companies committed to serving international markets must be creative, pursuing different pricing strategies during different periods. Appropriate strategies practised by a broad cross-section of multinationals are presented in Table 7.1.

Centralized pricing decisions

International pricing decisions are centralized in most global companies. There are several reasons for this:

(1) Increasing globalization of markets requires greater uniformity of prices across markets. The existence of differing prices from country to country often leads to grey-market imports, that is the sourcing of a product from low-price countries by unauthorized intermediaries for sale in high-price countries. This results in the creation of a distribution channel parallel to authorized channels but not under the control of the manufacturer in any way.

(2) Global companies encounter the same competitors in many markets, requiring globally coordinated competitive strategies. A fragmented strategy often leads to suboptimal results.

(3) At some companies, pricing is closely related to production-volume planning. Since volume planning is usually done at the corporate level, it requires centrally directed prices.

(4) Typically, the parent company wants to forecast its annual revenues world-wide. Therefore, it must be able to estimate the sales of all its operations, including its overseas subsidiaries. This often dictates setting prices centrally or, at least, imposing some guidelines for the prices to be set by subsidiaries.

(5) Many corporations seek tight control over pricing of their 'global' brands, that is, those aimed at a homogeneous market segment in many countries and positioned similarly from one market to another. To create a uniform

Table 7.1   International pricing strategies under varying currency conditions.

When the domestic currency is weak	When the domestic currency is strong
Stress price benefits	Engage in nonprice competition by improving quality, delivery and aftersale service
Expand product line and add more costly features	Improve productivity and engage in vigorous cost reduction
Shift sourcing manufacturing to domestic market	Shift sourcing and manufacturing overseas
Exploit export opportunities in all markets	Give priority to exports to countries with relatively strong currencies
Use a full-costing approach, but employ marginal-cost pricing to penetrate new or competitive markets	Trim profit margins and use marginal-cost pricing pricing
Speed repatriation of foreign-earned income and collections	Keep the foreign-earned income in host-country; slow down collections
Minimize expenditures in local or host-country currency	Maximize expenditures in local or host-country currency
Buy needed services (advertising, insurance, transportation, and so on) in domestic market	Buy needed services abroad and pay for them in local currencies
Bill foreign customers in their own currency	Bill foreign customers in the domestic currency

Source: S. Tamer Cavusgil, Michigan State University.

image across national boundaries, not only the product, but the price, must be consistent. The price is normally set by corporate headquarters relative to the prices of competing local products in each market. The policy might state, for example, that the brand must always be premium priced relative to local products and that 'premium' is defined as, say, 20% above the price of the most expensive locally produced item. Such a policy limits local autonomy in setting prices. An example of a global brand priced in this manner is Grand Metropolitan's Smirnoff vodka. Gillette is another company that seeks a global brand image for its products (see Case 6.1).

Also important to a company's pricing policies and practices is the proximity of its overseas markets to one another. When markets are close geographically, a country subsidiary cannot set prices for its own market in isolation. No subsidiary can mark up the price to the point at which customers will seek to import the product rather than buy locally. Centralized pricing management by the parent company or a regional office is often the only way to prevent subsidiaries from undermining one another's pricing programmes.

Case 7.1 AT&T and Gillette

Telecommunications group AT&T has found that in pricing decisions central coordination is essential. Therefore, pricing is primarily the responsibility of business group product managers at headquarters. Once set, prices are adjusted locally within certain parameters to meet country-specific conditions. For instance, AT&T's International Communications Services (ICS) group must be particularly sensitive to both volume and technology in setting prices. But the largest controllable cost is settlement – the amount paid to foreign telecommunications agencies for completing calls. AT&T is continuing to negotiate lower settlement rates and lower international prices for customers. AT&T has reduced international prices more than 40% in the last 10 years.

At consumer products company Gillette, subsidiary executives have the authority to set their own prices as long as they stay within the centrally planned positioning strategy. Desired price relationships vis-à-vis competing brands and products are defined by product executives at headquarters. Within these parameters, subsidiary executives are responsible for setting prices in their own markets. 'Our local people realize that their objective is to sell the product at the highest price consistent with product development, the local competitive situation and central positioning strategies,' said Bruce Cleverly, vice president of marketing at Gillette North Atlantic's shaving and personal care group.

Decentralized pricing decisions

Although global companies generally maintain centralized control over local prices, they do allow subsidiaries to alter prices when warranted by local conditions. In some situations, subsidiaries may, in fact, receive complete pricing autonomy because of competitive considerations.

Headquarters executives cite the following reasons for giving subsidiaries or distributors leeway to set local prices:

- Timing. There may be a need for a quick response to price changes made by competitors.
- Relative market share. If the brand is one of many in a local market, the subsidiary will be forced to follow the prices set by the market leaders. Conversely, market leadership allows greater pricing freedom.

- End-user characteristics. If the local market is relatively poor, with most consumers at lower income levels, the local subsidiary may have to deviate from centrally determined pricing guidelines.
- Specific local cost factors. Value-added taxes and the costs of adapting a product to a particular market may demand greater price flexibility in some countries.
- Transportation costs. These vary widely from country to country owing to the nature of the distribution infrastructure, the extent of unionization in the transport industries and the stipulations in local distribution laws.
- Economic and financial conditions. Interest rates and inflation often cause local divisions to sway from corporate pricing guidelines. Local prices must reflect currency realities if earnings are to be eventually transferred to the home country.
- Capacity utilization. A subsidiary with excess capacity in a local market may choose to lower prices to boost demand, while tight capacity may suggest an advantage in charging higher prices.

A medium-sized multinational that has adopted a decentralized price policy is the Taiwan-based personal computer firm, Acer. The home office in Lungtan, Taiwan consults closely with its regional and country offices to determine market conditions and formulate general market strategy and objectives, such as targets for net revenue, market share and the growth rate for gross sales. Local distributors are also encouraged – and given autonomy in devising their own value-added solutions, which allow them in some cases to sell the same product for different prices depending on the nature of the total package.

According to Max Wu, vice president for marketing promotion, Acer's marketing and sales headquarters in Taiwan provides technical, logistical, promotional and finance services. However, on the basis of the above objectives as well as cost information provided by Lungtan, local subsidiaries receive virtually total autonomy in setting their retail prices.

Resolving centralization/decentralization conflicts

How do global corporations resolve the conflicting needs for centralization and decentralization of pricing decisions? Typically, the corporate office sets policy and issues general guidelines to which the overseas subsidiaries and distributors must adhere. The guidelines are typically written at the beginning of each fiscal year – or more often, if necessary. Pricing policies reflect both the general direction prices should take during the course of the year and the company's underlying global strategy. For instance, an American manufacturing company's 1990 policy was that prices were not to rise more than 1% over 1989 prices. The company adopted this policy in an attempt to fend off its chief rival, Japan's Komatsu.

Once a broad pricing strategy is set by a company's home office, subsidiaries and distributors are allowed to make adjustments locally because of the considerations listed above. In some companies, the degree of pricing flexibility given to the subsidiary is defined precisely. For example, headquarters may allow local prices to deviate 5–15% from the centrally established prices.

In practice, pricing freedom is transferred to local subsidiaries from headquarters through three main mechanisms:

- A system of discounts on sales to intermediate customers;
- Credit arrangements and terms of sale;
- Transfer prices charged to subsidiaries.

Most global companies start out by setting a single world-wide price, sometimes referred to as the list price. However, the effective price or the price charged to intermediate customers (for example overseas distributors, representatives, agents) is determined by a discount system. The discount rate varies for different customers and territories on the basis of competitive considerations, exchange rates, landing costs and so on. The discount structure, which is reviewed frequently, thus becomes a vehicle for transferring greater pricing autonomy to subsidiaries and intermediate customers. The company as a whole benefits as a result of a pricing system that is responsive to local needs. Similarly, credit terms and other variable conditions of sale have a direct impact on the final cost to subsidiaries and intermediate customers.

Finally, transfer prices charged to subsidiaries can also be adjusted to increase the subsidiaries' pricing flexibility.

Different approaches to price setting

Clearly, there is no single approach to international pricing that is best for every company and every situation. Nevertheless, at most companies a product's price starts with a 'floor price', which is the lowest possible price at which the product may be retailed or wholesaled (depending on the nature of the company). The floor price is derived from the total cost of bringing the product to market plus a corporate markup. Costs typically include R&D, raw materials, processing, transportation, distribution, marketing and administrative overhead.

Arriving at the correct floor price is not as easy as it seems. As the following examples suggest, the process is complicated because of differences in cost accounting practices, company policies (such as whether or not to factor in domestic overhead), global manufacturing and sourcing factors, and so on.

Seiko Epson, the Japanese computer peripherals manufacturer, sets floor prices at headquarters after considering costs, recommendations from executives in the company's various manufacturing divisions and country markets and a corporate profit markup target for the particular product. Starting from this figure, product division presidents at headquarters establish flexibility parameters. According to N. Niwa, deputy general manager of the firm's Marketing and Sales Division, low-end products – such as Epson's LQ-500 series printer – are usually restricted to a variability range of less than 5%, while the prices charged for high-end products like computers and laser-jet printers can range from 10–25% above or below the base price. Salespeople in headquarters are allowed to negotiate prices within these parameters with country-level sales affiliates. In view of the rapid technological change and rapid entry of new products in this industry, this sort of price flexibility is considered essential by marketing staff.

Hewlett-Packard leaves the responsibility for setting floor prices ('factory base prices'), which are derived from production costs, to the product divisions. In the past, factory base prices coincided with US prices, but that is no longer the case because of the development of overseas production facilities and sourcing. In calculating floor prices, a currency differential (premium) is added when necessary. Management then assesses the competition in major markets and builds an appropriate profit premium into the price.

One US manufacturing company sets the same list price (FOB ('free on board') factory) in the US and abroad. In arriving at the discount structure for its dealers, this industrial manufacturing multinational takes into account the exchange rate, local competition and a reasonable profit margin for the dealers. Final prices, which tend to be at the high end of the range in each product category, also reflect elements of the company's strengths in providing service, technical support and a comprehensive warranty.

Options in export pricing

Companies have three basic options in setting prices on exports:

(1) Rigid cost-plus pricing. The complexity of export pricing has caused many managers to cling to rigid cost-plus pricing, a formula that ensures margins but may push the final price so high that the company becomes uncompetitive in major markets. The foreign list price is set by adding international customer costs and a gross margin to domestic

manufacturing costs. The final price to the foreign customer includes administrative and R&D overhead costs, transportation, insurance, packaging, marketing, documentation and customs charges as well as profit margins for both the distributor and the manufacturer. Cost-plus pricing is a static element of the marketing mix, since it cannot be changed to any significant extent and ignores the issue of sales volume and total contribution to profits from overseas markets.

(2)   Flexible cost-plus pricing. This strategy sets list prices in the same way as the more rigid system but allows for price variations in special circumstances. For example, discounts may be applied to the final price, depending on the customer, the size of the order or the strength of local competition. Although there is more room to adapt export prices to local conditions, the primary objective of this approach is still to maintain profit margins. It, too, is thus an essentially static element of the marketing mix.

(3)   Dynamic incremental pricing. This method assumes that fixed costs are incurred regardless of the company's export sales performance. Therefore, it seeks to recover only variable and international customer costs in export prices while adding in a partial overhead factor rather than the full overhead load. This approach enables the company to sell its exports at very competitive prices, perhaps enlarging its market share.

Most companies that use dynamic incremental pricing do so only under special circumstances. For example, one US industrial MNC (multinational corporation) negotiates 'one-shot' deals with its distributors, offering them low prices when it has a sufficient quantity of the product, when the sales potential is good or when competitive pressure necessitates aggressive pricing.

In some cases, dynamic incremental pricing helps a company introduce a product to a market. Under this strategy, also known as 'penetration' pricing, the introductory, or 'market floor', price is the lowest possible. The objective is to gain as much market share as possible in the shortest time. Once the product attains a sufficient market share, prices tend to increase slowly.

Over the past few decades, Japanese and Korean multinationals in particular have successfully used penetration strategies in the US and in other Western markets, often inviting dumping charges by local marketers. When carried to extremes, however, as when a company charges a price lower than the cost of making the product or the product's domestic price, penetration pricing may run foul of local antidumping laws, which are in effect in many countries.

Whereas in penetration strategies introductory prices start low and slowly rise, in 'skimming' a company introduces the product into a market at an artificially inflated price, often while limiting distribution. This can be an effective method for launching innovative, high-tech items, such as advanced consumer electronics devices or trendy products. A certain segment of the market will pay premium prices to be first to have such things, which are usually introduced amid great excitement, highly visible advertising and extensive media coverage. As with a penetration strategy, the price slowly comes into line with the product's price in other countries. Dynamic incremental pricing also implies skimming when it coincides with a dominant market share position, as other companies cannot afford to ignore the price leader's practices. Several years ago, Cummins Engine reduced its engine prices dramatically in Europe, the Middle East and the Far East to about 70% of its previous prices. This strategy was successful in limiting the inroads made by the company's Japanese competition.

Transfer pricing policies

One of the thorniest problems global companies grapple with when they venture beyond their home-country borders is transfer pricing (also known as intracompany pricing). The prices at which units of the same company sell to each other have a far-reaching effect on the company's success because they influence everything from foreign subsidiary performance to executive compensation to tax obligations. There has never been a single 'best' way to set transfer prices, one that satisfies both the parent company and its foreign affiliates (not to mention the tax collectors in all countries concerned). Nor does any system meet all the needs of production, marketing and finance equally well.

Global companies attempt to manage their corporate families' internal prices primarily for two reasons. First, transfer pricing can become a vehicle for repatriating profits from those countries that have remittance controls. In the extreme case, funds may be blocked by the central bank, and transfer pricing may be the only means of getting earnings out of the country. Second, transfer pricing can be a way to shift profits out of high-tax countries and into low-tax ones. Underlying both objectives is the desire to foster corporation-wide efficiency. While individual units may show poor performance, the company as a whole can achieve optimal results by means of careful transfer pricing. For this reason, multinationals typically centralize transfer pricing under the direction of the chief financial officer.

Companies have a number of transfer pricing strategies available. Products can be sold to members of the same corporate family at cost or a variation of direct cost, at market prices, at inflated prices or at some combination of these. Some global corporations use different transfer pricing methods for different purposes, accepting the cost and complexity of maintaining more than one system. Others opt for the simplicity of a single approach, accepting the inevitable deficiencies of whatever system they choose. The following are among the possible alternatives.

Actual cost

Actual cost, which is sometimes viewed as the absence of a transfer price, can be used for intracompany transactions. Manufacturing facilities are treated as cost centres rather than profit centres, an approach that resolves many internal disputes over allocation of profits. A disadvantage of the method is that it leaves the cost centres with little inducement to make investments, leading to additional inefficiencies for the company as a whole. Another problem is that tax authorities generally do not accept this technique, unless some taxable profits are allocated to the supplying unit.

Standard cost

Standard cost, unlike actual cost, has the advantage of identifying efficiencies or inefficiencies in the supplying unit. It also facilitates 'management by exception' decision making, in which variations from standard cost signal the need for additional investigation and attention by management. A major shortcoming is that standard costing often requires management to make arbitrary assumptions and leaves the company vulnerable to expending time unproductively in debates on how to set the standards.

Modified cost

Modified cost is useful in promoting achievement of strategic objectives. For example, actual or standard costs are sometimes adjusted to encourage more extensive use of certain products or services. Companies that expect to have unused capacity for a time often lower their transfer prices in order to provide incremental contributions to the coverage of 'sunk' costs. Among the modifications available are variable costs (those costs of materials, labour and overheads that vary directly with the number of units produced), marginal costs (the costs of producing one more unit) and full absorption costs (costs that would not change if sales to other business units stopped, for example the cost of shared factory overheads).

Market price

Prevailing external market prices (arm's-length prices) are often viewed as the best transfer pricing mechanism for external reporting. Because this approach removes internal bias and facilitates validation, it appeals to outside parties, such as tax authorities. From a performance evaluation perspective, however, market prices may be unfair because they give the supplying business unit the entire profit on the transaction, including the benefit of any cost reductions due to global efficiencies. To share the advantage of lower costs equitably, transfer prices must be lower than market price.

Modified market price

Market prices can be adjusted to reflect specific characteristics of the goods or services involved. For example, they may be reduced to reflect lower marketing or distribution costs that occur in external markets. Ordinarily, this will help resolve perceived inequities among supplying and receiving business units. However, a supplying unit that has no excess capacity will still feel unfairly penalized if the lower price cuts into the profits it would otherwise earn on external sales. In such a case, the external profit is a relevant opportunity cost and it should be factored into the transfer price.

Negotiated price

Negotiated prices are determined by bargaining between the buying and selling units. Although some executives may argue that this technique results in an arm's-length transaction that is just as valid as an external market price, its use in evaluating the performance of subsidiaries has some risks. For instance, negotiators may fail to reach agreement, which could result in counterproductive and expensive procurement of goods and services from outside the firm. Another problem is that excessive internal competition can undermine the achievement of congruent goals among business units and result in a serious loss of cooperation.

Contract price

A variation of the negotiated price method is a price agreed upon at the time the firm's business plan is adopted. Such a 'contract' price eliminates variations that result from centralized sourcing decisions beyond the control of managers of foreign operations. One drawback of the method is that it does not pass on price hikes in raw materials to marketing units; as a result, it removes the marketing unit's incentive to recover any inflationary and foreign exchange losses through third-party pricing. However contract prices can be set to reflect capacity utilization and indexed.

Factors affecting transfer pricing policies

How do global companies choose from among these transfer pricing possibilities? Many factors are involved in deciding which transfer price to use and whether to use different prices for reporting external and internal performance. Sometimes one issue is of overriding importance to a company, clearly dictating a particular pricing system. More often, however, a company's situation is mixed, making the choice highly complex and probably contentious. For most companies, the decision involves some combination of the considerations discussed below.

Local taxes

Perhaps the most significant concern in setting transfer prices is the local tax rate and pertinent tax regulations. The use of transfer pricing to shift profits into local jurisdictions that have relatively lower corporate tax rates normally results in lower overall income taxes. However, high prices for capital assets increase the depreciation allowances for the business units that receive them. This lowers overall taxes when the assets are transferred from lower- to higher-rate jurisdictions.

An effective transfer pricing system should deal with changes in import–export duties, income taxes, excise taxes and so on, in a way that minimizes these taxes overall. Generally, lower transfer prices mean lower levies; prices in excess of certain thresholds may result in higher import duties, especially if they are assessed on an *ad valorem* basis. Similarly, keeping transfer prices low can reduce local value-added taxes. Value-added taxes are based on the value added within the taxing jurisdiction and are factored into the price at the next sales level.

Currency fluctuations

Transfer prices can be adjusted so as to balance the effect of fluctuating currencies when one subsidiary operates in an environment of low-level inflation and another in a climate of rampant inflation.

Subsidiary profits

Still another use of transfer pricing is to manipulate the profit position of a subsidiary. For example, startups often require substantial corporate assistance, which can be provided in the form of lower purchase prices from, or higher sales prices to, other company units. In this way, a market niche can be carved out more quickly for the startup and its long-term survival guaranteed.

Expense accounting

Transfer prices can also be used to advantage when the host government imposes restrictions on allowable deductions for expenses. Sometimes certain services, such as product development or strategic planning assistance, are provided to the subsidiary but cannot be charged because of restrictions. In that case, costs for those services can be recouped by increasing the transfer prices of com-ponents sold to the units.

Joint venture support

Similarly, transfer pricing can help recoup expenses from a joint venture, especially if there are restrictions on repatriation of profits. Lowering the prices of products and services to a parent reduces the outflow of funds from the home country, while raising the prices of purchases from the parent shifts funds to the home country. When government imposes local price controls, transfer

pricing practices may again help. Higher transfer prices on exports of intermediate goods from a parent to a subsidiary in such a market may help support
the case for an increase in the price of the final product.

Output capacity

Subsidiaries with substantial excess production capacity can set transfer prices
low enough to encourage additional internal consumption, but high enough to
cover the supplying unit's variable costs.

As implied by the above discussion, the ability to control internal prices
charged to subsidiaries affords the global corporation significant flexibility and
overall efficiency. Nevertheless, these benefits often come at a cost. First, there
is the complication of internal control measures. Manipulating transfer prices
makes it very difficult to determine the true profit contribution of a subsidiary.
Second, morale problems typically surface at a subsidiary whose profit performance has been made worse artificially. Third, because of cultural differences,
some subsidiary managements may react negatively to price manipulation.
Fourth, there is the concern over local regulations. Subsidiaries, as local businesses, must abide by the rules. Legal problems will arise if the subsidiary follows accounting standards that are not approved by the host government.
Indeed, in many countries, transfer pricing practices are often subject to close
review by local authorities.

Facing the European market

For many companies the coalescence of the European markets will make
pricing one of their biggest single headaches. Partly this is a reflection of the
economic disparities within the European Community and the grey-market
problems that arise when prices are too far out of line between countries – a
practice the EC would like to end, to the unhappiness of some companies.
According to one of its main tenets (*Financial Times*, 1992):

> 'At the present time, price discrimination between national markets is
> widespread and substantial, to the considerable cost of consumers.
> Competition policy must, for the market to be fully integrated, make it
> clearly understood, for example, that parallel imports are to be wel-
> comed wherever undue price differences are seen to exists.'

Partly also, pricing is the litmus test of the company's management system. Local autonomy means nothing if prices are set centrally; conversely, if
the need to coordinate prices throughout Europe is the overriding factor, how
does the company give its product divisions and national subsidiaries the
decision-making autonomy that good customer service demands?

The problem is made worse by mounting public awareness of the price differences. Car manufacturers are under scrutiny over the substantial price differentials they manage to maintain between neighbouring countries. That may be one reason why their pricing decisions are generally centralized, as Claude Lacelle, director of commercial planning at Renault, explained:

> 'It's not the people in Austria or Spain, for example, who set their prices. On the basis of information they give us, we make proposals on pricing for new models or for price increases – according to a well-defined methodology which is the same for all countries – and submit them to the finance division. And we try to make our price proposals a good compromise between competitiveness and profitability . ... Our standard policy would be to compare a new model with the competition in the country concerned. We have data on products, prices and sales performance, so we can say we'll position ourselves here, here or here.'

According to NCR it

> 'prices to the local market, but we have to come up with multinational strategies through discounts. We'll be moving toward a single price structure, but we've got to give flexibility to local managers. What's happening is that local pricing is becoming very similar, the UK being one of the lowest in Europe, with several countries like Italy and Germany easing downward.'

The pressure for comparable pricing in different European markets will hit margins, which explains some of the manufacturers' reluctance to change. But taking the initiative in a desirable direction may be preferable. L'Oréal, for example, with its generally decentralized structure, recognizes that across its range of hair care, perfume and pharmaceutical products, prices have been coming together for several years. Therefore, in the past five years,

> 'harmonization has been speeded up deliberately – but by consensus . ... Prices are decided according to common denominators of concept, product technique and method of use by the consumer, and position in the local market. For modern products, price levels are becoming more uniform. There's a good example, Studio Line, a brand which is absolutely the same in 40 different countries . . . in terms of packaging, product technique and price level.'

Problems can arise not just with fluctuations in the exchange rates, but with discounts, credit terms, ordering patterns, delivery conditions and so on, all of which affect the margin finally made, but all of which have to be negotiated locally. John Ankeny, Levi Strauss's European marketing services director, expected to see a move to a common price for Levi jeans over the next two years, and he already charges his national subsidiaries a standard transfer price. But in the fashion trade, discounts can vary in bizarre ways, and 'I don't even want to know.'

In industrial markets, where multinational customers are slowly learning to buy the goods in whichever country the price is lowest, there is some urgency in closing the gaps, at least to within tolerable limits. At one engineering company, the pricing strategy is reviewed across Europe every year, and thereafter, 'we're happy if national subsidiaries operate within plus or minus 12%. That absorbs exchange rate wobbles, and is below the pain threshold of major customers.'

Other companies, however, may have to pay rather more attention to their competitors, some of which may be in no way inhibited by European pricing strategies. Compaq introduced a range of PCs to compete with the down-market Far Eastern competition in many of its territories, but its main pre-occupation is IBM, whose prices it uses as a marker. 'Sometimes we're higher than IBM,' it reported, 'and we avoid positioning ourselves underneath.' Rank Xerox issues pricing guidelines from the centre, which it intends should keep its products within 10% of key competitors and yield a 50–60% gross margin. The subsidiaries 'only come back to us if they can't meet the guidelines – if, for example, competitive prices are too low.'

The risk is, of course, that two rivals following that policy can chase each other down the price spiral. The consequences of getting the price structure wrong in that or other ways can be serious, and will become more so as customers take more interest in differences. The need for up-to-date, accurate and internationally comparable data is therefore growing fast, in this area as elsewhere.

Undoubtedly, pricing will continue to gain significance for global companies over the next decade. With intensified competition and interdependency of markets, global managers will find management of prices even more challenging. The challenges will involve attainment of better coordination of world-wide prices by corporate headquarters, achievement of the delicate balance between corporate and local control of prices, quicker response to marketplace changes, avoidance of grey-market or parallel-importing activity and development of alternatives to often costly price competition.

These challenges imply new or improved practices on the part of global companies. For example, an efficient, smooth and rapid system of communicating with subsidiary managers or distributors is essential. Those companies operating in so-called global industries such as telecommunications, construction equipment or medical equipment need to devise efficient mechanisms for monitoring competition world-wide and disseminating relevant information to the corporate family in a timely manner.

Pricing globally also remains an organizational challenge. Increasingly, it is an area where input from different functional divisions and the regions allows for better decision making. Nevertheless, many companies make critical pricing decisions without necessary consultation with all units concerned.

Pricing executives will also have to develop a better appreciation of the intimate relationships between price and other elements of the marketing mix. Pricing decisions cannot be reached in isolation from other dimensions of the offer such as product quality, aftersale service, follow-up sales opportunities, credit terms, and so on. Price represents only a dimension in the bundle of benefits perceived by the customer. Interpreting customers' perceptions of value for the product remains a formidable but necessary task. Pricing decisions which are based on a good understanding of perceived value – both from the perspective of the intermediaries and final customers – are more likely to succeed.

Summary

- The globalization of marketing has put tremendous pressure on multinational pricing systems. Over the past few decades, as companies moved from purely domestic operations to exporting and then to overseas manufacturing and marketing, they had to transform their pricing structures.

- Pricing decisions cannot be made in isolation, since pricing interacts with and affects all other marketing policy variables.

- Multinationals take great time and care in establishing pricing policies and setting prices for international customers. In addition to the basic factors of production cost, demand and competition that must be considered, pricing decisions for the global market must take into account such variables as exchange rate fluctuations and duties, as well as external costs, for example documentation, freight and insurance.

- Although global companies generally maintain centralized control over local prices, they do allow subsidiaries to alter prices when warranted by local conditions. In some situations, subsidiaries may, in fact, receive complete pricing autonomy because of competitive considerations.

- Conflicts between centralized and decentralized pricing decisions tend to be resolved by having the corporate office set policies and issue general guidelines to which overseas subsidiaries and distributors must adhere.

- Companies have three options in setting prices on exports: rigid cost-plus pricing, flexible cost-plus pricing and dynamic incremental pricing.

- One of the thorniest problems global companies grapple with when they venture beyond their home-country borders is transfer pricing (also known as intracompany pricing). The prices at which units of the same company sell to each other have a far-reaching effect on the company's success because they influence everything from foreign subsidiary performance to executive compensation to tax obligations.

- Many factors are involved in deciding which transfer price to use and whether to use different prices for reporting external and internal performance. Sometimes one issue is of overriding importance to a company, clearly dictating a particular pricing system. More often, however, a company's situation is mixed, making the choice highly complex and probably contentious.

- For many companies the coalescence of the European markets will make pricing one of their biggest single headaches. Partly this is a reflection of the economic disparities within the European Community and the grey-market problems that arise when prices are too far out of line between countries – a practice the EC would like to end, to the unhappiness of some companies. Partly also, pricing is the litmus test of the company's management system.

Checklist

As pricing decision making grows increasingly complex, does your company:

(1) Have a comprehensive understanding of the relationships between price and other elements of the marketing and promotional mix?

(2) Use the right variables when arriving at prices for foreign customers?

(3) Make sure pricing decisions are made in the right place to reflect the multi-dimensional strategic requirements?

(4) Have guidelines to diffuse the conflicting needs of centralization and decentralization of pricing decisions?

(5) Use pricing as an active component of international competitive strategy?

(6) Have a well-defined strategy toward transfer pricing?

(7) Devise a pricing policy for the European single market, particularly in light of the desire of the EC to harmonize prices throughout the Community?

Reference

The European Commission. (1988). The Economics of 1991: the Cecchini Report on the European Market, March. Quoted in the *Financial Times*, 5 March 1992

Managing information and culture

8

Marketing and information technology

Introduction

The slow arrival of IT into that last bastion of IT ignorance, the marketing function, has deep implications for marketing both strategically and tactically. Closing the information loop so that real-time, integrated data about customers flows around the company effectively ends reliance on inert geographical structures and enables the corporation to 'think global, act local' in the truest sense.

The application of IT to marketing at all levels will enable information to function as the central nervous system in the corporate organism, reacting to stimuli from both within and without the structure. That information is formatted for use for individual departments, like marketing, sales, accounts, and so on, which update it and exploit it. It then filters up to the top point, where it is used in strategic planning. These broad plans are translated into more specific objectives, and passed down to more specific points.

This chapter examines the issues involved in exploiting information technology in marketing, including:

- The central role of information
- Creating a marketing information system
- IT and the organization
- Information flow and the network
- Information and control
- Collecting the data
- Believing the data
- Shifting the information boundaries.

The central role of information

Most companies are only slowly beginning to grasp the need to coordinate the enormous amounts of information they gather. They are comfortable with IT in the manufacturing and financial functions because they can judge its effect on raising productivity levels. But they feel far less secure about the role of information systems in their marketing strategies. The problem is, as Edwina Dunn of DunnHumby Associates pointed out, 'There are not a lot of people who understand what marketing *and* what computers are about.'

What all companies say they want from IT is to get closer to their customers and deal with them as efficiently and competitively as possible, whether those customers buy coffee or construction plants. Checking what the customer wants and preferably anticipating it is usually paid lip-service as the most important function in the organization. People are only just realizing that this process will not necessarily make the most short-term profit. But it is the most important process for ensuring that they will still be around in five years' time. Exploiting IT will be a competitive necessity in the 1990s, according to a five year analysis done by the Sloan School of Management at the Massachusetts Institute of Technology (MIT) (see Case 8.1).

Case 8.1   The MIT programme

The Management in the 1990s Research Programme (MIT90s) was set up in the mid-1980s to investigate business turbulence, and IT's role in both causing it and dealing with it from a managerial point of view. It was sponsored by both industry and governmental agencies. These findings are from a report put out by one of the earliest sponsors, computer group ICL (1990).

The aim of the project was 'to develop a better understanding of the managerial issues of the 1990s and how to deal most effectively with them, particularly as these issues revolve around anticipated advances in information technology.'

The main findings were:

(1)   Turbulence in the business environment will continue – in fact, it could increase.

continues

continued

(2)   Improvements in IT capability will continue. However, there is no evidence that IT alone provides sustainable competitive advantage. The benefits come from a constructive combination of IT with structure and with people who can exploit the information and way of working IT can bring.

(3)   The core of the business must be rethought and processes re-engineered.

(4)   Integration provides the main opportunities for improving business effectiveness. This goes beyond combining databases or using a common database but means achieving a close and effective working relationship between various parts of an organization.

(5)   Flexible networked organizations need to be created.

(6)   Data and information will be a major problem area. Much information is currently dispersed, inconsistent, incompatible and inaccessible.

(7)   The nature of work is changing. That has implications for education, training and work design.

(8)   Managers must be agents of change. This does not mean responding to change but exploiting it. Senior management need to predict and intercept change, and to stimulate transformation in advance of events.

(9)   There are new roles for organizational leadership. It is no longer acceptable to be preoccupied with maintaining the *status quo*. Leaders have to predict requirements for change, and plan and implement them.

(10) Line managers must take up roles of leadership. Empire building or protecting the patch has to end.

The report outlined what it called four enabling conditions for these findings to have any value:

- The provision of leadership with a shared vision of the way ahead for the whole organization;
- Flexible human resources practices which among other things encourage managers to think long term and encourage risk taking;
- Investment in education and training;
- The existence of a readily available IT infrastructure.

There are some fundamental problems to be overcome in making IT work in marketing at both the strategic and tactical level:

- Over the last decade installation of IT has been driven by cost-saving and productivity-improvement measures. Automation, rather than information enhancement, has been the focal point;

- The costs and benefits of that automation process have been more easily measurable and hence justifiable compared to spending huge sums installing a network to enhance business strategic decision taking;
- Ignorance and misunderstanding of the creative application of IT is still depressingly prevalent at the top of many international companies, while middle managers worry it will undermine their roles. This is probably something that will only be solved when today's technology-literate youngsters begin to move into business;
- The structure of the organization itself can work against a coordinated, object-oriented use of IT: many companies have grown up in a piecemeal fashion;
- While more companies trumpet the virtues of being 'marketing-led' too many are still internally focused rather than customer-driven;
- There is a lack of understanding about what comes under IT. Do companies coordinate purchases of facsimile machines, for example? Or even know how many there are in the company?
- While great progress has been made in developing more open systems to boost networking and allow different systems to communicate, there is still a lack of flexibility and accessibility. This can have implications for takeovers and mergers: in the UK, a merger between two building societies was called off partly because of their lack of IT compatibility and the investment that would have been needed to overcome it.

As Peter Stauvers, strategic marketing manager at IT networking specialist Case Communications, pointed out,

'Companies find it hard to value information. Accountants don't understand the costs of getting it, and the value of exploiting it. It is still a numbers game. Companies are doing office automation to get rid of the typing pool. But few can see its use for competitive advantage, unless, like airlines, it means bums on seats.'

The winners in applying IT to marketing strategies will be the companies that recognize it as a means to an end, not the end in itself, since IT solutions can rapidly be copied by the competition. One of the early pioneers, and a commonly quoted case study of how to use information systems (IS) for competitive advantage is McKesson, one of the largest wholesale suppliers in the US of hospital goods. In the early 1980s it began to use IT to create an order-taking system, by putting personal computers on customers' desks. That was followed by linking the system back into the warehouse to use it to generate re-orders, which shortened delivery times.

The information was then used to give customers an analysis of their stock flow by marrying in accounting data. This also meant that McKesson could judge customers' fast or slow moving lines and charge for the information. The company then went one stage further and got even closer to their customers by

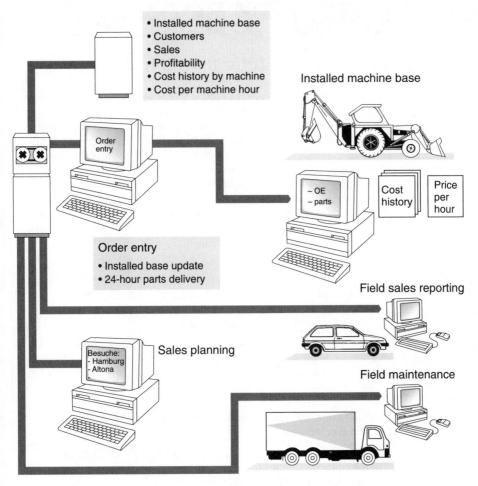

Figure 8.1   Zeppelin: managing the installed machine base. *Source:* The Index Group.

moving third-party medical insurance: since most drugs were supplied against insurance packages, it took over the job from the customers of collecting the insurance.

German Caterpillar dealer Zeppelin is a more recent illustration of how to tame IT (Figure 8.1). Zeppelin uses its massive but flexible database to keep track of its 20,000 customers and the big pieces of complicated earth-moving equipment it sells to them. Because detailed maintenance records are kept, the company can tell customers when, for instance, their machines are not operating at the optimum levels of efficiency and suggest solutions. All the information is easily accessible at branch level. Zeppelin's competitive advantage is expertise and knowledge.

Case 8.2 BA: Information technology

British Airways spends more than £100 million a year on information management. The former director of marketing and operations, Liam Strong, had three main concerns: getting value for money, persuading his people to 'own' the technology and not feel it has been thrust upon them, and having an IT architecture in the 1990s that will take advantage of the increased firepower which both mini- and micro-computers now offer. 'It is basic to what we do.'

'Most people have networks that were designed in the 1970s and have developed like patchwork quilts. If you have the courage to go back and redesign it completely, the benefits are enormous. And that is what we are doing', he said, 'reconfiguring all our databases so that we have genuinely integrated information.' The trick is using it:

> 'You know that your competitors have the same information as you do, so the issue becomes how you use it. It becomes a question of speed, skill and understanding. It is not a question of information being power – it is about analysis, deduction from the information, and how you use it to integrate the business.'

BA is an extraordinarily data-rich business and has been a heavy user of data processing for a long time. Strong called IT a 'facilitator': it enabled the company not only to track its performance but it would help push its services further, from more automation in the terminals to value-added ground/air links.

It offered another great advantage, in Strong's opinion: it allowed companies to cope with size:

> 'As organizations get larger and larger one of the issues from our point of view is how big can we get and still control the business cost-effectively? IT can help deal with that, while addressing both the service infrastructure and cost reduction through quality planning. It has already improved capacity management dramatically; the next step is database marketing.'

Creating a marketing information system

One of the most fundamental parts of a marketing IT strategy is the exploitation of increasingly integrated marketing information systems which are driven from a powerful central database – or several linked databases – of current and prospective customers. For many companies, information lies in unconnected and uncoordinated pockets throughout the organization. There is 'hard' data about markets, products, competition, brand profitability and so on which can be gathered from both within and from outside the company. There is also 'soft' information, gathered in all sorts of formal and informal ways, from sales contacts, distributors, or service engineers. It is the ability to manipulate this on a real-time basis that can give a definable edge over the competition.

Definition of terms

Database: An organized set of files providing a common pool of information for one, several or many users.

Marketing database: An organized set of files, providing a common pool of information for users about customers, their characteristics, needs, desires, buying methods, uses and consumption of a company's products/services. More comprehensive versions include information about competitors, prospects and other external or environmental variables affecting the organization.

Database marketing: A strategy for using an organized set of files, containing the best available information about potential and existing customers – their characteristics, needs, desires, buying methods, uses and consumption of products/services – in order to satisfy each individual customer more effectively and profitably.

Marketing information system: A system for coordinating marketing efforts in support of strategic marketing goals through the collection, analysis, interpretation and communication of relevant market information, both within an organization and within that organization's task environment.

Insurance companies are classic cases of an industry crying out for the application of systems that allow both coordination and updating of customer files on a real-time basis. Their customers will usually get quotations from not only their current insurance company, but from several others when they want a policy for something new. There is little likelihood that the original company's central customer file – if there even is one – will record that the customer asked for a quote, but did not take it up. Nor will it have recorded what the policy was for – like a second home in France, say. This information would not only be invaluable in profiling the customer, but would mean the company could target its new products more tightly.

Building up a comprehensive database means going to the very core of the business. First, find out what information your business habitually records and how good it is. The only way to do that is NOT by looking at a printout but by going and talking to the people who are inputting the information:

- Go to central data entry and talk to people entering records. How good are the forms? How much of the information is put in by default because it was not supplied and the system must have an entry? Is there a huge pile of cards waiting to go in?
- Go to the distributors you sell through. If you have added a few customer profile questions to purchase cards, are they being answered or ignored because they add to delays?
- What do sales people know that is not in the system? Who earns the most bonus? Why? Are they keeping better, additional files on customers?
- Do you know how to define a 'good' customer for a particular product?

The report by the IT consultancy OASiS on the management of marketing information (see Definition of terms, page 235) found that while the amount of information held about customers by the 193 companies it surveyed varied considerably, overall the information was more quantitative than qualitative.

Customer Databases: % Companies Holding Information On:	
Value of sales	75%
Industry classification	74%
Product usage	73%
Frequency of orders by product	65%
Financial status	64%
Purchase influencers	57%
Use of products supplied by competition	56%
Account profitability	52%
Demographic information	51%
Account profitability by line	46%
Personal interests	0%

Source: OASiS, 1989.

But the 'softer' information could help the company have a much more in-depth understanding of the market by building up individual customer profiles which could then be combined into groups and segmented, the report concluded.

The lack of cross-fertilization between different parts of the corporate empires is a great barrier to the optimal use of corporate intelligence. What IT consultancies increasingly find themselves being asked to do is help companies integrate all the information into a database accessible to different parts of

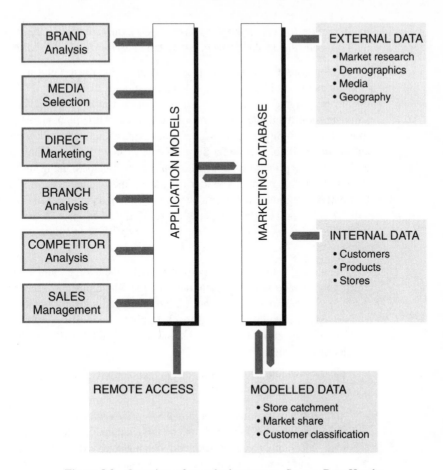

Figure 8.2   Overview of a marketing system. *Source:* DunnHumby.

the company in a tailored fashion to break down organizational barriers. So customer information, recorded at the sharp edge of sales, can be fed into planning the next generation of products and services, while modern brand management programmes, for example, can be a powerful aid to making marketing decisions (see Figure 8.2). The accounting systems can also be linked in and used as a basis for developing new techniques for analysing profitability, like profit per sales executive or per customer.

Stauvers of Case believed there are two main issues in database marketing:

- While there is a lot of computer processing power around, the software is not friendly enough: 'The whole database can be put on a desk. But what do you do with it? The labs love it. But it doesn't help the average business person,' he pointed out.

- To get customer profiling to work properly, the information a company has on its customers should be cross-matched with external databases.

Automating the marketing process itself is the most daunting challenge companies face in IT applications. This does not mean just using IT for modelling to investigate a number of 'what-if' marketing scenarios. The range of software tools available for the evaluation of marketing plans increases all the time, now including expert systems and neural networks. Comprehensive automation will not only be far more complex, but will demand that companies go back to first principles about what marketing means to them. It should lead to what Dr Robb Wilmot, founder of OASiS and former head of ICL, called 'computer-integrated marketing' to link in other techniques like computer-aided design/computer-aided manufacture (CAD/CAM), just-in-time (JIT) and total quality management (TQM). But, as OASiS' consultant Mike Perkin pointed out,

> 'Marketing is such a complex function that when you try and automate it you are talking about re-engineering the whole business (see Figure 8.3). You cannot deal with the strategy without thinking about how that strategy will be implemented. And if you deal with the systems without thinking about the processes that make up those systems, you are doomed to failure.'

The big problem is that most organizations have just happened and not been designed, according to Wilmot:

> 'To create a marketing-led organization *sometimes* can be achieved by adding more processes to those already extant, but rarely does this work. More often you're better off starting over with a clean sheet of paper and designing new processes and systems from scratch – but this presents tremendous change management challenges to leadership.'

OASiS has drawn up a list of critical recommendations for integrating marketing:

- Ensure there is a company champion for the system to oversee and push through both the technical and educational development;
- Make the approach business goal-directed to determine what information is necessary to support overall business aims;
- Carry out the integration of marketing information systems as part of the corporate information strategy, not as a piecemeal exercise;
- Invest in developing a shared model of the marketing process within the organization from the outset, in order to understand how the various elements of the marketing system will work together;
- Make all employees part of the marketing process by developing a combination of information management skills and marketing awareness;
- Realize the change in organizational culture required to implement the new customer-centred marketing;

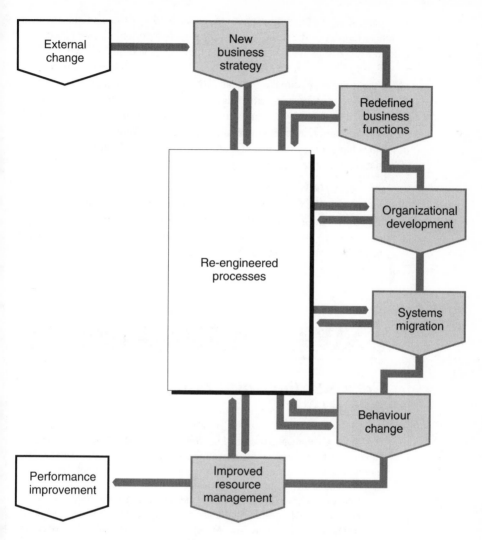

Figure 8.3   Re-engineering business. *Source:* OASiS.

- Carry out implementation in realistic and manageable stages, beginning with those operations which have the greatest potential for adding value to marketing in relation to the competition;
- Be realistic and pragmatic but be determined.

A big barrier to successful implementation is that most companies are not dealing with greenfield IT sites. They have accumulated masses of stand-alone systems and mini-networks, along with the big number crunchers in central data processing units. The major UK retail banks are one of the most prominent examples of the price to be paid for early automation: most core branch accounting systems were written in the late 1960s and are still what the businesses run on. But banks, much as they dread it, have known since the late 1970s that they have to make the leap into more relational databases which can cross-fertilize customer information (most banks still do not even record customers by name but by account number) and link up money transmission processes, commercial accounts and mortgages into individual customer files.

But what do they do, asked David Rumble, PA Consulting's director of information industries sector:

> 'Stop work? Take it branch by branch and install new systems while still running the old? For the last few years many of them have been shying away from what will be a formidable task. The most likely solution will be to build the new system in the background and run the old one at the same time and do it over several years.'

Case 8.3 Barclays: Information technology

The banking sector was one of the first to espouse IT in the shape of big mainframes. But that technology has moved on so quickly they are confronted with enormous investments to replace ageing equipment and systems. The time has come to make a quantum leap forward.

John Cheese, marketing director of the personal sector at Barclays, said that the banks recognize this. But he did not mitigate the problems; 'We are not starting from a greenfield site. We cannot just sit down and stop – we still have to open our doors on Monday at 9:30 and we still have to keep providing statements and so on, while at the same time trying to radically change the way we operate.' He compared it to operating on the patient while he was walking around the room.

Within the next five years the application of technology will have several major implications:

- It will have a profound impact on the way the bank operates, as powerful relational databases pull previously disparate strands of information from thousands of sources together;
- It will give marketing people 'the power to understand the needs of individual customers in a way never done before,' said Cheese;

continues

continued

- Allied to sophisticated direct marketing techniques, it will be a source of competitive advantage.

It will not appear that dramatic from the customer's point of view, Cheese believed, except in an evolutionary sense of enhancing a relationship that can last 40 years. After all, banks probably have more consumer data than almost any other industry – but it is data, as Cheese pointed out, which the industry finds incredibly difficult to convert to usable information, that Holy Grail of all marketers. 'The vast majority of our customers are amazed that we do not understand their needs better on an individual basis,' he believed.

The technology does exist but banks are keeping their thoughts quiet on how they will apply it in order not to give any secrets away and damage any competitive edge. What its use will *not* do, insisted Cheese, is be a sinister application of all that sensitive information.

Most of the technological tools are in place for attacking the automation of the marketing function. Relational databases, multimedia presentation systems, advanced communication and optical storage techniques can be applied to every aspect of the marketing system. But a big drawback is that in so many companies IT and marketing people communicate badly, if at all. While marketing people have to be increasingly financially hard-edged, there is still much of what they do which is often difficult to reduce to the logical structure with which IT system engineers, both within the company and in outside suppliers, like to work.

'Basically, IT people need to understand marketing. What they really need to understand is that marketing people are their customers and they need to get closer to them. But it goes deeper than that. It is not just the difficulty of understanding what we want out of marketing systems. It is that the world is changing so fast that we will *never* get it right. By the time IT builds a system marketing needs those needs will have changed',

said PA's Rumble. That means designing systems that understand flexibility: 'It is basically a different way of thinking that recognizes that this system will never be right and will always be following a bit behind. We need to have some way of systematically bodging it.'

The great danger is not to let the avalanche of data overwhelm innovation and creativity: people need to know *how* to think, rather than *what* to think, because, Rumble argued:

- In the real world you will never have all the information at the same time;
- People are crucial to the equation – it is no use making a decision if you cannot get it carried out;
- Too much data can lead you to believe the world is organized. It isn't. You need to have people who can stand back and look at the big picture.

Case 8.4 Zanussi

Zanussi UK marketing director Francis Huggins believed his company is fortunate that its data processing (dp) manager 'is a real person. That makes a fundamental difference.' The basic operation of the company is built around a large database so it is crucial to have a good dp department that can access information in whatever form marketing needs: 'It is driven by personalities. Computer people tend to talk in computer lingo, and so do marketing people. You have to take that into account.'

Huggins used IT both as an information and communications tool. He did not want to be drowned in information, however, so he kept strict control over the amount of information he allowed himself in order to keep it manageable. IT also made it easier to communicate quickly with people in other parts of the world – white goods manufacturer Zanussi is part of Electrolux – without having to spend all his time in a plane. 'But there is really nothing like a face-to-face meeting, and until IT is developed to the point where you can have a multi-image meeting environment, where the chairs around a table are replaced by monitors, it will still be a tool.'

Will IT change the way he works over the next few years? Huggins reckoned that in terms of the company's ability to act in the marketplace, the technology was as advanced as it needs to be: 'More would be nice, but do I really want it?' Where it would have a significant impact, however, was helping the group become more homogeneous – something particularly important to companies that grow by acquisition and are faced with the problem of making all operations work with compatible systems.

Another welcome innovation will be the increasing use by electrical goods retailers of Electronic Point of Sale (EPOS), so that, rather than wait three and a half weeks after a four-week sales period, all retailers can know within a week, or even sooner, sales by model, price, store and region: 'And the more closely linked manufacturers and retailers are, the more valuable that type of technology will be to both parties.'

Since the early 1980s an increasing number of companies have been investing heavily in some sophisticated software packages, which 'sit on top' of other IT systems, and provide a means of quickly and directly accessing core data, to the specification of the user. Called Executive Information Systems (EIS), these packages were initially designed for senior management, but in many instances have become widespread throughout companies because they are so easy to use and can communicate key information clearly and creatively. They are ideal packages for effecting a company-wide understanding of marketing issues, and as a means of integrating accounting, sales and production information held on various data systems around the organization. The process of buying and implementing EIS provides a useful focus on what are the key business indicators for a company, and how better management of information can improve competitive information. EIS are at the centre of successful businesses as diverse as British Airways, Frito-Lay, Pratt & Whitney and Hertz.

The US is probably the most advanced in using computers in marketing to improve customer care because the sheer size of the market has demanded IT solutions.

The following are a few selected examples *(Index Group, Inc.* 1990):

(1)   S. C. Johnson Wax has reduced the time it takes to deliver customer orders by 40% through an information system that links people in sales, customer service, manufacturing, distribution, credit and finance, shipping and warehouse operations. The system means the company can focus on customers and it breaks down barriers between internal functions.

(2)   Commonwealth Bank in central Pennsylvania has built a database of important information about trust account customers, which means that several authorized people in the bank other than the trust officer can answer customer questions quickly. The system also helps the bank investigate customer investment tastes and cross-sell other financial products. In addition, the system tracks the performance of trust officers, who can now handle a 50% increase in work.

(3)   Computer maker Digital Equipment Corporation feeds in customer information to telephone representatives at its three major US service centres on their computer terminals. The reps screen the calls and send them to the appropriate hardware and software experts at the centres. Most problems can be handled over the phone. If not, appropriate engineers are contacted electronically and ordered to the customer's site. It means expertise can be located quickly.

According to what has been considered a seminal article on the need to automate marketing in the *Harvard Business Review* (Moriarty and Swartz, 1989),

'For many companies, postponement of automation of the marketing function may seem to be a good way of skirting a difficult decision, but this do-nothing posture condemns the organization to being a marketing laggard. It may also be a costly mistake. Early adopters of MSP (marketing and sales productivity) systems have gained superior competitive advantage. Compared with their 'manual' competitors, they perform selling tasks with greater economy and impact. They know the customers better and can tailor their sales communications to supply just the right amount of sales stimulus at just the right time. Overall, they craft and control their marketing programmes more intelligently. In the long run, the competitive barriers they establish may change the nature of marketing in their industries.'

IT and the organization

The vision of a European market that is single in name but awash with cultural diversities is providing the incentive for many companies to rethink how they operate in Europe as part of global restructuring. IT should play the leading role. Most company networks still operate as islands in different countries. The goal is to link them all up, since only the most advanced networks will enable companies to cope with the sheer scale which Europe alone demands. These links will form what Kirt Mead, vice president at the UK office of US-based IT consultancy Index called the 'global company's corporate DNA': ubiquitous software and data structures (Figure 8.4).

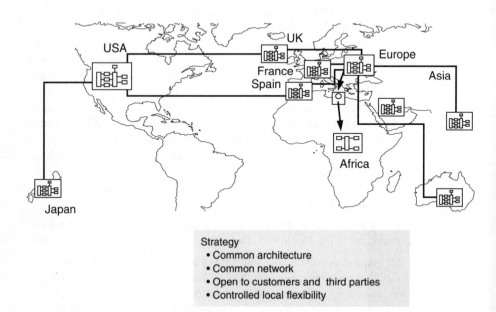

Figure 8.4   Standard software architecture: the global company's DNA. *Source:* The Index Group.

Technological links mean that companies can give the illusion of appearing local while centralizing essential functions. For customers, the subsidiaries in different European countries will seem autonomous. But they have the same products, the same financial systems, a European-wide logistics network, and IT tied into a central mainframe in Holland. Customers ordering products with a personal computer in Germany think they are dealing with a local company. But orders are being filed across three borders. Those orders will be in German, and so will the packaging: but, like a stage set, the local appearance is a facade (Figure 8.5). Mead used the metaphor of Charlemagne revisited. While from a marketing point of view companies want to appear in the Bismarckian sense as national states proud of their language, history and culture, behind the facade the logistics operate on a level European platform (Figure 8.6). This, declared Mead, helps companies manage one of the modern oxymorons: 'dispersed centralization'.

Big, multinational companies like Ford which have always viewed Europe as one, are a long way down the road with European sourcing, product development and production patterns. That is probably not the case with the companies that have been well-served by big home markets in countries like Germany, France and the UK. Those which, on the other hand, have long had to export because of a lack of a large enough domestic market, like Switzerland, will be further along in tackling the problems of linking on an international scale.

The technology is becoming advanced enough to establish these sophisticated links with the onset of open systems architecture and standards. There are still some barriers, however, including running data across borders: except for the UK, the European Postal, Telegraph and Telephone administrations (PTTs) are still run as national monopolies. Mead called them 'the last medieval organizations in Europe.' To overcome this, companies are turning to computer experts like IBM to run their data networks for them privately – and at great expense. While over time costs will come down as the PTTs get pushed into modernity, the idea of subcontracting the management of the organizations' entire network to outside experts will make increasing sense.

Unfortunately, controlling and coordinating European operations will demand better and more detailed information systems than most companies have at present. Modern information technology systems promise major benefits, but only to those who are prepared to adapt their structures to match and who have thought through its fundamental purpose.

Decentralization, matrix structures, task forces and networks all depend in a very intimate way on the corporate control system, the flow of management information and, thus, the potential of IT. The OASiS consultancy regards information, organization and strategy as the three corners of a corporate triangle. The failure of any one of these three elements will thwart the success of the other two. Other consultants make the point that their clients frequently fail to appreciate the distorting effect their control systems can have on the progress of the business.

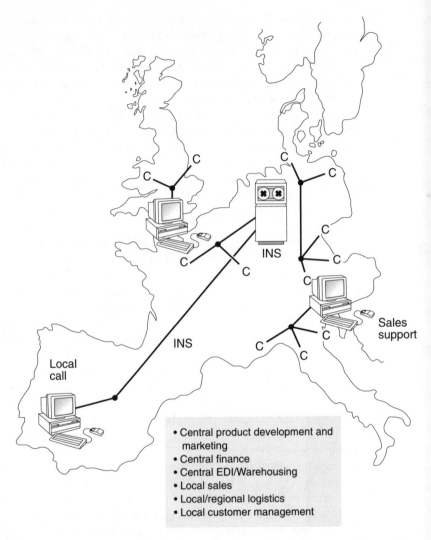

Figure 8.5 Medical products: the illusion of national companies. *Source:* The Index Group.

That has always been the case, and there are probably few companies whose controls have adequately kept pace with or anticipated the development of the business. But the evolution of a modern European structure, with its delicate balance of central and local authority, demands a parallel development in information systems. Team working and networking, in particular, assume that all members have ready access to the data they need and can communicate efficiently with each other. The implications of that assumption are enormous. One

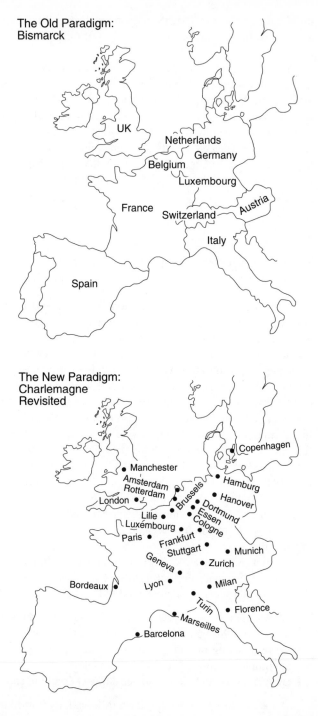

The Old Paradigm:
Bismarck

The New Paradigm:
Charlemagne
Revisited

Figure 8.6   Structure: from Bismarck to Charlemagne. *Source:* The Index Group.

multinational client of OASiS in the petrochemical industry is in the midst of a four-year programme costing hundreds of millions of dollars to implement 18 major information systems in 16 countries.

Many companies will be forced to make a thorough overhaul of their control and information systems. Electrolux is well on the way. Its 'Electrolux Forecasting & Supply' system is linking some 70 appliance companies in 13 European countries with an IT network. Ultimately, all manufacturing, supply and marketing operations will be provided with real-time data on production, sales, stocks and market activity. As a senior financial executive pointed out, 'With the large number of companies we have, to control them, we must have a uniform reporting system which is correct and tells us how the company is doing.'

Information flow and the network

As companies move toward more lateral and flexible structures, the data availability and flow become of critical importance. The problem that strikes many is that the existing information flow is primarily vertical – from sales branches and warehouses to regional offices to national offices to European offices and to headquarters. Differences in definitions or accounting standards may be accommodated as the data are consolidated, and the totals stored in the central data banks, usually in a form to suit the accounts department.

More flexible marketing structures may therefore demand radical change in information systems, particularly if the company is aiming to allow executives access to sales and marketing data across the group. The growing use of personal computers and workstations connected into local area networks potentially allows every executive to pull out the information needed from any part of the company, work on it, send the result to the other members of a task force in three different countries for further work and modification, then implement the agreed result. It is a tempting vision, but much work needs to be done to reach that state.

Even a company as sophisticated in data handling as NCR admits that its present management information system is inadequate for its future purposes. Said senior European vice president Fred Newall,

'We need common support systems because it eliminates problems of discussion. We've tried in the past to adjust to local systems, but now we're evolving our administration along open Unix system lines. At the moment, national companies can talk to each other, but on a hierarchical basis, and there's no peer-to-peer communication.'

A lot is achieved at NCR, claimed Newall, by informal networks of people who have had long experience in the company and know how it works. He gained his knowledge when he spent a year acting as executive assistant to the chairman and president.

The systems problems that NCR faces are widespread. Colgate–Palmolive, for example, has realized the need for major changes. Said European president Brian Bergin: 'We have to rewire all our operations, between departments and across Europe – they all tend to be vertical. It's difficult to overestimate the need for databases. I'm appalled how far we've got to go.' A further complication in his case is that Europe has to link into the US and the rest of the world. Ideally, a uniform, global system might be the right goal, but the additional complexities that would be entailed would possibly not justify the cost.

US computer manufacturer Digital Equipment claims that it has been networking internally for the past 10 years, backing its detailed matrix management system. Of its present employees two-thirds are on the network and can communicate with each other across the world. 'It's one of our biggest sales tools,' boasted an executive. 'Networking like this makes the world smaller, but tougher for manufacturers.' At Hewlett-Packard up to a million messages a day go whizzing around its 92,000 employees. Kodak also now uses electronic mail, and in the US – and soon in Europe – a computerized voice message system with an answer-back facility. This, European research director Bob Worden considered, 'has changed our communications style in a revolutionary manner in the past five years. There are no more telephone messages. Even so, a lot of improvements are still needed in management information.' One of the benefits of electronic mail over the telephone that he has noted (apart from time and labour savings) was that the system alleviated the language problem: because executives with a weak command of English can save the messages on their personal computers, they have the opportunity to clarify the meaning and compose an appropriate reply.

Evidently, the benefits of sophisticated IT systems are not going to be realized without very different styles of operation, just as the style of operation cannot be changed without major improvements to the IT system. 'If you have a good network,' considered IBM Europe's director of organization, Agnès Roux-Kiener, 'you can have 25 people reporting in to one manager. We've managed to cut out two layers of management between the salesman and the chief executive.' IBM is still working on its internal information system – 'the rules and document system are being developed; everything has to be consistent.'

However, Mike Perkin of OASiS warned:

'There's a growing realization that the technical developments are the easy bit. What is harder is to change the way people work. The shakeup affects everyone and is very painful. You will get gaps and things falling through them, so you have to be doubly clear why the new structure is good. I'm optimistic – I see a greater willingness after a reorganization to share information and work as a team. But what we've found is that companies need the same marketing skills internally as they use externally: What is the product, the system, the information process, job roles, threats and so on? Why should the staff buy it? How should the product be adapted to win the internal market?'

There is a growing realization among companies that unless they manage to extract the benefits offered by IT and the associated structural changes, they will face a serious and increasing competitive disadvantage.

A corollary of the radical changes in the information flow round the sales and marketing structures is the implication for companies' order processing and warehousing operations. Both, of course, are integral parts of the information network, but once common systems have been established in Europe or even throughout the group, the processing points can be placed anywhere in the network, offering further opportunities for dispersion of the central management.

The internal market should see the dismantling of large numbers of regulations that have so far obstructed multinational distribution. As NCR's Newall complained, 'It's relatively easy to move goods from country to country; it's the secondary moves and adjustments that are the problem.' NCR is therefore planning a centralized distribution system using just-in-time (JIT) techniques to keep inventory levels to a minimum. Similarly, with administration, 'there's no reason why we shouldn't bill everyone from Amsterdam, say,' American Express does that already, from its computer centre in Brighton, on England's south coast. But it foresees the day when only the database is central; the generation of accounts could be localized.

Rank Xerox, too, is planning a JIT distribution system based on its factory at Venray in southern Holland, with the aim of distributing its copiers directly from there to the customer. For the French small-appliances company Moulinex, the priorities and product sizes may be different but the need to rationalize the system is just as great. Group sales director Gilbert Torelli said that the newly revitalized company was considering all variables of the marketing mix – products, pricing, advertising, distribution – and 'I'm sure that distribution is going to be the biggest factor. When I talk about logistics, at the moment we have warehouses everywhere, in each country. Depending on how things develop, perhaps we eventually won't need that.'

Black & Decker is not alone in seeing distribution as a positive, competitive weapon, and in the opinion of European head Roger Thomas, there was no reason to accept current standards – 'warehousing is an admission of failure.' At the moment, said Thomas, 'we can give stores a three-day service, but why not a 24-hour service – and can we do it from only three or four warehouses?'

Ironically, ICI reckons its distribution system gives it a competitive edge at the moment because it is rather better at negotiating the obstacles than its chemical competitors. When the barriers come down, that advantage will disappear, but this will give the company the opportunity to cut the number of warehouses, clerical staff and the time taken between receipt of order and delivery to the customer – of critical importance with speciality or effect chemicals, where (unlike commodities) daily orders and 24-hour delivery are accepted as normal.

However a company's information system is organized, of course, its efficient functioning depends on the people operating it.

Information and control

The crucial issue is what information the system should carry, and, behind that, what sort of control companies wish to exercise. The role of the centre in respect of its subsidiaries has already been discussed in some detail. In its judgement of a subsidiary's performance, central management has to decide:

- Whether it is able, or obliged, to accept a country manager's or divisional director's view on how well the operation is doing;
- Or whether it needs to come to its own conclusion based on the information supplied, or judged against other similar operations or some external source;
- What action it needs to take if the results are not up to expectations.

In the view of Marcus Alexander of London-based consultants GAH, the basic control system should help to provide a means of judging a subsidiary's performance for a particular product by providing local managers with the ability to see the advantage of being part of the greater whole, the incentive to draw on its strengths, and the opportunity to do so.

Alexander cited the case of a retail group which decided to make each store manager responsible for profit. 'The initial reaction was to cut things that could influence the result. But the brighter managers started to pull resources out of head office to help them increase their profit.'

Systems analysts expect managers to be able to specify the data they need to do their jobs, but that is rarely the case, particularly in a fast-changing business. Historical financial information is one thing; 'soft' order totals, sales activity, market trend and economic information and so on, are quite another. As the report *From Hierarchy to Network* published by the Conference Board Europe (1989) warns:

'The availability of information makes it tempting for senior managers to bypass or invade the territories of their subordinates. This can feel like lack of trust. We have always to be clear why we need to dispense information: are we telling, counting or trusting? It has to be clear to all concerned. One study in one organization discovered that 40% of its information costs were due only to the need for reassurance at the top.'

Japanese companies' very detailed but informal system of reporting has the advantage of not being rigid and specific in the manner of some Western companies. The Doyle (1986) study (see Chapter 2) on subsidiaries operating in the UK concluded:

> 'The Americans relied much more on detailed and formal controls. Most employed standard planning and budgeting systems, and reported to international product and marketing committees . ... The Japanese did not favour the standardized planning systems; instead they relied on continuous informal monitoring. All subsidiaries indicated that reporting was a daily or constant process, with the telephone as the main mode of communication with Japan. Headquarters were invariably viewed as extremely well informed of activities, problems and progress.'

US and UK companies, Doyle concluded, focused on financial measures such as budgeted profit and return on investment targets, and did not monitor performance at the market or product-line level – giving, in his view, an inevitably short-term flavour to their policies. Japanese firms were more concerned with market share targets and strategy, and local managers knew the company was committed to long-term growth. While it is doubtful whether such strictures could be applied to 3M or even IBM, in spite of the strong emphasis on profit, the effect of control systems on the way the company's structure operates and develops is not in doubt.

As companies widen their focus beyond their national subsidiaries, and coordinate their marketing and sales activities, whether through product divisions or in other ways, the control system has to change also. Taking a global view on some or all of the products requires global information on them. Subsidiaries frequently still do not analyse their profits by product line, and even where they do accounting differences sometimes make it difficult to relate the Italian figure to the French or Swedish. But without accurate data of that kind, an issue can be judged at national level only according to national profit criteria, and cannot be isolated from national overheads. Therefore, the central product manager or director can assume only an advisory role, and must leave the ultimate decision to the country manager.

Collecting the data

'To get an accurate assessment of marketing costs is a particularly thorny issue,' found OASiS consultant Mike Perkin. 'Systems have usually grown up on accounting lines and are therefore transaction-oriented. You're calling for a company to make a major departure on centralized accounting to view the operation on functional, vertical market lines.' Rather than adapt the existing system, some companies have decided to scrap it and start again, with all the risks and expense that entails – hence the major expenditure by one of the oil companies referred to above.

'All nationalities work differently, so when you operate in so many different countries, it's not just the systems that have to change but the way you take an order, handle stock, and run the distribution and accounts,' said Perkin. When setting up a new operation like Chep's pallet hire in Germany, such details can be made universal from the start. Compaq was also careful to adopt common terms and conditions for its computer dealers right round the world, including discounts, payment terms and promotional expenditure. It has faced problems with some big dealers, but an important benefit is that data are comparable from Minneapolis to Madrid. The lack of comparability can be a major obstacle. As one senior Colgate–Palmolive executive found in the early 1980s, 'We couldn't make any sense out of the data we had. For a given product line, it was collected and analyzed in countries all around the world under different assumptions and with different methods.'

There is an accompanying risk. For the system to accommodate every oddity in every country, it has to be comprehensive, and can become too clumsy and time consuming for the operators, who will then short-circuit it if they can. On the other hand, simplification may conceal the very differences that spell success or failure. Market research information, in particular, is notoriously difficult to relate from one country to another, partly for reasons of demography, partly methodology (see Chapter 5). But some US multinationals' attempts to impose their own research methodology on, for example, advertising effectiveness have not been noticeably more effective. That is one important reason for retaining local management with enough skill to interpret the data and enough authority to adapt or even abandon the rules when the occasion demands.

At Black & Decker, European chief Roger Thomas found that 'asking subsidiaries for more sales was a waste of time,' partly because they are already well motivated to sell as much as the trade will bear, but partly too because 'you can also "buy" forward sales with discounts. So we measure sales out (from the retailers), not sales in, and the pipeline stock.' Those data are harder to collect, but the company has had many years' experience of assessing the level of retail sales from the number of guarantee cards that customers return, and basing its production programmes on them rather than its own invoiced sales.

One industrial company that claims to have an effective, bottom-up management information system in place is John Crane, part of the UK engineering company, TI Group. Crane has 60,000 items on its product list – seals for all sorts of moving machinery – and its national subsidiaries all use common software which details sales, prices, costs and so on, by product. 'We roll up performance with each major customer weekly and monthly,' said a senior central executive. 'If margins are too low, perhaps because of discounts, we can take action.'

Like several other companies, Crane is also using a common (CAD) system to stimulate the generation of new ideas throughout the group, simplify and speed up their development, and prevent duplication. Like many companies, Crane is concerned to increase the rate of innovation and throughput without adding staff, whether in the subsidiaries or the centre. Modern technology offers the prospect of whisking design proposals, draft specifications, costings and almost any quantity of accompanying data to wherever in the world it is needed. Thorn EMI's lighting division, before its aborted sale to GTE of the US, was planning to spend £20 million on upgrading its CAD/CAM system over the next few years so that, for example, an architect in Milan could specify the product design, which would then be made in Germany or the UK. 'We have the computing power to do it now, but it's not yet good enough,' commented an executive. As in other companies, such a system will be effective only if common standards are in force in technical, financial and operational terms.

In management terms, such systems have a two-way effect: the centre is able to keep in much closer contact with conditions at the battle front, and the local sales and marketing executives are provided with precise and up-to-date information about pricing estimates, deliveries, the feasibility of variants and so on. Providing salesmen with laptop or handheld computers has a similar effect. Some of Lego's toy sales staff have been using handheld computers for some years to collect and record retailers' order levels, sales and stocks. The information can then be processed by the subsidiary and fed into the central computers to provide a more detailed and immediate picture of sales trends than would be feasible in other ways.

Carefully planned, such systems can also give the salesman much more authority when talking to customers. In a case in which OASiS consultant Mike Perkin was recently involved,

> 'The salesman can be thousands of miles away but is given a clear picture of prices, credit limits and other details. That represents a significant increase in delegated authority, but it demands that the price-setting process and the rules for establishing the high and low limits have to be clear and widely understood.'

Decision making can thus be pushed right down the line and literally next to the customer, and intermediate executive layers avoided. For the system to be effective, the centre must be well prepared with a thoroughly researched strategy and the necessary expertise to apply it, and the salespeople well trained as to the exercise of their power and the limits of their competence. But the benefits to the customer in terms of prompt and accurate quotations or delivery dates are obvious.

Believing the data

It is a fact of corporate life that the information submitted by subsidiaries to headquarters will reflect the expectations, and the bonuses, attached to it. If the centre believes that service engineers should make a minimum of five calls per day or that debtors be cut to an average 60 days, that is what, within three months or so, the data will actually show. If a bonus depends on it, the period will be reduced by a month. That may seem too cynical, but dishonesty is not necessarily implied: the basic facts, or the way the data are collected, are often open to interpretation, and it is only human nature to interpret them in the most favourable way if a lot hangs on the outcome. The underlying reality may be different.

The problem extends beyond information. One executive with long experience at a big multinational remarked: 'If you want to apply a policy to 20 subsidiaries, some will be simply incompetent, others will not do as they are told.' The more the centre tries to 'manage' its subsidiaries and draw them into a global strategy, the worse the problem could become. 'Once the basic belief in a control system breaks down, you're in a mess,' warned GAH consultant Marcus Alexander, who saw one solution to lie in giving subsidiaries the obligation to pull the resources they need from the centre, rather as Glaxo does. In that way, the prized global strategy may not be so neat and tidy, and progress may be a bit slower, but at least the centre will have more confidence that apparent progress is real.

Few companies would openly admit to difficulties of this kind – it would be surprising if they did, and quite possible that they were unaware that they existed. But the importance of trust in a complex international structure cannot be overemphasized, principally between individuals but also in the data and research that they produce. Colgate–Palmolive's European president, Brian Bergin, for example, affirmed that 'in a changing European environment, integrity is very important. There's a lot of game playing in any organization, but it has to be minimized, and data mustn't be used as an excuse for the differences between markets.' One of his solutions was to make sure that executives did not lose touch with their markets, and got out into the field at least once a week. Other companies have stressed the importance of their senior executives knowing each other and having worked together over a long period.

Shifting the information boundaries

To gain real competitive advantage from IT, integration of systems has to begin to move through the entire supply chain, from primary suppliers through to distributors/retailers and on to the customer. This process begins to turn traditional notions of supplier/manufacturer/distributor relationships around from one characterized by conflict and suspicion to one of 'partnership', where the sum of the parts results in a much stronger and more competitive unit. Many companies will find it initially painful to share information with organizations formally regarded as adversaries. But unless they do there will always be a danger of a weak link in the chain having a deleterious affect on quality and service.

That means that electronic data exchange (EDI) is set to become as essential to doing business in the global village as the telephone and facsimile machines are now. Truly transparent information flows both inter- and intra-companies will break down traditional boundaries as never before. Many multinational companies like Ford and DuPont, as well as major retailers in the US and UK, already insist that their suppliers link in with their EDI systems to eliminate duplicated and wasteful paperwork.

EDI is an umbrella term that covers any system based on the transfer of data from computer to computer with agreed message standards, like electronic point of sale (EPOS) and electronic funds transfer at point of sale (EFTPOS). It replaces paperwork in areas like ordering, invoicing, payments, customs, reservations and so on. It evolved from the end of the 1960s when customs and freight forwarders began to investigate ways to make communications faster and more efficient. It has since been extended to other sectors: the international financial community uses an EDI network called Swift to clear international payments, while retailers, car manufacturers and chemical industries in Europe have all been working to set up European-wide EDI networks both between themselves and their suppliers in anticipation of the emergence of the Single Market.

Considering that unnecessary delays in paperwork are reckoned to have cost EC companies up to £7 billion a year, it is hardly surprising that many groups have chosen to share the costs and work toward establishing common standards instead of waiting for internationally agreed ones to be set up. These are coming, however: in 1987 the United Nations produced the EDIFACT standard for global use and is working toward integrating the standards followed by systems like Swift and the UK retail industry's Tradacoms. It is generally accepted that over time isolated EDI 'islands' will become connected and an international EDI network will emerge and be as prevalent as the telephone system. Some estimates predict that by 1995 400,000 companies will be using EDI, about 50% of them in the US, 35% in Europe and 15% in Asia, including Japan.

The implications for the push toward being 'global/local' are obvious. A continuous electronic dialogue will act as the central nervous system not just of companies but networks, enabling the communication of strategic goals and standards with local operations feeding back valuable market/customer information on a real-time basis. The umbilical cord connecting suppliers/manufacturers/retailers can start to have a major impact on things like inventory levels – and inventory is really a cost for lack of information – and service provision.

In these new groupings the supply chain becomes the unit of competition rather than the individual member companies. The partnerships, which have to be strategic and long-term, create a symbiotic relationship that works for all partners in the long run. Food retailing is a good example of how supplier companies can have little choice but to participate in a network: not only are retailers closer to the end customer, but their exploitation of increasingly sophisticated systems over the years has turned them into big, profitable operations in their own right which means they can act as the driving force in the supply chain. In the UK, for example, the top six grocery retailers account for almost three-quarters of food sales, and have developed successful competitive products under their own brand names.

Food retailers have been in the forefront of implementing IT not only to help with the sheer volume of transactions – a French superstore can push through one million items a day – but increasingly to flex their strategic marketing muscle. They have eagerly embraced developments like:

- Electronic point of sale (EPOS) based on the use of agreed bar codes;
- Electronic funds transfer at point of sale (EFTPOS);
- Automated warehousing and storage;
- EDI as a way to speed up communications with suppliers to improve the flow of goods and cut down drastically on paperwork.

Figure 8.7 illustrates the increasingly electronic nature of the retail cycle.

The ability to capture detailed information not only about which products are selling best and how fast, but increasingly who the buyers are, will supply retailers with a powerful source of competitive advantage. In the US information about individual customers gathered from store cards is already enabling the stores to send buyers details of promotions about frequently purchased products and develop 'frequent buyer' programmes. At 7-Eleven in Japan modern EPOS systems allow the checkout staff to key in information about a customer's sex and approximate age. Analysing the data means that each of the 4500 stores can tailor stock to local markets and compete more effectively with larger retailers. That has also worked through to improved inventory control since accurate decisions can be taken about what is moving.

Companies in other sectors have been quick to spot the potential value of such information: financial services company Citicorp has built a new generation of point-of-sale store systems with which it plans to collect the grocery purchase histories of up to 20 million households and use them to provide services to organizations like retailers and consumer packaged goods companies.

According to the MIT90s programme, there are a number of potential benefits from participating in a business network (Table 8.1):

- Operating efficiency may increase as a result of lower costs and improvements in service and quality.
- The financial structure can become less rigidly fixed, and shift between members in the network. Suppliers can take over the movement of inventory in a just-in-time system, for example.
- Market positioning may change as one company in the network begins to bias the business decisions of other members through the facilities, information and services the electronic network provides.

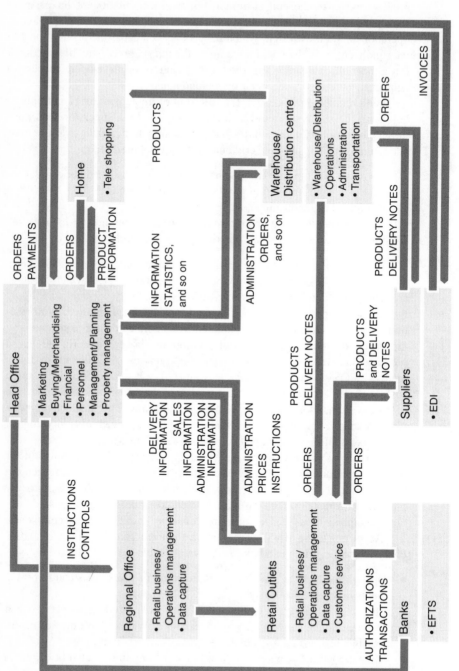

Figure 8.7 ICL's retail cycle. *Source:* ICL.

Table 8.1 MIT90s programme.

Business network roles	Benefits and sustainability				
	Operating efficiency	Financial structure	Market positioning	Participation conditions	Strategic capability
Transaction	Reduced costs and errors; temporary advantage	Reduces float; benefits drift upstream	Easy to do business but temporary first mover effects	Standards help participation but weaken linkage	Very limited potential
Inventory/ availability	Reduced errors; confirmation before placing orders	Just-in-time can cause upstream drift of inventory	Presentation effects; new product introductions	Special contracts and terms; volume commitments	Channel expansion
Process linkage	Simplification of procedures; long-term advantage	Potential for shared benefits	Process timing and simple customization long term	Process integration creates strong binding	Development of product derivatives and specials
Expertise link	Direct savings through close working and load sharing	Early exposure of opportunities	Fast channel for requirements in collaborations	Visibility of opportunities limited to participants	Collaborations enhancing joint capability

Sources: ICL Briefing, MIT90s.

- Conditions for belonging to the network may have pronounced benefits. Discount structures might become visible in exchange for commitment to certain volumes, for example.
- Enhanced business relationships may yield strategic capability so that the whole is greater than its parts. The airlines have created added value by linking in their computerized reservation systems with those of travel agencies, hotels, car hire firms and so on.

Summary

- The slow arrival of IT into that last bastion of IT ignorance, the marketing function, has deep implications for marketing both strategically and tactically. Closing the information loop so that real-time, integrated data about customers flows around the company effectively ends reliance on inert geographical structures and enables the corporation to 'think global, act local' in the truest sense.
- Most companies are only slowly beginning to grasp the need to coordinate the enormous amounts of information they gather. They are comfortable

with IT in the manufacturing and financial functions because they can judge its effect on raising productivity levels. But they feel far less secure about the role of information systems in their marketing strategies.

- One of the most fundamental parts of a marketing IT strategy is the exploitation of increasingly integrated marketing information systems which are driven from a powerful central database – or several linked databases – of current and prospective customers.

- A big barrier to successful implementation is that most companies are not dealing with greenfield IT sites. They have accumulated masses of stand-alone systems and mini-networks, along with the big number crunchers in central data processing units.

- The vision of a European market that is single in name but awash with cultural diversities is providing the incentive for many companies to rethink how they operate in Europe as part of global restructuring. IT should play the leading role. Most company networks still operate as islands in different countries. Modern information technology systems promise major benefits, but only to those who are prepared to adapt their structures to match and who have thought through their fundamental purpose.

- For systems to accommodate every oddity in every country, they have to be comprehensive, and can become too clumsy and time consuming for the operators, who will then short-circuit them if they can. On the other hand, simplification may conceal the very differences that spell success or failure.

- To gain real competitive advantage from IT, integration of systems has to begin to move through the entire supply chain, from primary suppliers through to distributors/retailers and on to the customer. This process begins to turn traditional notions of supplier/manufacturer/distributor relationships around from one characterized by conflict and suspicion to one of 'partnership', where the sum of the parts results in a much stronger and more competitive unit.

Checklist

As information collection and analysis begins to play an increasingly dominant role, does your company:

(1) Have a clear and coordinated approach to information technology (IT) in areas other than manufacturing and finance?

(2) Understood that IT is not just about automation but about ultimately increasing effectiveness across markets?

(3) Have plans to establish a marketing database to coordinate information about customers, markets and competitors?

(4) Have someone senior – whether in IT or in marketing – driving any marketing IT projects?

(5) Understand how to justify the resources that need to be spent developing systems?

(6) Encourage dialogue between the IT people and other less technically literate staff?

(7) Have a policy on creating EDI links and using information for competitive advantage?

References

Conference Board Europe. (1989). From hierarchy to network. *Research Monograph No. 2*. Brussels

ICL. (1990). *A Window on the Future*. An ICL Briefing for Management on the Findings of MIT90s. Bracknell: ICL

Index Group, Inc. (1990). How computers make customers king. *Insights*, 2(3), 4–5

Moriarty, R. T. and Swartz, G. S. (1989). Automation to boost sales and marketing. *Harvard Business Review*, Jan/Feb

The Management of Marketing Information. (1989). A report by OASiS in association with the Chartered Institute of Marketing

Wilmot, Dr R. (1990). *Marketing in the New Information Era – The New CIM*. OASiS

9

The human factor

Introduction

No company can hope to meet the challenges facing it without finding and motivating the right people to provide marketing expertise. Issues of recruitment at both the middle and senior level on an international scale are increasingly complex. The restructuring demanded by the European market in particular presents companies with a daunting personnel task in making managers of varying nationalities think European.

But while this has to be at the top of the agenda in the short term, it has to be underpinned by a long-term commitment to foster the corporate culture that makes everyone in the company face outward and think marketing and customers. An integral part of that effort is coming to terms with what the role of the marketing director and marketing department will be in a marketing-led organization. These are probably the hardest trials that those who run companies have to face. But they are also the most important. This chapter thus considers the following issues:

- Finding staff for global marketing
- Middle-management recruitment
- Top-level recruitment
- Establishing a Eurovision:
- Creating a marketing culture
- The role of the marketing director
- The evolution of the marketing department.

Finding staff for global marketing

The issue of staffing for effective global marketing involves at least two organizational levels of a multinational – the corporate and the foreign subsidiary – and perhaps more, if the company has a regional organization or a matrix system.

Increasingly, companies are making a concerted effort to include executives with diverse international backgrounds at the central corporate office. The input of people with strong hands-on experience in foreign marketing is equally important for companies that retain a large degree of decision making at the corporate office and those that are decentralized – but for different reasons.

In the former case, without the varied points of view contributed by executives from different countries, a distant headquarters' group can easily become parochial in its outlook and policies. In the latter case, because most decision-making authority remains in the field, there is often a need to have one or more knowledgeable people at headquarters to serve as liaison with marketing personnel in the foreign-based subsidiaries.

Although the question of whether top managers of foreign subsidiaries should be expatriates, local nationals or third-country nationals continues to fuel debate at parent companies, there is widespread agreement in theory – but less so in practice – that overseas marketing should be headed by a local executive. The rationale is compelling: marketing, unlike accounting, finance, R&D and even production, requires in-depth knowledge of the local market and the ability to communicate well with distributors and customers. In a literal sense, this means being fluent in the national language, but effective communication also requires there to be a mutuality of interests, traditions and cultural preferences.

At most multinationals the ideal senior marketing manager of a foreign-country operation is a citizen of that country whose career has been split between the parent company and the local affiliate. Such a person has worked (or at least been through a training programme) at parent-company headquarters or one of the parent company's domestic product divisions or both. This experience provides the knowledge of products, procedures and people effective international managers need, as well as steeping them in the corporate culture. The person will, of course, have spent a number of years in marketing positions in his or her own country and, perhaps, in other countries as well.

Such international diversity, however, is a rarity in today's corporate world. While executives from the parent company are spending more time at foreign subsidiaries, local executives from those subsidiaries do not have many opportunities to work at company headquarters. Howard V. Pearlmutter, chairman of the Multinational Enterprise Unit at the Wharton School of Business in Philadelphia, surveyed 150 of the largest global companies and found that barely 1% of senior headquarters' positions were filled by foreign nationals.

Foreign managers appear to be caught in a Catch-22 situation. Many parent-company executives contend that a lack of corporate experience is what limits foreign managers from reaching the upper echelons of the corporate hierarchy. But if, as the Pearlmutter survey indicates, most international companies do not offer these individuals opportunities to work at the home office, there is really no way they can gain the requisite background.

Many corporate executives believe that recruitment, rather than promotion, is the main problem in getting local nationals into senior positions at overseas subsidiaries. One reason cited by experts is nationalistic chauvinism. That is, US companies tend to view Americans as being the best qualified, UK companies believe the same thing about Britons, and so on.

Middle-management recruitment

Where do companies recruit global managers for midlevel positions? For most companies, the first source of supply is their own lower-management ranks. A growing number of multinationals are stepping up their internal management development efforts at the subsidiary level, viewing this as a more cost-effective route than continually going outside to find new recruits.

However, the demand for top-calibre product managers, salespeople, sales managers, market researchers and all the rest of the specialists needed in a sophisticated marketing operation virtually forces companies to tap outside sources. European business schools, such as the European Institute for Business Administration (INSEAD) based in Fontainebleau, France, the London Business School (LBS), City University Business School and the University of Warwick in the UK, and Bocconi in Milan, have all begun to churn out a new generation of global managers, as have a growing number of other European and US colleges and universities, which are developing international business curricula. Supply, however, cannot keep up with demand.

To deal with the shortage of local managers in many countries without sending more home-country expatriates overseas, companies are increasingly turning to third-county nationals. Some corporate personnel managers view Italian and Scandinavian managers as the most adaptable and innovative Europeans. 'Because of the small size of the markets, Scandinavian and Italian companies tend to emphasize foreign languages and internationalism far more than the larger European countries,' said Ahmed Aykac, director of the senior executive programme at the Geneva-based International Management Development Institute (IMD).

In addition to recent business school graduates and third-country nationals, midlevel marketing managers at other companies are the prime source of local executive talent for foreign subsidiaries. Companies use the full range of methods to attract experienced local marketing personnel, including ads in local newspapers and international publications, such as *The Wall Street Journal* and *The Economist*, executive recruiters (for higher-paid positions) and word of mouth.

Case 9.1 The Colgate–Palmolive global marketing training programme

Few companies pour as much money and management expertise into training marketing managers as New York-based Colgate–Palmolive. Although much smaller than Lever Brothers and Procter & Gamble, Colgate derives 60% of its revenue from abroad. The company prides itself on its ability to penetrate new markets (sometimes before its giant competitors arrive) and maintain good profitability. To retain its position as one of the world's pre-eminent consumer products companies, Colgate decided years ago to develop a programme to assure itself of a steady supply of superior marketers with the skills to operate almost anywhere.

The 'Global Marketing Training Programme' Colgate created, which gives its participants a two-year immersion in global marketing, has acquired considerable prestige since its establishment. Admission is highly competitive and is sought by some of the brightest BAs and MBAs from the world's best colleges and business schools. Successful applicants must have not only excellent academic credentials but also leadership skills, fluency in at least one other language in addition to English and some international-living experience, for example a year of study in a country other than the applicant's own.

The programme itself consists of assignments in various departments at Colgate, with a strong emphasis on marketing functions. A typical rotation would include some time in finance and manufacturing and larger blocks of time at Colgate's ad agency, in market research and in product management. Seven months of the programme are spent as a field salesperson in the US, with the trainees actually performing the job rather than merely accompanying regular salespeople on their rounds.

According to R. Alicia Whitaker, director of management and organization development, the programme gave trainees the basic skills global marketing managers need. The participants learned to use computers, devise budgets, formulate sales promotion strategies, manage work groups and so on. They also began to develop relationships that would help them when they started to operate in the international environment.

continues

continued

> Most of Colgate's new marketing 'graduates' are sent to markets in developing countries. Some are initially assigned to work in the US, but they, too, are soon posted overseas. Because non-US markets are so important to Colgate, it does not automatically bring its international marketers back to the US after a foreign assignment, as do many other multinationals. Often, the marketers go directly from one overseas post to another, becoming, in essence, career internationalists.

Top-level recruitment

Many companies want the top three to four people at each foreign subsidiary, including the head of marketing, to have risen through the ranks at the parent company. They feel that these individuals have the best grasp of the company's philosophy, culture and business practices.

The major drawback to filling the highest positions with local nationals can be the tendency of such executives to lack corporate scope. Several corporate executives said that local nationals often view their own operating entity as all-encompassing, rather than as simply one part of the overall corporation. The primary way companies address this concern is to rotate the most promising foreign executives among various foreign subsidiaries and between subsidiaries and corporate headquarters. This exposure to multiple business environments helps to break down parochial attitudes and foster a more global view.

The following highlight the way some companies handle the international staffing issue:

- At Nobel Industries, a diversified Swedish industrial manufacturing company, subsidiary presidents are viewed as the chief marketers in their countries of operation. Most subsidiary presidents are Swedish expatriates, whose main marketing task is to make sure that decisions and strategies benefit the company as a whole, not just the local subsidiary. However, mid-level marketing and sales executives in each country are usually local nationals. In Nobel's Japanese subsidiary, for example, the president is a Swedish expatriate, while almost everyone else in the subsidiary, including all sales, advertising and distribution managers are Japanese. Nobel's management feels that this arrangement gives the company the best of both worlds.
- Hewlett-Packard claims that 98% of its overseas marketing personnel are local nationals. In fact, according to William Johnson, vice president of

marketing, the few expatriates who may be on a foreign subsidiary's staff are, by and large, there to provide technical assistance rather than marketing expertise. Country managers also tend to be indigenous. This is changing in an evolutionary way as European nationals move within Europe, Asians move within Asia and Europeans and Asians move between their home region and the US.

- Siemens, the German manufacture of industrial equipment, finds that while it may be advantageous to the company to staff subsidiaries with local nationals, it is not always possible. Several foreign subsidiary divisions have been in existence for only a few years. 'The division structure has not yet developed to the point where a local national can step in and take over,' explained a Siemens spokesperson.

- Seiko Epson, a Japanese computer and peripherals maker, is in a similar position. It would like to fill its foreign-based senior marketing vacancies with local nationals but does not find enough who have adequate corporate experience. 'We are trying to give authority and responsibility to the local people, but there are simply not enough of them to fill every executive opening,' explained Norio Niwa, deputy general manger of marketing and sales. Of Epson's five sales divisions in Europe, three have presidents who are local nationals, while the other two have Japanese managers. The company has plans eventually to eliminate Japanese expatriates and staff top to bottom with local nationals.

- Baxter Healthcare attempts to fill senior marketing personnel vacancies with local nationals. In times of rapid growth, when company operations are expanding, this becomes quite difficult, and Baxter then turns to foreign expatriates to fill top positions. 'We try to fill local senior vacancies with local people. If no suitable local candidate can be located, little regard is given to where the person is from,' explained Bob Hurley, vice president of human resources for Baxter's Global Businesses group. Hurley cited two examples: a Norwegian currently headed the company's German subsidiary and a Briton was the number two marketing executive in Japan.

Case 9.2   A recruiter's perspective

'There is no such thing as a national market anymore,' said Virgil Baldi, a vice president in the New York office of Korn/Ferry International, the world's largest executive recruiting firm, with 40 offices in 19 countries:

continues

continued

'Everything is international now. A company may start out being in one country, but it may be acquired tomorrow by another company in another country. Suddenly, it's someone's foreign subsidiary. Or, as is happening in the EC countries and in Eastern Europe, the market itself may expand to include other countries. Overnight a marketing manager who used to be responsible for just one country finds he's selling to 12 or more.'

A recruiter for two decades, he spent about three-quarters of his time in searches that extended beyond a single country's border. Korn/Ferry as a whole conducts more than 2000 executive searches each year, of which about 20% are for placements in marketing, sales and advertising. Many of these roughly 400 searches are international in scope.

Some of Baldi's observations about recruiting international marketers follow:

On the backgrounds companies seek: In marketing, it's almost essential to have solid experience in the company's product line. For example, a company that sells chemicals normally doesn't want a marketing manager who has never worked in the chemical industry even if the applicant has great credentials. Obviously, the company does want someone with international experience, and many companies want someone who is comfortable working in a matrix-type organization, with both product and country or regional responsibilities.

Of course, there are exceptions to every rule. For example, there was one US-based software company looking for an international marketing manager without previous experience in the software field. It was looking for someone from the *hardware* side of the industry, because hardware marketers – who probably trained at IBM, Wang or another big computer firm – typically have better knowledge of the overall computer business. This software company is also atypical in that it doesn't care if the candidate has any international experience at all. What it is most concerned about is that he or she have a great deal of energy and be prepared to travel 75% of the time, since the job mainly involves working with dealers and reps overseas.

On the importance of prior international experience and foreign language capability: Despite exceptions like the software company, most big multinationals want their marketing executives to have previously lived and worked abroad. This is important for both positions at overseas operations and those on the international staff at the parent-company headquarters. Facility in at least one foreign language is highly desirable, but not essential. As English increasingly becomes the world-wide language of business, ability to speak another language is perhaps less important than it was some years ago. But even a smattering of another language can create immense goodwill and help to bridge the cultural gaps.

On pay packages for international marketers: Today, especially in Europe where the push is on for region-wide marketing strategies, true 'internationalist' marketers are at a premium. This is partly a consequence of the

continues

continued

realization of US companies that they must be competitive not only in products, but also in people.

Senior European marketing executives with, say, 10–15 years' experience and fluency in more than one language are in great demand right now. Beyond substantial base salaries and benefits, marketers at the general manager or executive vice president level of a subsidiary can command bonuses, stock options or phantom stock and, often, an employment contract. This could guarantee either employment for a certain number of years or a certain level of income.

Marketing salaries around the world are rising at about the same rate as other executive pay, although in specific cases, the packages are very, very rich.

On the relative merits of expatriates, local nationals and third-country nationals: Because the transfer of expatriates from the parent company to an overseas location has become so expensive, many multinationals seek to phase out that activity as much as possible. Years ago, US companies in particular thought that nobody but an American could do 'it' right, whatever 'it' was. That is no longer the case. The smart companies realize that there are very competent local and third-country managers who cost less and, when it comes to marketing, often know more about the local scene than their American bosses.

In Europe, executives are becoming very mobile, especially as EC integration nears. There are very few cultural problems that would bar sending someone from one European country to another. In other parts of the world, such as Latin America and Asia, cultural sensitivities play a greater role. A Korean executive would probably not be well received in Japan, for example, either by his own company's workers or his customers. There are certain countries – and Japan is probably the most significant example – where a foreign company really needs local people in the key management jobs in order to succeed.

On the use of executive search firms internationally: The firms are engaged in a growing number of searches on behalf of the overseas subsidiaries of major companies as well as of the parent companies. For the subsidiaries, such a search would probably not be categorized as 'international', since it might well be confined to the local market. For example, Korn/Ferry's New York office might find a French marketing executive for the French subsidiary of a US or British company. Thus, many searches are done within a single country, although the more difficult ones tend to expand in ever-widening circles to cover the immediate region, then a wider region and finally the whole world, if necessary.

On the economics of using recruiters: Search firms charge about one-third of the annual compensation (including bonus) of the position being filled. Most also have a minimum fee as well. This varies from country to country. Because of the minimum fee, it usually isn't cost effective to engage a search firm for relatively low-level positions – for example, a brand manager in a country subsidiary making the equivalent of $40,000 in salary. Executive search makes economic sense at the higher salary levels – $100,000 and upwards.

Establishing a Eurovision

Any corporate restructuring exacts a heavy price in personnel terms, and in Europe-wide restructuring, the price may be even heavier. New structures depend for their success on the ability of executives to embrace the new methods and to realize the benefits. Companies have to recognize that not everyone is suited to the kind of organization that they need to build up, either because of the nature of the organization itself, or an inability to take a broad international view. As a result, radical organizational change may imply a change of some of the personnel needed to run the operation.

Whatever the precise nature of the hurdles, many companies have gone to some lengths to help their staff jump over them. The reorganization of Thorn EMI's lighting division came out of careful planning by the group's personnel and organization development director and three days of meetings among the managers to thrash out the details. It was ironic that the whole division was sold shortly afterward. If these two companies operated in only one country, the changes would be testing enough for corporate systems and the executives running them. The fact that the foreign dimension adds several more layers of complexity makes them traumatic.

OASiS consultant Mike Perkin, who specializes in the implementation of major information technology and reorganization projects, found that

> 'the shakeup can be very painful. The senior staff can usually cope because they can see and understand the final result. But the middle and junior staff can only see part of it and are in a much more difficult position. People cling to their geographical identity, and when that goes, their drive and commitment go. So the management has to be doubly clear why the new structure is good, and the messages have to be sold to the staff.'

For companies not involved in quite such cataclysmic changes, the personnel issues are still important. 'We have a heritage of too much diversity, and we have to stress the commonality now,' said Colgate–Palmolive European president Brian Bergin. 'We probably should bring people in, but that's difficult. So we prefer to remake ourselves, to look first among our own people. But we have to find a mechanism to achieve the same effect.' (See Case 9.1.)

Some companies have already established a strong cooperative culture, often traceable back to the company's origins. Electrolux, Nestlé, Canon, NCR and Kodak all display a sense of corporate teamwork – a 'roundtable in the mind', as the executive in another Japanese company described it. It is a quality that lends itself naturally to participation in international, flexible project teams and networks that global competition and IT appear to demand.

It is also a quality associated with ponderous bureaucracy at a time when the world markets are demanding speedy, flexible reactions, profit consciousness and lean management. The traditional power of well-motivated country managers is effective as long as markets can be considered in isolation; centralized structures work well for capital and research-intensive industries where the customer accepts what is offered. In searching for the best of all worlds, companies find that the solution lies as much in the executive's mind as in the structure and direction. Electrolux, Kodak and some others believe they have now got the balance about right. The record will provide the only final answer.

Meanwhile, for the many other companies that, like Colgate–Palmolive, believe they have some way to go before achieving that balance, staff issues in one form or another do loom large. At Hoechst, for example, its radical decentralization programme – into autonomous business units, many of them outside Germany – has been delayed by a shortage of suitably experienced managers. ICI and Levi Strauss have noted a significant increase in the reluctance of executives to move with the job. Perhaps the younger generation is, in some cases anyway, better prepared for a career in a European, rather than an American, German, French or any other business culture, but they have to be recruited with that view in mind, and that takes time.

It is partly for these reasons that many companies are spending more time on ways to increase the European vision and responsibilities of their executives, but with the minimum of disruption. The obvious step of simply transferring executives for a few years from their home subsidiaries to some others is relatively rare in the companies discussed in this book – judging by actions rather than intentions. The growing number of spouses with careers of their own, and the continuing problems of finding appropriate (and perhaps affordable) schooling for children are decisive factors for many executives.

Managements also face the sensitivities of local staff, the difficulties of career planning, and ensuring that executives can operate effectively on their foreign assignments and again when they return home. In some cases, there is simply a lack of the necessary central mechanism. The largest multinationals naturally find the process easier, and companies like ICI and Unilever have been transferring staff for years. However, even in these companies, staff transfers might need to be accelerated. 'Transfers are an attempt to break down the feudalism – if the country manager's got a foreign marketing director, he can't count on his loyalty any more,' said one consultant.

Developing Euromanagers

Roche, when it transfers staff, asserted that it simply aims to increase co-operation inside the group. A senior executive said the company

'wants its managers to have experience in different areas, not just in sales and marketing. Roche wants to create Euromanagers who have developed international experience through six-month to two-year assignments. International experience counts for a lot in determining management potential.'

L'Oréal is also a staff transfer enthusiast. Assistant director for consumer products Giles Roger claimed:

'Twenty years ago, a marketing director in France would hear from local marketing directors that "things are different here". But now everything is international, modern . . . because of European culture and the fact that we move around. European culture is being disseminated in the universities, the schools . . . when people come to us now, they already have three languages.'

There may be an element of Gallic enthusiasm in that response. Some companies find French executives the most reluctant of all Europeans to live outside their home country. Further, a career with a foreign multinational, with a promotion ladder leading inexorably toward Frankfurt or New York, may hold less attraction than some national institution, particularly for graduates of the élite French *grandes écoles*. Other nationalities, however cosmopolitan, face similar dilemmas, and Honeywell, while it expects its staff to be ready to live anywhere in Europe and would not normally appoint someone to a general management position without foreign experience, finds it necessary nonetheless to guarantee to move them back home afterwards.

A readiness to work in other countries for longer or shorter periods has always been a condition of employment for some companies with extensive overseas interests. The difference in Europe is that working in Milan or Malmö is coming to be regarded as equivalent to home. 'The highly successful executives accept that their home countries can't satisfy them,' claimed Jean-Pierre Rosso, Honeywell's European president, himself French but having spent most of his career in the US and Belgium.

The problems may be more acute for the middle fliers. Companies' top priority must always be to find and develop good business managers, but a facility for languages, and just as important, a sympathy with and understanding of other countries' cultures and customs are naturally of growing importance. In practice, most companies find that much can be achieved with a gradualist policy, which may actually help solve other personnel problems, as a Union Carbide spokesperson explained:

'Local salesmen often need to be offered further career opportunities but may not wish to transfer to another country, so some of the more senior people are given a European assignment as well. It is very motivating and not too expensive. In Germany, one salesman spends 30% of his time on the one product line for which he has European responsibility – this allows him to travel, breaks him in gently to international work – but he still keeps his major responsibility at home and does not have to be trans-ferred to Geneva. This way he can see if he is really ready for international work.'

Giving an executive a European as well as a national hat in this way is gaining in popularity for several reasons:

- It adds to the individual's job opportunities;
- It exposes him or her to the international dimension;
- It promotes the transfer of valuable ideas and skills between subsidiaries;
- It helps avoid the 'not invented here' mentality;
- It saves the rising costs of transferring executives to another country, and the overheads of another layer of management.

Inevitably, however, companies have also encountered a number of drawbacks:

- Responsibilities may become confused and rapid remedial action more difficult;
- The executive's prime role in his or her home subsidiary may be neglected;
- Salary and other costs may need to be apportioned, the system for which may be unavoidably complicated;
- The company management information system may need an overhaul to give the executive the data needed for him or her to take on the additional work;
- Considerable time may be spent in travelling and liaison meetings;
- New developments will take longer to spread round the group if one or two executives are relied on to take them from one subsidiary to the next.

For most companies, the pros are considered to outweigh the cons, and American Express, for one, makes extensive use of the system of giving staff additional, external responsibilities. The UK subsidiary may earn fees for the time its executives spend helping its European fellows, and according to the UK managing director, Alan Stark, 'the fees do well for both sides,' since the paying company saves the salaries of local experts. For the future, Amex is recruiting 'international-type MBAs to become a Europe-wide management resource,' but Stark found that 'although some sell themselves as European managers, they are not necessarily any better.' At a more senior level, Amex has a 'very valuable' group of managers who move from market to market, although the corporate policy is to employ national staff wherever possible – 'I'm the first Brit in this job,' remarked Stark.

3M as usual has pushed the system one step further. As well as giving suitable executives European assignments either individually or as a member of a team in 'resource sharing programmes', executives with potential are given the accolade of 'subsidiary-based international managers'. The formal identification acts as some incentive in itself, and they meet every year in Brussels to learn more about and discuss 3M's European progress and strategy. 'We've still got a long way to go,' thought European vice president Edoardo Pieruzzi, 'but I think we're on the move.'

Other companies seem to share his optimism. Reckitt & Colman, through its quarterly marketing meetings and a lead country system, finds that 'people's attitudes have changed. They're concentrating on the similarities, not the differences. You have to persist at harmonization, and moving from complexity to simplicity.' Heinz now claims that its 'thinking is much less insular – it's the sort of nonparochial thinking on every subject that we're trying to instill.' Information technology networks will help the process on: 'I want operating managers to see what's happening in Italy and France,' said Heinz's European senior vice president Paul Corddry. Equally, personal attitudes, skills and interest will be necessary to make the IT systems provide the benefits that they promise. Managing through project teams and through the network will make big demands on individuals' flexibility and adaptability.

Rewarding the good Europeans

Most companies accept that the system of rewards for its senior staff has a powerful part to play in shaping attitudes to a European structure. Country managers with large bonuses dependent on the profits of their subsidiaries cannot be expected to have much enthusiasm for changes that may strengthen the company but make bonuses harder to earn. Equally, a single group bonus is unlikely to be much of a motivator since the manager can do little to influence the outcome. Many companies (one exception is Moulinex where, following the management buyout, a large number of the employees hold shares) regard motivation of key individuals as vital, and one of the arguments for keeping national subsidiaries intact is that they provide a performance focus around which some kind of bonus system can be maintained. The trick is to ensure that local rewards do not undermine Europe-wide profits – neatly summing up the whole European structure debate.

Highly decentralized companies can afford to make country managers' bonuses dependent entirely on the results of their operations. Few, however, would go as far as the UK electronic instrumentation group Eurotherm, which has a policy of setting up an individual manager with a sizeable stake in a new subsidiary in a new market, and even establishing arm's-length transfer prices to ensure that the profits are realistic and the motivation fair and effective. The system works well, but the managers concerned are not expected to cooperate with each other in the way that many larger companies regard as essential.

Instead, some more complex reward system has to be found that will reflect and encourage the fulfilment of the central strategy. Roche managers are rewarded for performance against a number of factors, including budget achievement, launching of new products, staff development and profitability. But while each of those factors is calculated only on the performance of the subsidiary or business unit, the system cannot be said to encourage cooperation. Some companies have therefore settled for a combination of national and European or group bonuses.

Heinz goes one stage further, linking a substantial part of its European chief executives' rewards to a formula based on volume, profit and return on investment (ROI). Down the line, a formula is used linking total profits and individual goals according to a 15-point scale:

- 2 points corporate profit;
- 2 points European subsidiary group performance;
- 5 points individual subsidiary performance;
- 6 points individual performance.

The European subsidiary performance has only recently been inserted to encourage the European as well as the group and national company performance. The product line heads also receive bonuses based on profit and ROI, and the company has probably made more use of stock options among its staff than any other comparable US company. Some 16% of the equity is now in employee hands, and 'every key player in the organization is an owner of the company,' said Corddry. 'It ensures they focus on the corporate good, not their own affiliate. In meetings, when they discuss, say, the reallocation of marketing funds, people say "OK, let's do it. It'll affect my stock price".'

Dealing with the stresses of travel

Closer coordination of European operations, however achieved, unavoidably demands more travelling by key staff, and for many executives, this is a growing charge on their time. A certain amount of travelling may be desirable from a corporate as well as a personal point of view. 'Managing by walking around' has a long and honourable tradition, and many executives pointed out that the alternative to going to see for oneself was far worse. The sharp differences in conditions and attitudes across Europe demand regular visits by managers if they are to do their job properly. For every executive who travels too much, there will be one who travels too little.

John Ankeny, Levi Strauss's marketing services director, spent 85% of his time away from his Brussels base, visiting the European subsidiaries or the US headquarters. NCR's European senior vice president Fred Newall spent less than half his time in Europe, the rest fulfilling his role as a corporate NCR officer in Dayton, Ohio. The US and Japanese multinationals were at an obvious disadvantage in this respect, particularly where the European head had to present his region's case at headquarters as well as travelling round the European subsidiaries.

The same problem afflicted the Europeans, however. At Electrolux and Reckitt & Colman, some senior executives spent a third or half of their time visiting their European outposts, and Moulinex, with its new ambition to strengthen its European position and image, was heading in the same direction.

With the growth of international team working, dual responsibilities and management networks, the need for middle ranks of executives to travel more frequently was also growing, encouraged by companies anxious to break down the national barriers.

Too much travel easily becomes a burden for the executives and their families. It can sap energy as well as absorb large amounts of time, leaving them incommunicado for long periods and beyond management control. A heavy travel schedule, with its macho, hands-on image, can easily be mistaken for the reality of management, and can merely leave the local executives bemused and alienated. It has been dubbed by one critic as 'pigeon management', where the executive flies in, leaves a mess and flies out.

It may be that developments in information technology will save some travelling, either by providing more data and message systems direct to executives' terminals or through teleconferencing facilities. But for the time being at least, the need for executives at all levels to travel throughout Europe and beyond is likely to grow, with Central and Eastern Europe adding more markets, with their own peculiarities to be mastered. Meanwhile, the increasing congestion on the European air routes, as well as at the approaches to major cities, can be expected to exacerbate the problems. In fact, the effective span of European management may in future be limited more by airline schedules than by an executive's capacity to control and lead subordinates.

Companies' only remedy may be to take a more realistic view of the need to travel, or even to modify their structures and procedures. Either way, the fact that they are, in the end, made up of groups of people who need to be led, encouraged and made to feel wanted will ensure that there is an irreducible minimum of travel to be undertaken.

Creating a marketing culture

There can be no question that the effectiveness of companies' sales and marketing structures depends first and last on the people in them, and travel has a direct contribution to make. But it should not be allowed to obscure the deeper issues which all of the points outlined in this book are exposing. Recruitment and personnel issues obviously need a lot of time and energy spent on them. But a company's ability to out-perform its competitors in the long term depends on the creation of an outward-facing marketing culture that affects both the behaviour and values of everyone in the company.

Every company has some kind of culture, whether it is a positive or negative one; it is the ethos, the collection of values, that go to make the personality of the organization. It embraces the entire company and may be largely dependent on the personality of, and the tone set by, the chairman or chief executive.

Culture is not a rigid or even necessarily an obvious presence. It tends to get noticed at times of change, something that is paradoxically becoming something of a constant for many companies. Too many companies fall into the trap of restructuring to get closer to the customer without 'reculturing'. But changing the organizational shape is pointless without an accompanying philosophical shift. Nor will ordering a pretty new logo, or sending out jolly memos, do much to make a grumpy service engineer more pleasant and efficient, or ensure that a 'hotline' is readily answered.

Creating a sustainable marketing culture consists of the following crucial elements:

- Time. It can take from 5 to 10 years of solid commitment.
- Belief. The chief executive/chairman must believe in it, understand it, and want it. Without that, the effort is doomed to be short-term and superficial and will probably degenerate into a 'have a nice day' syndrome.
- Planning. A carefully thought out plan has to be devised to convert everyone in the company, and anyone else with whom it has a relationship, to the understanding that they are all working for the customer.
- Measurement. Developing some form of built-in measurement for reaching goals. Otherwise, how will you know if you have got there?
- Flexibility. Cultures appropriate to today's environment may be unsuitable or even deleterious in tomorrow's.

Case 9.3 Becoming more market-driven

One large UK company which embarked on an ambitious programme to drive a new marketing culture through the group a few years ago began by carrying out an audit of what would be needed to become more market-driven. Four main issues arose:

(1) The top priority was for training and education in terms of getting everyone to understand how to approach the marketplace, from the chairman right through to people like machine operators who had little contact with customers.
(2) Good practice needed to be shared.
(3) Marketing' had to be given the professional status it deserved. In many traditional UK-based manufacturing companies, marketing has been viewed as a 'maverick' activity, not on a par with professions like accountancy, the law or personnel.
(4) There had to be awareness and commitment in all functions and at all levels.

continues

continued

Customized training became one of the most important parts of the project. Moreover, a questionnaire was devised with the help of outside experts to allow managers to assess how attuned they were to the market, by asking about market objectives, competitors, customer knowledge and the wider business environment. Emphasis was placed on encouraging cross-company communication to promote innovation by sharing ideas.

One problem which all programmes like this encounter is knowing how well it is going. A company needs to be able to measure progress to see if it has to move faster, or focus on a particular aspect. This is even more important in a very large organization where every area is competing for funds. At the same time, the programme's executives should not spend their whole time measuring things. It is easy for them to delude themselves that they are achieving, when they are really only monitoring. Another danger is to forget these issues when times get hard.

At Federal Express, the US-based distribution carrier well known for a strong marketing culture driven by the chairman and founder, Fred Smith, corporate communications is a key part of the marketing function. The company's effort were rewarded in 1990 when it won the prestigious Malcolm Baldridge award established by the US government to stimulate companies to rival Japanese success. The award is not just about showing that the products or services are of high quality, but, more importantly, that they are being improved all the time. Constant improvement ties in with the Federal Express motto of 'people, service, profit'. It works on the basis that if the company hires, keeps and motivates good people, they will give good service. It is circular – it leads to better profit, better pay, more training.

British Airways has been singled out as one of the companies to implement a cultural change with a strong degree of success. Its cultural transformation has been a source of competitive advantage in an industry where making the difference is all about the reality behind the perception. As former director of marketing and operations Liam Strong said, at BA it had been clear from the very top that creating a service culture was the priority. But it cannot be a static activity: 'Now we are having to adjust that as we move into a deregulated Europe and a much more competitive international market and look at service in a cost-effective way. That is a much more difficult message to get across.' It demanded that internal marketing be as important as external marketing and that a link be created between customers and employees.

One important aspect in making a defined cultural shift which top management often disregards is the importance of treating employees as customers. There should be a good understanding of the relationship between customers, suppliers and the labour force. Given the rise of customer sovereignty, employees are customers of organizations as well as 'servants', so there has been a change in the balance of power. The role of the marketing-aware company is to use that understanding to market to its employees, both actual and potential, using the same principles and techniques it does to the outside.

Some of the modern forces pushing cultural change forward are the fashionable but nonetheless valid ideas encompassing total quality management (TQM). TQM is the most recent and favoured of corporate theories for changing and modifying company behaviour and practice on a long-term basis. The main method of achieving this is to ensure that the driving force of a company is customer satisfaction. In many ways it is simply common sense: if service to the customer in terms of both product and delivery is the way to win in a marketplace of decreasing product differentiation and more discerning consumers, then it makes eminent sense for a company to employ any method which has constant improvement as its objective.

TQM first came into existence through the statistical quality control methods for manufacturing developed in the US before World War II. It places the emphasis on getting things right the first time rather than finding defects during inspection at the end of the process or through receiving customer complaints. In service industries, TQM is concerned with enhancing service by marrying efficient systems and procedures with improved staff attitudes and behaviour. The atmosphere in which a TQM flourishes is based on a flat management structure which encourages open communication at all levels, clarity of direction, delegation and openness.

A great danger companies face when they decide to change the culture is to see it as a quick fix: 'Get me a new culture by Monday.' But if it is approached in that way, one of the few assured results will be employee scepticism ('The chairman has read another book') and cynicism. As BA's Strong pointed out, 'People take very seriously what you do, not what you say. Culture has to be about very simple messages so that people can see what is important. It might sound banal – but where most cultures fall down is that people get cynical.'

The role of the marketing director

What should the role of the senior marketing people be in creating a more market-focused organization? It should be pivotal. Marketing specialists, whether called marketing directors or not, can act as:

- Evangelists. They can spread the gospel of the market throughout the company, and ensure best practice.

- Integrators. They can be the link between the strategic vision and its practical implementation.
- Explorers. They should be hunting out their companies' future. The best should always be able to come up with at least five potentially lucrative business opportunities.
- Interpreters. They can explain the market to the company, and the company to the market.
- Advisors. Although more marketing experts are making it to the top, even they need specialists to act as staff consultants not only in marketing, but in areas like finance and personnel.

The difficulty arises when marketing specialists are brought on board to 'make a difference', but are confronted with ingrained habits formed by years of tradition at the top. This can happen in hidebound consumer goods companies. It has perhaps been most noticeable, however, in sectors like heavy industry and financial services. But change is coming, as Case 9.4 shows.

Case 9.4 Barclays

In the last five years the financial services industry has had to tackle the knotty problem of how to install a marketing-driven culture into its ethos. It has been, and still is, a struggle. Barclays Bank, one of the UK's three biggest clearing banks, believes that it, for one, is coming to grips with the issues: 'There is a recognition that marketing has to drive the company. It is probably not expressed in those terms, but the recognition that the needs of the customer drives what we do is a good definition of marketing,' said John Cheese, marketing director of the personal sector.

Barclays first filled the post of a marketing director overseeing the personal sector with an outside marketing specialist four years ago. Cheese joined about two years ago, having worked both in consumer goods marketing and financial services. What does he think has been the spur for banks to sharpen the marketing focus?

- Deregulation. That has led to blurred lines between all financial services companies, from banks and building societies to insurance companies, which means they are all poaching in each other's territory;
- Static markets in some areas like mortgages which has led to a fierce battle for market share and stronger competition for those growth markets like life insurance;

continues

continued

- Technology – all banks want to exploit what are probably the most information-packed customer databases of any sector.

Banks fulfil a complex assortment of functions: they are in one sense manufacturers – although they do not manufacture money, they do have to fund their balance sheets and put the product together and package it. There is also a wholesale element to their business, providing large credit lines and extensive money transmission services to major customers. And there is a retail aspect to their business as well, where they need to maintain a considerable high street presence. 'Marketing is not just taking a process that works in one industry and applying it to the last detail somewhere else,' said Cheese. 'It's more to do with having a basic philosophy to the way we do business.'

Cheese suspected that when the financial services sector looks back in five years' time it will consider that it was somewhat rigid in its attempt to import marketing skills: 'There has to be a philosophical and sympathetic transfer. You have to understand the fundamentals of banking, not necessarily in the procedural sense but you need to understand why people buy banking services.'

Cheese has not been convinced by arguments that banks have to become more like retailers and act as financial supermarkets: 'To talk about high street retailing and about supermarkets is to describe a sales process which is inordinately reactive – people go into the shop to buy things.' Banking products are not only different, but more sophisticated, he pointed out, so 'we need to provide advice and be more proactive in the way we sell our products to the customer.' Nor is there a need for large-scale diversification: 'the fundamental elements of the product range are in place.'

Cheese summed up his personal hobby horse about banks and marketing:

> 'To get competitive advantage we have all been applying the principles of marketing, but in reality what we have been doing is merely tinkering with the product range. We call what we have been doing product development. The truth is, I believe, that what we have been doing is nothing more that product proliferation. We *think* we have been applying the principles of marketing. But what we have been doing is tinkering with the product range. What we *think* we have been doing is product development. The reality is, I believe, that what we have been doing is product proliferation.'

How do banks push a marketing-driven energy right down to the teller – and keep it there? Cheese admitted it was not easy. It needed not only the total commitment of the top management but what was in effect a constant evolution and revolution in sales skills through training, encouraging and keeping constant pressure to effect change.

Marketing has come of age in banking in the sense that it is no longer eyed suspiciously as that mysterious department which seems to do little but produce glitzy advertising. The important issues facing them in the 1990s include:

continues

continued

- Eliminating the friction between the banking culture and the attempt to inculcate a better understanding of the growing demands of more sophisticated consumers;
- Dealing with tougher competition, not only from other financial services organizations but from other industries like retail;
- The Single Market/global market;
- The Japanese. We buy their cars and TVs happily – why not a bank account?

Marketing is becoming a far more complex discipline, where the mix of skills and responsibilities could vary quite dramatically from company to company. It is likely to prove daunting, as well as stimulating. Marketers face a number of challenges:

- The need to come to terms with finance. They will have to learn to understand profit not just in the sense of the bottom line, but the effects of the costs of dealing with customers;
- As the repository of market information, they will have to come to terms with the application of IT and its impact on organizational effectiveness and flexibility and not view it as a threat to their jobs;
- They will have to think more strategically, and be encouraged to do so from the top;
- They will have to play an active role in driving TQM and a customer-driven culture by being instrumental in breaking down little corporate empires, and using their practised communications skills to do so;
- They will have to be involved in structuring the company according to customers, not product, geography or function;
- They will have to understand not just their customers, but their customers' customers;
- They will need to act more like line operators than functional staff, while still acting as a centre of expertise;
- They will have to oversee the evolution of integrated promotional strategies that reflect the overall strategy;
- They will have to think and act as brand champions globally;
- They will need a far better understanding of other areas, particularly sales and production.

This probably sounds like a tall order, and more in keeping with what is expected of a modern chief executive. But that, indeed, is what good marketing directors should be: mini chief executives, who act as both the right and left hands of their chief who has the ultimate responsibility of keeping the organization on track.

The evolution of the marketing department

What about the marketing department? There are several ways it could evolve:

- It could become more of an implementation and coordination department, carrying out the more centrally held strategic goals;
- It could be a boffin department;
- It could be a breeding ground for managers;
- It could disappear since everyone is concerned with 'marketing'.

Getting rid of the marketing department is not quite so radical as it sounds. The assumption that marketing is what happens in a marketing department can be dangerous because in a competitive world marketing has to be about what happens everywhere in an organization. But it will probably exist in some form. While 'marketing' people should be spread throughout the organization, there should be a small department of highly qualified, highly paid and highly effective doers who act with the energy of a crack SAS team on all the relationships with customers and suppliers.

As IT specialists Case Communications' strategic marketing manager Peter Stauvers noted, 'In the early 1980s we had product managers, and then everyone read [Michael] Porter so we had marketing managers, and in the 1990s we will have business people.' He believed that, as has happened at Case, big central marketing departments will get smaller and concentrate on examining long-term trends as marketing people get more dispersed through-out the business. 'Artificially created marketing departments can hold business back and stop other people taking responsibility for marketing. If you have your strategy right from the start, you shouldn't really need it,' he believed.

Portrait of a marketing department

A 1990 survey by consultants DunnHumby of just over 100 big UK adver-tisers showed, among other things, that many of them see the role of the marketing department as merely a promotional one. Between 80% and 97% of managers said that they were responsible for:

- Monitoring competitor marketing activity
- Management and measurement of products

continues

continued

- Above-the-line advertising
- Sales promotion and point of sale
- Market research
- Monitoring advertising effectiveness
- Media selection
- Market planning
- Market segmentation
- New product development.

Between 58% and 69% had responsibility for:

- Choosing and motivating channels of distribution
- Direct marketing customers
- Direct marketing prospects
- Improved customer knowledge and care.

Finally, 7–39% had control over:

- Sales management, quotas and measurement
- Control and management of the sales force
- Telemarketing, inbound and outbound.

Then they were asked to rate the importance of those activities to the company on a scale between 1 (irrelevant) and 9 (important). Ironically, the ones at the top of the list are those over which marketing in general has little control:

- Customer care/knowledge (7.8)
- Sales force management (7.5)
- Sales management and quotas (7.1)
- Channels distribution (7)
- Product measurement (7).

Liam Strong, now at the Sears group, believed that the role of marketing would be less clear cut as the business as a whole becomes more market-led, rather than marketing-led, and other functions form views about marketing. Moreover, it is becoming a more complex discipline where the mix of skills and responsibilities can vary quite dramatically company by company:

'Ultimately marketing is there to interpret the market to the company and interpret the company to the marketplace. Someone has to be responsible for that. The marketing function plays the role between the general management team and the rest of the business in terms of the conflicting challenges of profitability versus investment in the market-place. It has to be a trade-off between market needs, company needs, financial needs, investment needs. The successful ones are those that are most business-focused and really understand that.'

He believed that the marketing department should have a coordinating role, pulling together multifunctional teams to solve business problems, rather than just handling technical aspects of the business mix. Before he left BA, sales and marketing had been more closely integrated, while the managers in the marketing department were to be assessed by brand profit contributions to make them more alert to the business, rather than simply administering marketing programmes.

As marketing becomes the strategic function of the company as a whole, in some companies the marketing department is bound to lose some of the power over devising the promotional programmes it once had. As Nestlé general manager and executive vice president, marketing, Camillo Pagano, said,

> 'Since marketing is the basic business function the final responsibility for marketing communications is at the top. Sometimes the younger people get discouraged about it, and complain about lack of autonomy. We are not asking them to have autonomy. They will have it when they are at the top.'

He believed that, certainly in his industry, young marketers have to have experience of business at the sharp end:

> 'When you talk to Sainsbury, you are talking to businessmen, you are not talking about fishing. What you need to discuss is business, because the orders nowadays go through computers. This is where the marketing function is changing radically. And it is a huge challenge. You have to go from people that have been accustomed to classical advertising.'

If US trends are anything to go by, the days in consumer goods companies when the brand manager was king, are indeed over. The focus now is increasingly on technical specialists who have specific functional expertise in areas like trade relations, integrated communications, market research and so on. As Fiona Gilmore, director of brand and corporate identity consultancy Springpoint said,

> 'Many consumer goods companies are saying: we have had too many junior people dabbling in senior decision making, who stay for only two years and mess up the brand positioning. They realize they might lose out on motivating junior people, who will still get good basic training but won't have the responsibility they used to have. There will be more doers, but senior marketing people will take the decisions on all important aspects, including product design. The whole thing is going back up the line as companies recognize that they are dealing with brands on a European and global basis.'

Barclay's Cheese believed that although marketing support roles could change and the marketing department be repositioned, there would always be a need to have people who understand marketing in its fullest functional sense because:

'You still need to know which specialists to employ and how to integrate them. You cannot have the specialist tales wagging the company dog.'

Summary

- No company can hope to meet the challenges facing it without finding and motivating the right people to provide marketing expertise. Issues of recruitment at both the middle and senior level on an international scale are increasingly complex, with the restructuring demanded by the European market in particular presenting companies with a daunting personnel task, making managers of varying nationalities think European.

- Increasingly, companies are making a concerted effort to include executives with diverse international backgrounds at the central corporate office.

- Many corporate executives believe that recruitment, rather than promotion, is the main problem in getting local nationals into senior positions at overseas subsidiaries. One reason cited by experts is nationalistic chauvinism. That is, US companies tend to view Americans as being the best qualified, UK companies believe the same thing about Britons, and so on.

- For most companies, the first source of supply for midlevel positions is their own lower-management ranks. A growing number of multinationals are stepping up their internal management development efforts at the subsidiary level, viewing this as a more cost-effective route than continually going outside to find new recruits.

- Many companies want the top three to four people at each foreign subsidiary, including the head of marketing, to have risen through the ranks at the parent company.

- Any corporate restructuring exacts a heavy price in personnel terms, and in Europe-wide restructuring, the price may be even heavier. New structures depend for their success on the ability of executives to embrace the new methods and to realize the benefits.

- Most companies accept that the system of rewards for its senior staff has a powerful part to play in shaping attitudes to a European structure.

- With the growth of international team working, dual responsibilities and management networks, the need for middle ranks of executives to travel more frequently is also growing, encouraged by companies anxious to break down the national barriers. But too much travel easily becomes a burden for the executives and their families.

- A company's ability to out-perform its competitors in the long term depends on the creation of an outward-facing marketing culture that affects both the behaviour and values of everyone in the company. And every company has some kind of culture, whether it is a positive or negative one.

- The role of marketing directors in a marketing-led company should be pivotal: they should be evangelists, integrators, explorers, interpreters, advisors.

- Marketing executives face daunting challenges in the 1990s, including the need to think more strategically and to come to terms with the financial implications of their jobs.

Checklist

In terms of creating a marketing-led culture, has your company:

(1) Established a consistent approach toward treatment of marketing executives at foreign subsidiaries?

(2) Encouraged executives from outside the headquarters to spend time there to get a feel for the corporate framework?

(3) Made a concerted effort to grow executives in order to create managers with a more global view?

(4) Assessed the personnel implications of European restructuring ?

(5) Put in place some system – rewards, for instance – to encourage a more European view on the part of national managers?

(6) Developed a view on the optimal structure of the marketing department to deal with the erosion of once-clear market boundaries?

(7) Made plain that there is a solid commitment on the part of the senior management to create and sustain a lasting marketing culture throughout the organization?

Reference

Use and altitudes to computers in marketing (1990). DunnHumby

Bibliography

General

Buzzell, R. D., Quelch, J. A. and Bartlett, C. (1992). *Global Marketing Management.* Reading MA: Addison-Wesley

Davidson, H. (1990). *Offensive Marketing.* Revised edition. Harmondsworth: Penguin

Goold, M. and Quinn, J. J. (1990). *Strategic Control: Milestones and Long-term Performance.* London: Economist Books/Hutchinson

Heller, R. (1987). *The Supermarketers.* New York: Truman Talley

The Henley Centre (1989). *Euro-strategies in the 1990s*

Kotler, P. (1988). *Marketing Management, Analysis, Planning and Control*, 6th edn. Englewood Cliffs NJ: Prentice-Hall

Ohmae, K. (1990). *The Borderless World.* London: Collins

Porter, M. (1980). *Competitive Strategy.* New York: Free Press

Porter, M., ed. (1986). *Competition in Global Industries.* Boston: Harvard Business School

Porter, M. (1990). *The Competitive Advantage of Nations.* London: Macmillan

Prahalad, C. and Doz, Y. (1987). *The Multinational Mission: Balancing Local Demands and Global Vision.* New York: Free Press

Branding

DeMooiji, M. K. and Keegan, W. J. (1991). *Advertising Worldwide.* Englewood Cliffs NJ: Prentice-Hall

Interbrand (1990). *Brands, An International Review.* London: Mercury Business Books

Macrae, C. (1991). *World Class Brands.* Wokingham: Addison-Wesley

Murphy, J., ed. (1987). *Branding: A Key Marketing Tool.* London: Macmillan

Murphy, J. (1990). *Brand Strategy.* Cambridge: Director Books

Olins, W. (1989). *Corporate Identity.* London: Thames & Hudson

Information technology

ICL. (1990). *A Window on the Future.* An ICL Briefing for Management on the Findings of MIT90s. Bracknell: ICL

The Management of Marketing Information (1989). A report by OASiS in association with the Chartered Institute of Marketing (1989)

EIU Management Guide, April (1991). *The Management Challenge of IT*

EIU Management Guide, May (1991). *Executive Information Systems*

Culture

Corporate Culture for Competitive Edge. Special report 1195. Economist Publications (1990)

Campbell, A. *et al.* (1990). *A Sense of Mission.* London: Economist Books/Hutchinson

Smythe, J., Dorward, C. and Reback, J. (1992). *Corporate Reputation.* London: Century Business

Index